Introduction to Computing

Explorations in Language, Logic, and Machines

David Evans
University of Virginia

For the latest version of this book and supplementary materials, visit:

http://computingbook.org

Version: August 15, 2011

Contents

List of Explorations

List of Figures

Image Credits

Most of the images in the book, including the tiles on the cover, were generated by the author.

Some of the tile images on the cover are from flickr creative commons licenses images from: ell brown, Johnson Cameraface, cogdogblog, Cyberslayer, dmealiffe, Dunechaser, MichaelFitz, Wolfie Fox, glingl, jurvetson, KayVee.INC, michaeldbeavers, and Oneras.

The Van Gogh *Starry Night* image from Section 1.2.2 is from the Google Art Project. The Apollo Guidance Computer image in Section 1.2.3 was released by NASA and is in the public domain. The traffic light in Section 2.1 is from iStockPhoto, and the rotary traffic signal is from the Wikimedia Commons. The picture of Grace Hopper in Chapter 3 is from the Computer History Museum. The playing card images in Chapter 4 are from iStockPhoto. The images of Gauss, Heron, and Grace Hopper's bug are in the public domain. The Dilbert comic in Chapter 4 is licensed from United Feature Syndicate, Inc. The Pascal's triangle image in Excursion 5.1 is from Wikipedia and is in the public domain. The image of Ada Lovelace in Chapter 6 is from the Wikimedia Commons, of a painting by Margaret Carpenter. The odomoter image in Chapter 7 is from iStockPhoto, as is the image of the frustrated student. The Python snake charmer in Section 11.1 is from iStockPhoto. The Dynabook images at the end of Chapter 10 are from Alan Kay's paper. The xkcd comic at the end of Chapter 11 is used under the creative commons license generously provided by Randall Munroe.

Preface

This book started from the premise that Computer Science should be taught as a liberal art, not an industrial skill. I had the privilege of taking 6.001 from Gerry Sussman when I was a first year student at MIT, and that course awakened me to the power and beauty of computing, and inspired me to pursue a career as a teacher and researcher in Computer Science. When I arrived as a new faculty member at the University of Virginia in 1999, I was distraught to discover that the introductory computing courses focused on teaching industrial skills, and with so much of the course time devoted to explaining the technical complexities of using bloated industrial languages like C++ and Java, there was very little, if any, time left to get across the core intellectual ideas that are the essence of computing and the reason everyone should learn it.

With the help of a University Teaching Fellowship and National Science Foundation grants, I developed a new introductory computer science course, targeted especially to students in the College of Arts & Sciences. This course was first offered in Spring 2002, with the help of an extraordinary group of Assistant Coaches. Because of some unreasonable assumptions in the first assignment, half the students quickly dropped the course, but a small, intrepid, group of pioneering students persisted, and it is thanks to their efforts that this book exists. That course, and the next several offerings, used Abelson & Sussman's outstanding *Structure and Interpretation of Computer Programs* (SICP) textbook along with Douglas Hofstadter's *Gödel, Escher, Bach: An Eternal Golden Braid.*

Spring 2002 CS200 Pioneer Graduates

Back row, from left: Portman Wills (*Assistant Coach*), Spencer Stockdale, Shawn O'Hargan, Jeff Taylor, Jacques Fournier, Katie Winstanley, Russell O'Reagan, Victor Clay Yount. Front: Grace Deng, Rachel Dada, Jon Erdman (*Assistant Coach*).

I am not alone in thinking SICP is perhaps the greatest textbook ever written in any field, so it was with much trepidation that I endeavored to develop a new textbook. I hope the resulting book captures the spirit and fun of computing exemplified by SICP, but better suited to an introductory course for students with no previous background while covering many topics not included in SICP such as languages, complexity analysis, objects, and computability. Although this book is designed around a one semester introductory course, it should also be suitable for self-study students and for people with substantial programming experience but without similar computer science knowledge.

I am indebted to many people who helped develop this course and book. Westley Weimer was the first person to teach using something resembling this book, and his thorough and insightful feedback led to improvements throughout. Greg Humphreys, Paul Reynolds, and Mark Sherriff have also taught versions of this course, and contributed to its development. I am thankful to all of the Assistant Coaches over the years, especially Sarah Bergkuist (2004), Andrew Connors (2004), Rachel Dada (2003), Paul DiOrio (2009), Kinga Dobolyi (2007), Jon Erdman (2002), Ethan Fast (2009), David Faulkner (2005), Jacques Fournier (2003), Richard Hsu (2007), Rachel Lathbury (2009), Michael Lew (2009), Stephen Liang (2002), Dan Marcus (2007), Rachel Rater (2009), Spencer Stockdale (2003), Dan Upton (2005), Portman Wills (2002), Katie Winstanley (2003 and 2004), and Rebecca Zapfel (2009). William Aiello, Anna Chefter, Chris Frost, Jonathan Grier, Thad Hughes, Alan Kay, Tim Koogle, Jerry McGann, Gary McGraw, Radhika Nagpal, Shawn O'Hargan, Mike Peck, and Judith Shatin also made important contributions to the class and book.

My deepest thanks are to my wife, Nora, who is a constant source of inspiration, support, and wonder.

Finally, my thanks to all past, present, and future students who use this book, without whom it would have no purpose.

Happy Computing!

David Evans
Charlottesville, Virginia
August 2011

Spring 2003

Spring 2004

Spring 2005

1 Computing

In their capacity as a tool, computers will be but a ripple on the surface of our culture. In their capacity as intellectual challenge, they are without precedent in the cultural history of mankind.
Edsger Dijkstra, 1972 Turing Award Lecture

The first million years of hominid history produced tools to amplify, and later mechanize, our physical abilities to enable us to move faster, reach higher, and hit harder. We have developed tools that amplify physical force by the trillions and increase the speeds at which we can travel by the thousands.

Tools that amplify intellectual abilities are much rarer. While some animals have developed tools to amplify their physical abilities, only humans have developed tools to substantially amplify our intellectual abilities and it is those advances that have enabled humans to dominate the planet. The first key intellect amplifier was language. Language provided the ability to transmit our thoughts to others, as well as to use our own minds more effectively. The next key intellect amplifier was writing, which enabled the storage and transmission of thoughts over time and distance.

Computing is the ultimate mental amplifier—computers can mechanize any intellectual activity we can imagine. Automatic computing radically changes how humans solve problems, and even the kinds of problems we can imagine solving. Computing has changed the world more than any other invention of the past hundred years, and has come to pervade nearly all human endeavors. Yet, we are just at the beginning of the computing revolution; today's computing offers just a glimpse of the potential impact of computing.

There are two reasons why everyone should study computing:

1. Nearly all of the most exciting and important technologies, arts, and sciences of today and tomorrow are driven by computing.
2. Understanding computing illuminates deep insights and questions into the nature of our minds, our culture, and our universe.

It may be true that you have to be able to read in order to fill out forms at the DMV, but that's not why we teach children to read. We teach them to read for the higher purpose of allowing them access to beautiful and meaningful ideas.
Paul Lockhart, *Lockhart's Lament*

Anyone who has submitted a query to Google, watched *Toy Story*, had LASIK eye surgery, used a smartphone, seen a Cirque Du Soleil show, shopped with a credit card, or microwaved a pizza should be convinced of the first reason. None of these would be possible without the tremendous advances in computing over the past half century.

Although this book will touch on on some exciting applications of computing, our primary focus is on the second reason, which may seem more surprising.

Computing changes how we think about problems and how we understand the world. The goal of this book is to teach you that new way of thinking.

1.1 Processes, Procedures, and Computers

information processes

Computer science is the study of *information processes*. A process is a sequence of steps. Each step changes the state of the world in some small way, and the result of all the steps produces some goal state. For example, baking a cake, mailing a letter, and planting a tree are all processes. Because they involve physical things like sugar and dirt, however, they are not pure information processes. Computer science focuses on processes that involve abstract information rather than physical things.

The boundaries between the physical world and pure information processes, however, are often fuzzy. Real computers operate in the physical world: they obtain input through physical means (e.g., a user pressing a key on a keyboard that produces an electrical impulse), and produce physical outputs (e.g., an image displayed on a screen). By focusing on abstract information, instead of the physical ways of representing and manipulating information, we simplify computation to its essence to better enable understanding and reasoning.

procedure

algorithm

A *procedure* is a description of a process. A simple process can be described just by listing the steps. The list of steps is the procedure; the act of following them is the process. A procedure that can be followed without any thought is called a *mechanical procedure*. An *algorithm* is a mechanical procedure that is guaranteed to eventually finish.

A mathematician is a machine for turning coffee into theorems.
Attributed to Paul Erdös

For example, here is a procedure for making coffee, adapted from the actual directions that come with a major coffeemaker:

1. Lift and open the coffeemaker lid.
2. Place a basket-type filter into the filter basket.
3. Add the desired amount of coffee and shake to level the coffee.
4. Fill the decanter with cold, fresh water to the desired capacity.
5. Pour the water into the water reservoir.
6. Close the lid.
7. Place the empty decanter on the warming plate.
8. Press the ON button.

Describing processes by just listing steps like this has many limitations. First, natural languages are very imprecise and ambiguous. Following the steps correctly requires knowing lots of unstated assumptions. For example, step three assumes the operator understands the difference between coffee grounds and finished coffee, and can infer that this use of "coffee" refers to coffee grounds since the end goal of this process is to make drinkable coffee. Other steps assume the coffeemaker is plugged in and sitting on a flat surface.

One could, of course, add lots more details to our procedure and make the language more precise than this. Even when a lot of effort is put into writing precisely and clearly, however, natural languages such as English are inherently ambiguous. This is why the United States tax code is 3.4 million words long, but lawyers can still spend years arguing over what it really means.

Another problem with this way of describing a procedure is that the size of the description is proportional to the number of steps in the process. This is fine for simple processes that can be executed by humans in a reasonable amount of time, but the processes we want to execute on computers involve trillions of steps. This means we need more efficient ways to describe them than just listing each step one-by-one.

To program computers, we need tools that allow us to describe processes precisely and succinctly. Since the procedures are carried out by a machine, every step needs to be described; we cannot rely on the operator having "common sense" (for example, to know how to fill the coffeemaker with water without explaining that water comes from a faucet, and how to turn the faucet on). Instead, we need mechanical procedures that can be followed without any thinking.

computer

A *computer* is a machine that can:

1. Accept input. Input could be entered by a human typing at a keyboard, received over a network, or provided automatically by sensors attached to the computer.
2. Execute a mechanical procedure, that is, a procedure where each step can be executed without any thought.
3. Produce output. Output could be data displayed to a human, but it could also be anything that effects the world outside the computer such as electrical signals that control how a device operates.

A computer terminal is not some clunky old television with a typewriter in front of it. It is an interface where the mind and body can connect with the universe and move bits of it about.
Douglas Adams

Computers exist in a wide range of forms, and thousands of computers are hidden in devices we use everyday but don't think of as computers such as cars, phones, TVs, microwave ovens, and access cards. Our primary focus is on *universal computers,* which are computers that can perform *all* possible mechanical computations on discrete inputs except for practical limits on space and time. The next section explains what it discrete inputs means; Chapters 6 and 12 explore more deeply what it means for a computer to be universal.

1.2 Measuring Computing Power

For physical machines, we can compare the power of different machines by measuring the amount of mechanical work they can perform within a given amount of time. This power can be captured with units like *horsepower* and *watt.* Physical power is not a very useful measure of computing power, though, since the amount of computing achieved for the same amount of energy varies greatly. Energy is consumed when a computer operates, but consuming energy is not the purpose of using a computer.

Two properties that measure the power of a computing machine are:

1. *How much information* it can process?
2. *How fast* can it process?

We defer considering the second property until Part II, but consider the first question here.

1.2.1 Information

information

Informally, we use *information* to mean knowledge. But to understand information quantitatively, as something we can measure, we need a more precise way to think about information.

The way computer scientists measure information is based on how what is known changes as a result of obtaining the information. The primary unit of information is a *bit*. *One bit* of information *halves* the amount of uncertainty. It is equivalent to answering a "yes" or "no" question, where either answer is equally likely beforehand. Before learning the answer, there were two possibilities; after learning the answer, there is one.

bit

We call a question with two possible answers a *binary question*. Since a bit can have two possible values, we often represent the values as **0** and 1.

binary question

For example, suppose we perform a fair coin toss but do not reveal the result. Half of the time, the coin will land "heads", and the other half of the time the coin will land "tails". Without knowing any more information, our chances of guessing the correct answer are $\frac{1}{2}$. One bit of information would be enough to convey either "heads" or "tails"; we can use **0** to represent "heads" and 1 to represent "tails". So, the amount of information in a coin toss is one bit.

Similarly, one bit can distinguish between the values 0 and 1:

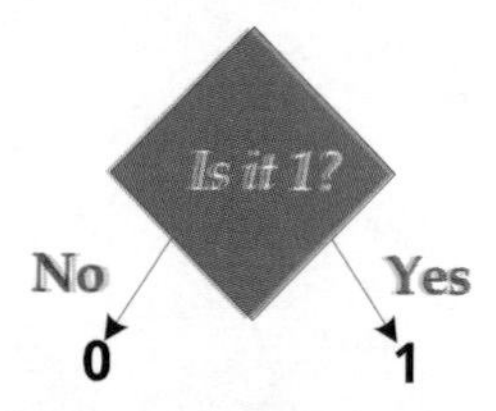

Example 1.1: Dice

How many bits of information are there in the outcome of tossing a six-sided die?

There are six equally likely possible outcomes, so without any more information we have a one in six chance of guessing the correct value. One bit is not enough to identify the actual number, since one bit can only distinguish between two values. We could use five binary questions like this:

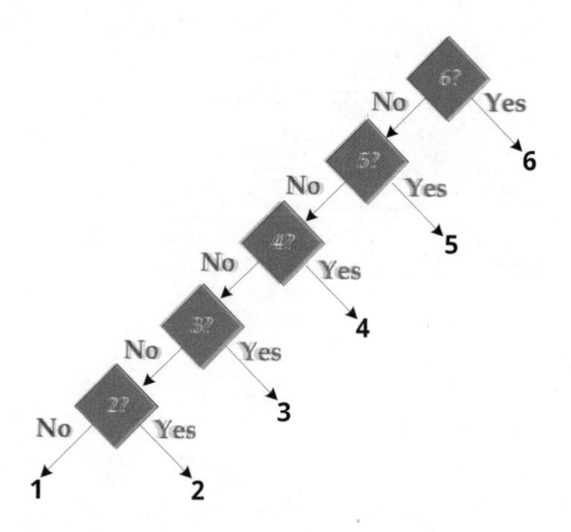

This is quite inefficient, though, since we need up to five questions to identify the value (and on average, expect to need $3\frac{1}{3}$ questions). Can we identify the value with fewer than 5 questions?

Our goal is to identify questions where the "yes" and "no" answers are equally likely—that way, each answer provides the most information possible. This is not the case if we start with, "Is the value 6?", since that answer is expected to be "yes" only one time in six. Instead, we should start with a question like, "Is the value at least 4?". Here, we expect the answer to be "yes" one half of the time, and the "yes" and "no" answers are equally likely. If the answer is "yes", we know the result is 4, 5, or 6. With two more bits, we can distinguish between these three values (note that two bits is actually enough to distinguish among *four* different values, so some information is wasted here). Similarly, if the answer to the first question is no, we know the result is 1, 2, or 3. We need two more bits to distinguish which of the three values it is. Thus, with three bits, we can distinguish all six possible outcomes.

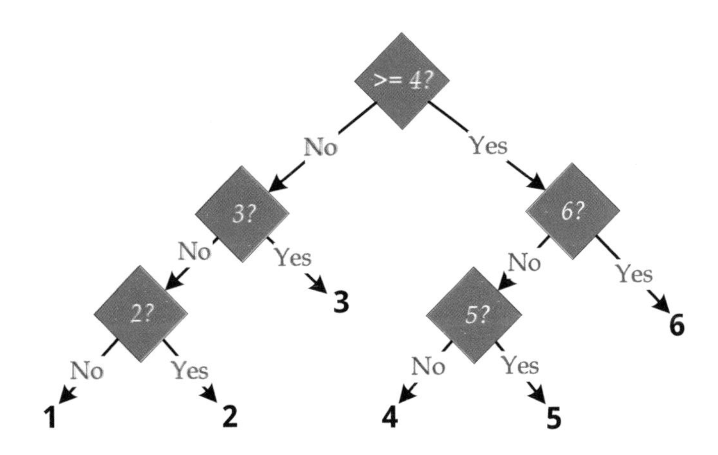

Three bits can convey more information that just six possible outcomes, however. In the binary question tree, there are some questions where the answer is not equally likely to be "yes" and "no" (for example, we expect the answer to "Is the value 3?" to be "yes" only one out of three times). Hence, we are not obtaining a full bit of information with each question.

Each bit doubles the number of possibilities we can distinguish, so with three bits we can distinguish between $2 * 2 * 2 = 8$ possibilities. In general, with n bits, we can distinguish between 2^n possibilities. Conversely, distinguishing among k possible values requires $\log_2 k$ bits. The *logarithm* is defined such that if $a = b^c$ then $\log_b a = c$. Since each bit has two possibilities, we use the logarithm base 2 to determine the number of bits needed to distinguish among a set of distinct possibilities. For our six-sided die, $\log_2 6 \approx 2.58$, so we need approximately 2.58 binary questions. But, questions are discrete: we can't ask 0.58 of a question, so we need to use three binary questions.

logarithm

Trees. Figure 1.1 depicts a structure of binary questions for distinguishing among eight values. We call this structure a *binary tree*. We will see many useful applications of tree-like structures in this book.

binary tree

Computer scientists draw trees upside down. The *root* is the top of the tree, and the *leaves* are the numbers at the bottom (0, 1, 2, ..., 7). There is a unique path from the root of the tree to each leaf. Thus, we can describe each of the eight possible values using the answers to the questions down the tree. For example, if the answers are "No", "No", and "No", we reach the leaf 0; if the answers are "Yes", "No", "Yes", we reach the leaf 5. Since there are no more than two possible answers for each node, we call this a *binary* tree.

We can describe any non-negative integer using bits in this way, by just adding additional levels to the tree. For example, if we wanted to distinguish between 16 possible numbers, we would add a new question, "Is is $>= 8$?" to the top of the tree. If the answer is "No", we use the tree in Figure 1.1 to distinguish numbers between 0 and 7. If the answer is "Yes", we use a tree similar to the one in Figure 1.1, but add 8 to each of the numbers in the questions and the leaves.

depth The *depth* of a tree is the length of the longest path from the root to any leaf. The example tree has depth three. A binary tree of depth d can distinguish up to 2^d different values.

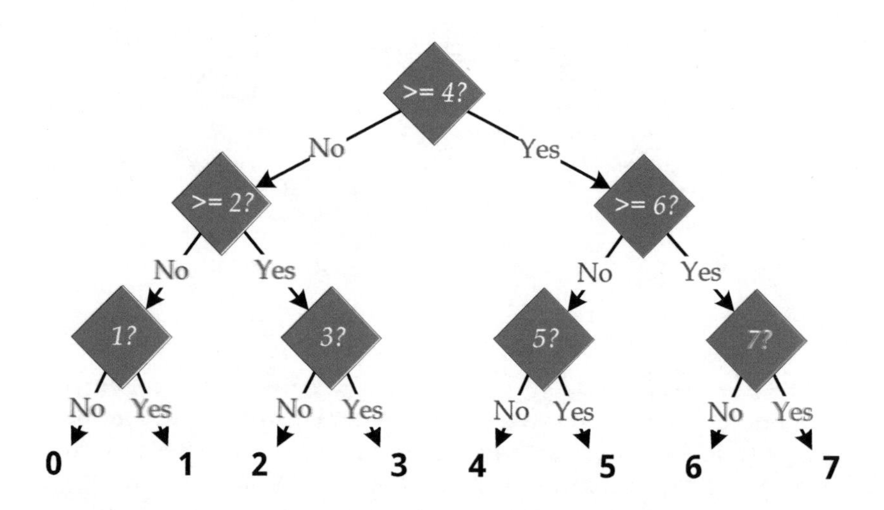

Figure 1.1. Using three bits to distinguish eight possible values.

Units of Information. One *byte* is defined as eight bits. Hence, one byte of information corresponds to eight binary questions, and can distinguish among 2^8 (256) different values. For larger amounts of information, we use metric prefixes, but instead of scaling by factors of 1000 they scale by factors of 2^{10} (1024). Hence, one *kilobyte* is 1024 bytes; one *megabyte* is 2^{20} (approximately one million) bytes; one *gigabyte* is 2^{30} (approximately one billion) bytes; and one *terabyte* is 2^{40} (approximately one trillion) bytes.

Exercise 1.1. Draw a binary tree with the minimum possible depth to:

a. Distinguish among the numbers $0, 1, 2, \ldots, 15$.

b. Distinguish among the 12 months of the year.

Exercise 1.2. How many bits are needed:

a. To uniquely identify any currently living human?

b. To uniquely identify any human who ever lived?

c. To identify any location on Earth within one square centimeter?

d. To uniquely identify any atom in the observable universe?

Exercise 1.3. The examples all use binary questions for which there are two possible answers. Suppose instead of basing our decisions on bits, we based it on *trits* where one trit can distinguish between three equally likely values. For each trit, we can ask a ternary question (a question with three possible answers).

a. How many trits are needed to distinguish among eight possible values? (A convincing answer would show a ternary tree with the questions and answers for each node, and argue why it is not possible to distinguish all the values with a tree of lesser depth.)

b. [*] Devise a general formula for converting between bits and trits. How many trits does it require to describe b bits of information?

Exploration 1.1: Guessing Numbers

The guess-a-number game starts with one player (the *chooser*) picking a number between 1 and 100 (inclusive) and secretly writing it down. The other player (the *guesser*) attempts to guess the number. After each guess, the chooser responds with "correct" (the guesser guessed the number and the game is over), "higher" (the actual number is higher than the guess), or "lower" (the actual number is lower than the guess).

a. Explain why the guesser can receive slightly more than one bit of information for each response.

b. Assuming the chooser picks the number randomly (that is, all values between 1 and 100 are equally likely), what are the best first guesses? Explain why these guesses are better than any other guess. (Hint: there are two equally good first guesses.)

c. What is the maximum number of guesses the second player should need to always find the number?

d. What is the average number of guesses needed (assuming the chooser picks the number randomly as before)?

e. [*] Suppose instead of picking randomly, the chooser picks the number with the goal of maximizing the number of guesses the second player will need. What number should she pick?

f. [**] How should the guesser adjust her strategy if she knows the chooser is picking adversarially?

g. [**] What are the best strategies for both players in the adversarial guess-a-number game where chooser's goal is to pick a starting number that maximizes the number of guesses the guesser needs, and the guesser's goal is to guess the number using as few guesses as possible.

Exploration 1.2: Twenty Questions

20Q Game
Image from ThinkGeek

The two-player game *twenty questions* starts with the first player (the *answerer*) thinking of an object, and declaring if the object is an animal, vegetable, or mineral (meant to include all non-living things). After this, the second player (the *questioner*), asks binary questions to try and guess the object the first player thought of. The first player answers each question "yes" or "no". The website http://www.20q.net/ offers a web-based twenty questions game where a human acts as the answerer and the computer as the questioner. The game is also sold as a $10 stand-alone toy (shown in the picture).

a. How many different objects can be distinguished by a perfect questioner for the standard twenty questions game?

b. What does it mean for the questioner to play perfectly?

c. Try playing the 20Q game at http://www.20q.net. Did it guess your item?

d. Instead of just "yes" and "no", the 20Q game offers four different answers: "Yes", "No", "Sometimes", and "Unknown". (The website version of the game also has "Probably", "Irrelevant", and "Doubtful".) If all four answers were equally likely (and meaningful), how many items could be distinguished in 20 questions?

e. For an Animal, the first question 20Q sometimes asks is "Does it jump?" (20Q randomly selected from a few different first questions). Is this a good first question?

f. [★] How many items do you think 20Q has data for?

g. [★★] Speculate on how 20Q could build up its database.

1.2.2 Representing Data

We can use sequences of bits to represent many kinds of data. All we need to do is think of the right binary questions for which the bits give answers that allow us to represent each possible value. Next, we provide examples showing how bits can be used to represent numbers, text, and pictures.

Numbers. In the previous section, we identified a number using a tree where each node asks a binary question and the branches correspond to the "Yes" and "No" answers. A more compact way of writing down our decisions following the tree is to use 0 to encode a "No" answer, and 1 to encode a "Yes" answer and describe a path to a leaf by a sequence of 0s and 1s—the "No", "No", "No" path to 0 is encoded as 000, and the "Yes", "No", "Yes" path to 5 is encoded as 101. This is known as the *binary number system*. Whereas the decimal number system uses ten as its base (there are ten decimal digits, and the positional values increase as powers of ten), the binary system uses two as its base (there are two binary digits, and the positional values increase as powers of two).

binary number system

There are only 10 types of people in the world: those who understand binary, and those who don't.
Infamous T-Shirt

For example, the binary number 10010110 represents the decimal value 150:

Binary:	1	0	0	1	0	1	1	0
Value:	2^7	2^6	2^5	2^4	2^3	2^2	2^1	2^0
Decimal Value:	128	64	32	16	8	4	2	1

As in the decimal number system, the value of each binary digit depends on its position.

By using more bits, we can represent larger numbers. With enough bits, we can represent any natural number this way. The more bits we have, the larger the set of possible numbers we can represent. As we saw with the binary decision trees, n bits can be used to represent 2^n different numbers.

Discrete Values. We can use a finite sequence of bits to describe *any* value that is selected from a *countable* set of possible values. A set is *countable* if there is a way to assign a unique natural number to each element of the set. All finite sets are countable. Some, but not all, infinite sets are countable. For example, there appear to be more integers than there are natural numbers since for each natural number, n, there are two corresponding integers, n and $-n$. But, the integers are in fact countable. We can enumerate the integers as: $0, 1, -1, 2, -2, 3, -3, 4, -4, \ldots$ and assign a unique natural number to each integer in turn.

countable

Other sets, such as the real numbers, are uncountable. Georg Cantor proved this using a technique known as *diagonalization*. Suppose the real numbers are enumerable. This means we could list all the real numbers in order, so we could assign a unique integer to each number. For example, considering just the real numbers between 0 and 1, our enumeration might be:

diagonalization

1	.00000000000000 . . .
2	.25000000000000 . . .
3	.33333333333333 . . .
4	.6666666666666 . . .
. . .	. . .
57236	.141592653589793 . . .
. . .	. . .

Cantor proved by contradiction that there is no way to enumerate all the real numbers. The trick is to produce a new real number that is not part of the enumeration. We can do this by constructing a number whose first digit is different from the first digit of the first number, whose second digit is different from the second digit of the second number, etc. For the example enumeration above, we might choose .1468....

The kth digit of the constructed number is different from the kth digit of the number k in the enumeration. Since the constructed number differs in at least one digit from every enumerated number, it does not match any of the enumerated numbers exactly. Thus, there is a real number that is not included in the enumeration list, and it is impossible to enumerate all the real numbers.[1]

Digital computers[2] operate on inputs that are discrete values. Continuous values, such as real numbers, can only be approximated by computers. Next, we

[1]Alert readers should be worried that this isn't quite correct since the resulting number may be a different way to represent the same real number (for example, .1999999999999 . . . = .20000000000 . . . even though they differ in each digit). This technical problem can be fixed by placing some restrictions on how the modified digits are chosen to avoid infinite repetitions.

[2]This is, indeed, part of the definition of a digital computer. An *analog computer* operates on continuous values. In Chapter 6, we explain more of the inner workings of a computer and why nearly all computers today are digital. We use *computer* to mean a *digital computer* in this book. The property that there are more real numbers than natural numbers has important implications for what can and cannot be computed, which we return to in Chapter 12.

consider how two types of data, text and images, can be represented by computers. The first type, text, is discrete and can be represented exactly; images are continuous, and can only be represented approximately.

Text. The set of all possible sequences of characters is countable. One way to see this is to observe that we could give each possible text fragment a unique number, and then use that number to identify the item. For example we could enumerate all texts alphabetically by length (here, we limit the characters to lowercase letters): a, b, c, . . ., z, aa, ab, . . ., az, ba, . . ., zz, aaa, . . .

Since we have seen that we can represent all the natural numbers with a sequence of bits, so once we have the mapping between each item in the set and a unique natural number, we can represent all of the items in the set. For the representation to be useful, though, we usually need a way to construct the corresponding number for any item directly.

So, instead of enumerating a mapping between all possible character sequences and the natural numbers, we need a process for converting any text to a unique number that represents that text. Suppose we limit our text to characters in the standard English alphabet. If we include lower-case letters (26), upper-case letters (26), and punctuation (space, comma, period, newline, semi-colon), we have 57 different symbols to represent. We can assign a unique number to each symbol, and encode the corresponding number with six bits (this leaves seven values unused since six bits can distinguish 64 values). For example, we could encode using the mapping shown in Table 1.1. The first bit answers the question: "Is it an uppercase letter after **F** or a special character?". When the first bit is 0, the second bit answers the question: "Is it after **p**?".

a	000000
b	000001
c	000010
d	000011
...	...
p	001111
q	010000
...	...
z	011001

A	011010
B	011011
C	011100
...	...
F	011111
G	100000
...	...
Y	110010
Z	110011

space	110100
,	110101
.	110110
newline	110111
;	111000
unused	111001
...	...
unused	111110
unused	111111

Table 1.1. Encoding characters using bits.

This is one way to encode the alphabet, but not the one typically used by computers. One commonly used encoding known as ASCII (the American Standard Code for Information Interchange) uses seven bits so that 128 different symbols can be encoded. The extra symbols are used to encode more special characters.

Once we have a way of mapping each individual letter to a fixed-length bit sequence, we could write down any sequence of letters by just concatenating the bits encoding each letter. So, the text CS is encoded as 011100 101100. We could write down text of length n that is written in the 57-symbol alphabet using this encoding using $6n$ bits. To convert the number back into text, just invert the mapping by replacing each group of six bits with the corresponding letter.

Rich Data. We can also use bit sequences to represent complex data like pictures, movies, and audio recordings. First, consider a simple black and white picture:

Since the picture is divided into discrete squares known as *pixels*, we could encode this as a sequence of bits by using one bit to encode the color of each pixel (for example, using 1 to represent black, and 0 to represent white). This image is 16x16, so has 256 pixels total. We could represent the image using a sequence of 256 bits (starting from the top left corner):

pixel

```
0000011111100000
0000100000010000
0011000000001100
0010000000000100
       ...
0000011111100000
```

What about complex pictures that are not divided into discrete squares or a fixed number of colors, like Van Gogh's *Starry Night*?

Different wavelengths of electromagnetic radiation have different colors. For example, light with wavelengths between 625 and 730 nanometers appears red. But, each wavelength of light has a slightly different color; for example, light with wavelength 650 nanometers would be a different color (albeit imperceptible to humans) from light of wavelength 650.0000001 nanometers. There are arguably infinitely many different colors, corresponding to different wavelengths of visible light.[3] Since the colors are continuous and not discrete, there is no way to map each color to a unique, finite bit sequence.

[3]Whether there are actually infinitely many different colors comes down to the question of whether the space-time of the universe is continuous or discrete. Certainly in our common perception it seems to be continuous—we can imagine dividing any length into two shorter lengths. In reality, this may not be the case at extremely tiny scales. It is not known if time can continue to be subdivided below 10^{-40} of a second.

On the other hand, the human eye and brain have limits. We cannot actually perceive infinitely many different colors; at some point the wavelengths are close enough that we cannot distinguish them. Ability to distinguish colors varies, but most humans can perceive only a few million different colors. The set of colors that can be distinguished by a typical human is finite; any finite set is countable, so we can map each distinguishable color to a unique bit sequence.

A common way to represent color is to break it into its three primary components (red, green, and blue), and record the intensity of each component. The more bits available to represent a color, the more different colors that can be represented.

Thus, we can represent a picture by recording the approximate color at each point. If space in the universe is continuous, there are infinitely many points. But, as with color, once the points get smaller than a certain size they are imperceptible. We can approximate the picture by dividing the canvas into small regions and sampling the average color of each region. The smaller the sample regions, the more bits we will have and the more detail that will be visible in the image. With enough bits to represent color, and enough sample points, we can represent any image as a sequence of bits.

Summary. We can use sequences of bits to represent any natural number exactly, and hence, represent any member of a countable set using a sequence of bits. The more bits we use the more different values that can be represented; with n bits we can represent 2^n different values.

We can also use sequences of bits to represent rich data like images, audio, and video. Since the world we are trying to represent is continuous there are infinitely many possible values, and we cannot represent these objects exactly with any finite sequence of bits. However, since human perception is limited, with enough bits we can represent any of these adequately well. Finding ways to represent data that are both efficient and easy to manipulate and interpret is a constant challenge in computing. Manipulating sequences of bits is awkward, so we need ways of thinking about bit-level representations of data at higher levels of abstraction. Chapter 5 focuses on ways to manage complex data.

1.2.3 Growth of Computing Power

The number of bits a computer can store gives an upper limit on the amount of information it can process. Looking at the number of bits different computers can store over time gives us a rough indication of how computing power has increased. Here, we consider two machines: the Apollo Guidance Computer and a modern laptop.

The Apollo Guidance Computer was developed in the early 1960s to control the flight systems of the Apollo spacecraft. It might be considered the first *personal computer*, since it was designed to be used in real-time by a single operator (an astronaut in the Apollo capsule). Most earlier computers required a full room, and were far too expensive to be devoted to a single user; instead, they processed jobs submitted by many users in turn. Since the Apollo Guidance Computer was designed to fit in the Apollo capsule, it needed to be small and light. Its volume was about a cubic foot and it weighed 70 pounds. The AGC was the first computer built using integrated circuits, miniature electronic circuits that can perform simple logical operations such as performing the logical *and*

AGC User Interface

of two values. The AGC used about 4000 integrated circuits, each one being able to perform a single logical operation and costing $1000. The AGC consumed a significant fraction of all integrated circuits produced in the mid-1960s, and the project spurred the growth of the integrated circuit industry.

The AGC had 552 960 bits of memory (of which only 61 440 bits were modifiable, the rest were fixed). The smallest USB flash memory you can buy today (from SanDisk in December 2008) is the 1 gigabyte Cruzer for $9.99; 1 gigabyte (GB) is 2^{30} bytes or approximately 8.6 billion bits, about 140 000 times the amount of memory in the AGC (and all of the Cruzer memory is modifiable). A typical low-end laptop today has 2 gigabytes of RAM (fast memory close to the processor that loses its state when the machine is turned off) and 250 gigabytes of hard disk memory (slow memory that persists when the machine is turned off); for under $600 today we get a computer with over 4 million times the amount of memory the AGC had.

Moore's law is a violation of Murphy's law. Everything gets better and better.
Gordon Moore

Improving by a factor of 4 million corresponds to doubling just over 22 times. The amount of computing power approximately doubled every two years between the AGC in the early 1960s and a modern laptop today (2009). This property of exponential improvement in computing power is known as *Moore's Law*. Gordon Moore, a co-founder of Intel, observed in 1965 than the number of components that can be built in integrated circuits for the same cost was approximately doubling every year (revisions to Moore's observation have put the doubling rate at approximately 18 months instead of one year). This progress has been driven by the growth of the computing industry, increasing the resources available for designing integrated circuits. Another driver is that today's technology is used to design the next technology generation. Improvement in computing power has followed this exponential growth remarkably closely over the past 40 years, although there is no law that this growth must continue forever.

Although our comparison between the AGC and a modern laptop shows an impressive factor of 4 million improvement, it is much slower than Moore's law would suggest. Instead of 22 doublings in power since 1963, there should have been 30 doublings (using the 18 month doubling rate). This would produce an improvement of one billion times instead of just 4 million. The reason is our comparison is very unequal relative to cost: the AGC was the world's most expensive small computer of its time, reflecting many millions of dollars of government funding. Computing power available for similar funding today is well over a billion times more powerful than the AGC.

1.3 Science, Engineering, and the Liberal Arts

Much ink and many bits have been spent debating whether computer science is an art, an engineering discipline, or a science. The confusion stems from the nature of computing as a new field that does not fit well into existing silos. In fact, computer science fits into all three kingdoms, and it is useful to approach computing from all three perspectives.

Science. Traditional science is about understanding nature through observation. The goal of science is to develop general and predictive theories that allow us to understand aspects of nature deeply enough to make accurate quantitative predications. For example, Newton's law of universal gravitation makes predictions about how masses will move. The more general a theory is the better. A key, as yet unachieved, goal of science is to find a universal law that can describe all physical behavior at scales from the smallest subparticle to the entire universe, and all the bosons, muons, dark matter, black holes, and galaxies in between. Science deals with real things (like bowling balls, planets, and electrons) and attempts to make progress toward theories that predict increasingly precisely how these real things will behave in different situations.

Computer science focuses on artificial things like numbers, graphs, functions, and lists. Instead of dealing with physical things in the real world, computer science concerns abstract things in a virtual world. The numbers we use in computations often represent properties of physical things in the real world, and with enough bits we can model real things with arbitrary precision. But, since our focus is on abstract, artificial things rather than physical things, computer science is not a traditional natural science but a more abstract field like mathematics. Like mathematics, computing is an essential tool for modern science, but when we study computing on artificial things it is not a natural science itself.

In a deeper sense, computing pervades all of nature. A long term goal of computer science is to develop theories that explain how nature computes. One example of computing in nature comes from biology. Complex life exists because nature can perform sophisticated computing. People sometimes describe DNA as a "blueprint", but it is really much better thought of as a program. Whereas a blueprint describes what a building should be when it is finished, giving the dimensions of walls and how they fit together, the DNA of an organism encodes a process for growing that organism. A human genome is not a blueprint that describes the body plan of a human, it is a program that turns a single cell into a complex human given the appropriate environment. The process of evolution (which itself is an information process) produces new programs, and hence new species, through the process of natural selection on mutated DNA sequences. Understanding how both these processes work is one of the most interesting and important open scientific questions, and it involves deep questions in computer science, as well as biology, chemistry, and physics.

The questions we consider in this book focus on the question of what can and cannot be computed. This is both a theoretical question (what can be computed by a given theoretical model of a computer) and a pragmatic one (what can be computed by physical machines we can build today, as well as by anything possible in our universe).

Scientists study the world as it is; engineers create the world that never has been.
Theodore von Kármán

Engineering. Engineering is about making useful things. Engineering is often distinguished from crafts in that engineers use scientific principles to create their designs, and focus on designing under practical constraints. As William Wulf and George Fisher put it:[4]

> *Whereas science is analytic in that it strives to understand nature, or what is, engineering is synthetic in that it strives to create. Our own favorite description of what engineers do is "design under constraint". Engineering is creativity constrained by nature, by cost, by concerns of safety, environmental impact, ergonomics, reliability, manufacturability, maintainability–the whole long list of such "ilities". To be sure, the realities of nature is one of the constraint sets we work under, but it is far from the only one, it is*

[4]William Wulf and George Fisher, A Makeover for Engineering Education, *Issues in Science and Technology*, Spring 2002 (http://www.issues.org/18.3/p_wulf.html).

seldom the hardest one, and almost never the limiting one.

Computer scientists do not typically face the natural constraints faced by civil and mechanical engineers—computer programs are massless and not exposed to the weather, so programmers do not face the kinds of physical constraints like gravity that impose limits on bridge designers. As we saw from the Apollo Guidance Computer comparison, practical constraints on computing power change rapidly — the one billion times improvement in computing power is unlike any change in physical materials[5]. Although we may need to worry about manufacturability and maintainability of storage media (such as the disk we use to store a program), our focus as computer scientists is on the abstract bits themselves, not how they are stored.

Computer scientists, however, do face many constraints. A primary constraint is the capacity of the human mind—there is a limit to how much information a human can keep in mind at one time. As computing systems get more complex, there is no way for a human to understand the entire system at once. To build complex systems, we need techniques for managing complexity. The primary tool computer scientists use to manage complexity is *abstraction*. Abstraction is a way of giving a name to something in a way that allows us to hide unnecessary details. By using carefully designed abstractions, we can construct complex systems with reliable properties while limiting the amount of information a human designer needs to keep in mind at any one time.

abstraction

Liberal Arts. The notion of the *liberal arts* emerged during the middle ages to distinguish education for the purpose of expanding the intellects of free people from the *illiberal arts* such as medicine and carpentry that were pursued for economic purposes. The liberal arts were intended for people who did not need to learn an art to make a living, but instead had the luxury to pursue purely intellectual activities for their own sake. The traditional seven liberal arts started with the *Trivium* (three roads), focused on language:[6]

- Grammar — "the art of inventing symbols and combining them to express thought"
- Rhetoric — "the art of communicating thought from one mind to another, the adaptation of language to circumstance"
- Logic — "the art of thinking"

The Trivium was followed by the *Quadrivium*, focused on numbers:

- Arithmetic — "theory of number"
- Geometry — "theory of space"
- Music — "application of the theory of number"
- Astronomy — "application of the theory of space"

All of these have strong connections to computer science, and we will touch on each of them to some degree in this book.

I must study politics and war that my sons may have liberty to study mathematics and philosophy. My sons ought to study mathematics and philosophy, geography, natural history, naval architecture, navigation, commerce, and agriculture, in order to give their children a right to study painting, poetry, music, architecture, statuary, tapestry, and porcelain.
John Adams, 1780

Language is essential to computing since we use the tools of language to describe information processes. The next chapter discusses the structure of language and throughout this book we consider how to efficiently use and combine

[5]For example, the highest strength density material available today, carbon nanotubes, are perhaps 300 times stronger than the best material available 50 years ago.

[6] The quotes defining each liberal art are from Miriam Joseph (edited by Marguerite McGlinn), *The Trivium: The Liberal Arts of Logic, Grammar, and Rhetoric*, Paul Dry Books, 2002.

symbols to express meanings. Rhetoric encompasses communicating thoughts between minds. In computing, we are not typically communicating directly between minds, but we see many forms of communication between entities: interfaces between components of a program, as well as protocols used to enable multiple computing systems to communicate (for example, the HTTP protocol defines how a web browser and web server interact), and communication between computer programs and human users. The primary tool for understanding what computer programs mean, and hence, for constructing programs with particular meanings, is logic. Hence, the traditional trivium liberal arts of language and logic permeate computer science.

The connections between computing and the quadrivium arts are also pervasive. We have already seen how computers use sequences of bits to represent numbers. Chapter 6 examines how machines can perform basic arithmetic operations. Geometry is essential for computer graphics, and graph theory is also important for computer networking. The harmonic structures in music have strong connections to the recursive definitions introduced in Chapter 4 and recurring throughout this book.[7] Unlike the other six liberal arts, astronomy is not directly connected to computing, but computing is an essential tool for doing modern astronomy.

Although learning about computing qualifies as an illiberal art (that is, it can have substantial economic benefits for those who learn it well), computer science also covers at least six of the traditional seven liberal arts.

1.4 Summary and Roadmap

Computer scientists think about problems differently. When confronted with a problem, a computer scientist does not just attempt to solve it. Instead, computer scientists think about a problem as a mapping between its inputs and desired outputs, develop a systematic sequence of steps for solving the problem for any possible input, and consider how the number of steps required to solve the problem scales as the input size increases.

The rest of this book presents a whirlwind introduction to computer science. We do not cover any topics in great depth, but rather provide a broad picture of what computer science is, how to think like a computer scientist, and how to solve problems.

Part I: Defining Procedures. Part I focuses on how to define procedures that perform desired computations. The nature of the computer forces solutions to be expressed precisely in a language the computer can interpret. This means a computer scientist needs to understand how languages work and exactly what phrases in a language mean. Natural languages like English are too complex and inexact for this, so we need to invent and use new languages that are simpler, more structured, and less ambiguously defined than natural languages. Chapter 2 focuses on language, and during the course of this book we will use language to precisely describe processes and languages are interpreted.

The computer frees humans from having to actually carry out the steps needed to solve the problem. Without complaint, boredom, or rebellion, it dutifully ex-

[7] See Douglas Hofstadter's *Gödel, Escher, Bach* for lots of interesting examples of connections between computing and music.

ecutes the exact steps the program specifies. And it executes them at a remarkable rate — billions of simple steps in each second on a typical laptop. This changes not just the time it takes to solve a problem, but qualitatively changes the kinds of problems we can solve, and the kinds of solutions worth considering. Problems like sequencing the human genome, simulating the global climate, and making a photomosaic not only could not have been solved without computing, but perhaps could not have even been envisioned. Chapter 3 introduces programming, and Chapter 4 develops some techniques for constructing programs that solve problems. To represent more interesting problems, we need ways to manage more complex data. Chapter 5 concludes Part I by exploring ways to represent data and define procedures that operate on complex data.

Part II: Analyzing Procedures. Part II considers the problem of estimating the cost required to execute a procedure. This requires understanding how machines can compute (Chapter 6), and mathematical tools for reasoning about how cost grows with the size of the inputs to a procedure (Chapter 7). Chapter 8 provides some extended examples that apply these techniques.

Part III: Improving Expressiveness. The techniques from Part I and II are sufficient for describing all computations. Our goal, however, it to be able to define concise, elegant, and efficient procedures for performing desired computations. Part III presents techniques that enable more expressive procedures.

Part IV: The Limits of Computing. We hope that by the end of Part III, readers will feel confident that they could program a computer to do just about anything. In Part IV, we consider the question of what can and cannot be done by a mechanical computer. A large class of interesting problems cannot be solved by any computer, even with unlimited time and space.

Themes. Much of the book will revolve around three very powerful ideas that are prevalent throughout computing:

Recursive definitions. A recursive definition define a thing in terms of smaller instances of itself. A simple example is defining your ancestors as (1) your parents, and (2) the ancestors of your ancestors. Recursive definitions can define an infinitely large set with a small description. They also provide a powerful technique for solving problems by breaking a problem into solving a simple instance of the problem and showing how to solve a larger instance of the problem by using a solution to a smaller instance. We use recursive definitions to define infinite languages in Chapter 2, to solve problems in Chapter 4, to build complex data structures in Chapter 5. In later chapters, we see how language interpreters themselves can be defined recursively.

Universality. Computers are distinguished from other machines in that their behavior can be changed by a program. Procedures themselves can be described using just bits, so we can write procedures that process procedures as inputs and that generate procedures as outputs. Considering procedures as data is both a powerful problem solving tool, and a useful way of thinking about the power and fundamental limits of computing. We introduce the use of procedures as inputs and outputs in Chapter 4, see how generated procedures can be packaged with state to model objects in Chapter 10. One of the most fundamental results in computing is that any machine that can perform a few simple operations is powerful enough to perform any computation, and in this deep sense, all mechanical computers are equivalent. We introduce a model of computation in Chapter 6, and reason about the limits of computation in Chapter 12.

Abstraction. Abstraction is a way of hiding details by giving things names. We use abstraction to manage complexity. Good abstractions hide unnecessary details so they can be used to build complex systems without needing to understand all the details of the abstraction at once. We introduce procedural abstraction in Chapter 4, data abstraction in Chapter 5, abstraction using objects in Chapter 10, and many other examples of abstraction throughout this book.

Throughout this book, these three themes will recur recursively, universally, and abstractly as we explore the art and science of how to instruct computing machines to perform useful tasks, reason about the resources needed to execute a particular procedure, and understand the fundamental and practical limits on what computers can do.

2

Language

Belittle! What an expression! It may be an elegant one in Virginia, and even perfectly intelligible; but for our part, all we can do is to guess at its meaning. For shame, Mr. Jefferson!
European Magazine and London Review, 1787
(reviewing Thomas Jefferson's *Notes on the State of Virginia*)

The most powerful tool we have for communication is language. This is true whether we are considering communication between two humans, between a human programmer and a computer, or between a network of computers. In computing, we use language to describe procedures and use machines to turn descriptions of procedures into executing processes. This chapter is about what language is, how language works, and ways to define languages.

2.1 Surface Forms and Meanings

A *language* is a set of surface forms and meanings, and a mapping between the surface forms and their associated meanings. In the earliest human languages, the surface forms were sounds but surface forms can be anything that can be perceived by the communicating parties such as drum beats, hand gestures, or pictures.

language

A *natural language* is a language spoken by humans, such as English or Swahili. Natural languages are very complex since they have evolved over many thousands years of individual and cultural interaction. We focus on *designed* languages that are created by humans for some a specific purpose such as for expressing procedures to be executed by computers.

natural language

We focus on languages where the surface forms are text. In a textual language, the surface forms are linear sequences of characters. A *string* is a sequence of zero or more characters. Each character is a symbol drawn from a finite set known as an *alphabet*. For English, the alphabet is the set $\{a, b, c, \ldots, z\}$ (for the full language, capital letters, numerals, and punctuation symbols are also needed).

string

alphabet

A simple communication system can be described using a table of surface forms and their associated meanings. For example, this table describes a communication system between traffic lights and drivers:

Surface Form	Meaning
Green	Go
Yellow	Caution
Red	Stop

Communication systems involving humans are notoriously imprecise and subjective. A driver and a police officer may disagree on the actual meaning of the *Yellow* symbol, and may even disagree on which symbol is being transmitted by the traffic light at a particular time. Communication systems for computers demand precision: we want to know what our programs will do, so it is important that every step they make is understood precisely and unambiguously.

The method of defining a communication system by listing a table of

$$< \textit{Symbol, Meaning} >$$

pairs can work adequately only for trivial communication systems. The number of possible meanings that can be expressed is limited by the number of entries in the table. It is impossible to express any *new* meaning since all meanings must already be listed in the table!

Languages and Infinity. A useful language must be able to express *infinitely* many different meanings. Hence, there must be a way to generate new surface forms and guess their meanings (see Exercise 2.1). No finite representation, such as a printed table, can contain all the surface forms and meanings in an infinite language. One way to generate infinitely large sets is to use repeating patterns. For example, most humans would interpret the notation: "1, 2, 3, ..." as the set of all natural numbers. We interpret the "..." as meaning keep doing the same thing for ever. In this case, it means keep adding one to the preceding number. Thus, with only a few numbers and symbols we can describe a set containing infinitely many numbers. As discussed in Section 1.2.1, the language of the natural numbers is enough to encode all meanings in any countable set. But, finding a sensible mapping between most meanings and numbers is nearly impossible. The surface forms do not correspond closely enough to the ideas we want to express to be a useful language.

2.2 Language Construction

To define more expressive infinite languages, we need a richer system for constructing new surface forms and associated meanings. We need ways to describe languages that allow us to define an infinitely large set of surface forms and meanings with a compact notation. The approach we use is to define a language by defining a set of rules that produce exactly the set of surface forms in the language.

Components of Language. A language is composed of:

- *primitives* — the smallest units of meaning.
- *means of combination* — rules for building new language elements by combining simpler ones.

The primitives are the smallest meaningful units (in natural languages these are known as *morphemes*). A primitive cannot be broken into smaller parts whose meanings can be combined to produce the meaning of the unit. The means of combination are rules for building words from primitives, and for building phrases and sentences from words.

Since we have rules for producing new words not all words are primitives. For example, we can create a new word by adding *anti-* in front of an existing word.

The meaning of the new word can be inferred as "against the meaning of the original word". Rules like this one mean anyone can invent a new word, and use it in communication in ways that will probably be understood by listeners who have never heard the word before.

For example, the verb *freeze* means to pass from a liquid state to a solid state; *antifreeze* is a substance designed to prevent freezing. English speakers who know the meaning of *freeze* and *anti-* could roughly guess the meaning of *antifreeze* even if they have never heard the word before.[1]

Primitives are the smallest units of *meaning*, not based on the surface forms. Both *anti* and *freeze* are primitive; they cannot be broken into smaller parts with meaning. We can break *anti-* into two syllables, or four letters, but those sub-components do not have meanings that could be combined to produce the meaning of the primitive.

Means of Abstraction. In addition to primitives and means of combination, powerful languages have an additional type of component that enables economic communication: *means of abstraction.*

Means of abstraction allow us to give a simple name to a complex entity. In English, the means of abstraction are *pronouns* like "she", "it", and "they". The meaning of a pronoun depends on the context in which it is used. It abstracts a complex meaning with a simple word. For example, the *it* in the previous sentence abstracts "the meaning of a pronoun", but the *it* in the sentence before that one abstracts "a pronoun".

In natural languages, there are a limited number of means of abstraction. English, in particular, has a very limited set of pronouns for abstracting people. It has *she* and *he* for abstracting a female or male person, respectively, but no gender-neutral pronouns for abstracting a person of either sex. The interpretation of what a pronoun abstract in natural languages is often confusing. For example, it is unclear what the *it* in this sentence refers to. Languages for programming computers need means of abstraction that are both powerful and unambiguous.

Exercise 2.1. According to the *Guinness Book of World Records*, the longest word in the English language is *floccinaucinihilipilification*, meaning "The act or habit of describing or regarding something as worthless". This word was reputedly invented by a non-hippopotomonstrosesquipedaliophobic student at Eton who combined four words in his Latin textbook. Prove Guinness wrong by identifying a longer English word. An English speaker (familiar with floccinaucinihilipilification and the morphemes you use) should be able to deduce the meaning of your word.

Exercise 2.2. Merriam-Webster's word for the year for 2006 was *truthiness*, a word invented and popularized by Stephen Colbert. Its definition is, "truth that comes from the gut, not books". Identify the morphemes that are used to build *truthiness*, and explain, based on its composition, what *truthiness* should mean.

[1] Guessing that it is a verb meaning to pass from the solid to liquid state would also be reasonable. This shows how imprecise and ambiguous natural languages are; for programming computers, we need the meanings of constructs to be clearly determined.

Exercise 2.3. According to the Oxford English Dictionary, Thomas Jefferson is the first person to use more than 60 words in the dictionary. Jeffersonian words include: (a) authentication, (b) belittle, (c) indecipherable, (d) inheritability, (e) odometer, (f) sanction, (g) vomit-grass, and (h) shag. For each Jeffersonian word, guess its derivation and explain whether or not its meaning could be inferred from its components.

Dictionaries are but the depositories of words already legitimated by usage. Society is the workshop in which new ones are elaborated. When an individual uses a new word, if ill formed, it is rejected; if well formed, adopted, and after due time, laid up in the depository of dictionaries.
Thomas Jefferson, letter to John Adams, 1820

Exercise 2.4. Embiggening your vocabulary with anticromulent words ecdysiasts can grok.

a. Invent a new English word by combining common morphemes.

b. Get someone else to use the word you invented.

c. [⋆⋆] Convince Merriam-Webster to add your word to their dictionary.

2.3 Recursive Transition Networks

This section describes a more powerful technique for defining languages. The surface forms of a textual language are a (typically infinite) set of strings. To define a language, we need to define a system that produces all strings in the language and no other strings. (The problem of associating meanings with those strings is more difficult; we consider it in later chapters.)

recursive transition network

A *recursive transition network* (RTN) is defined by a graph of nodes and edges. The edges are labeled with output symbols—these are the primitives in the language. The nodes and edge structure provides the means of combination.

One of the nodes is designated the start node (indicated by an arrow pointing into that node). One or more of the nodes may be designated as final nodes (indicated by an inner circle). A string is in the language if there exists some path from the start node to a final node in the graph where the output symbols along the path edges produce the string.

Figure 2.1 shows a simple RTN with three nodes and four edges that can produce four different sentences. Starting at the node marked *Noun*, there are two possible edges to follow. Each edge outputs a different symbol, and leads to the node marked *Verb*. From that node there are two output edges, each leading to the final node marked *S*. Since there are no edges out of *S*, this ends the string. Hence, the RTN can produce four strings corresponding to the four different paths from the start to final node: "Alice jumps", "Alice runs", "Bob jumps", and "Bob runs".

Recursive transition networks are more efficient than listing the strings in a language, since the number of possible strings increases with the number of possible paths through the graph. For example, adding one more edge from *Noun* to

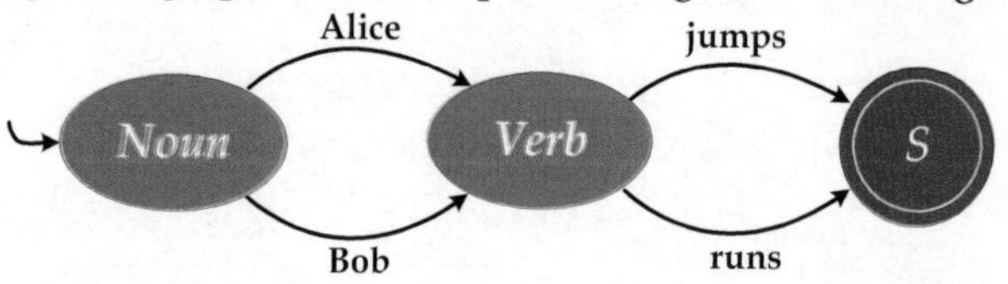

Figure 2.1. Simple recursive transition network.

Verb with label "Colleen" adds two new strings to the language.

The expressive power of recursive transition networks increases dramatically once we add edges that form cycles in the graph. This is where the *recursive* in the name comes from. Once a graph has a cycle, there are *infinitely* many possible paths through the graph!

Consider what happens when we add the single "and" edge to the previous network to produce the network shown in Figure 2.2 below.

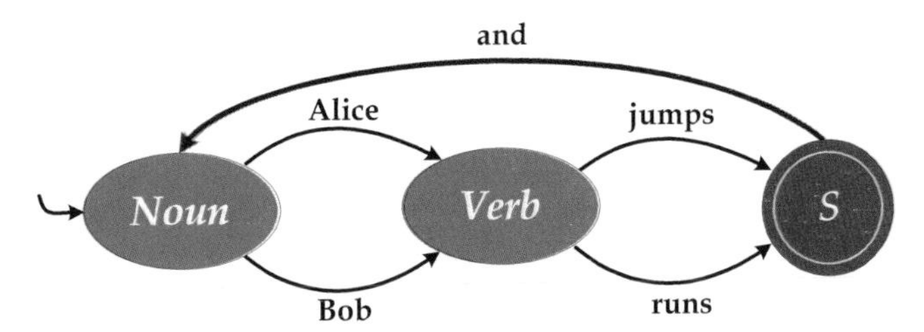

Figure 2.2. RTN with a cycle.

Now, we can produce infinitely many different strings! We can follow the "and" edge back to the *Noun* node to produce strings like "Alice runs and Bob jumps and Alice jumps" with as many conjuncts as we want.

Exercise 2.5. Draw a recursive transition network that defines the language of the whole numbers: 0, 1, 2, . . .

Exercise 2.6. How many different strings can be produced by the RTN below:

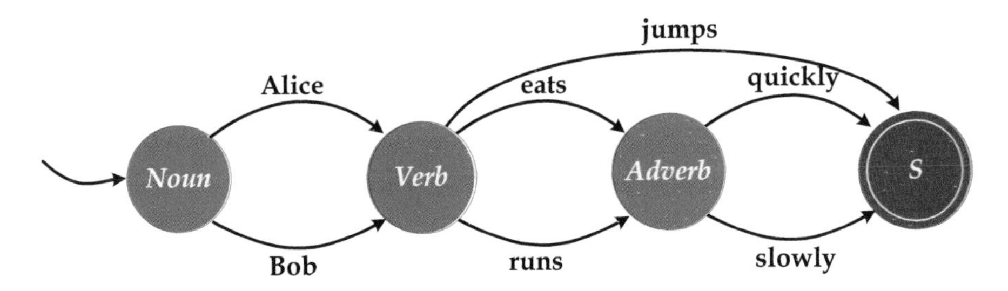

Exercise 2.7. Recursive transition networks.

a. How many nodes are needed for a recursive transition network that can produce exactly 8 strings?

b. How many edges are needed for a recursive transition network that can produce exactly 8 strings?

c. [★★] Given a whole number n, how many edges are needed for a recursive transition network that can produce exactly n strings?

Subnetworks. In the RTNs we have seen so far, the labels on the output edges are direct outputs known as *terminals*: following an edge just produces the symbol on that edge. We can make more expressive RTNs by allowing edge labels to also name *subnetworks*. A subnetwork is identified by the name of its starting node. When an edge labeled with a subnetwork is followed, the network traversal jumps to the subnetwork node. Then, it can follow any path from that node to a final node. Upon reaching a final node, the network traversal jumps back to complete the edge.

For example, consider the network shown in Figure 2.3. It describes the same language as the RTN in Figure 2.1, but uses subnetworks for *Noun* and *Verb*. To produce a string, we start in the *Sentence* node. The only edge out from *Sentence* is labeled *Noun*. To follow the edge, we jump to the *Noun* node, which is a separate subnetwork. Now, we can follow any path from *Noun* to a final node (in this cases, outputting either "Alice" or "Bob" on the path toward *EndNoun*.

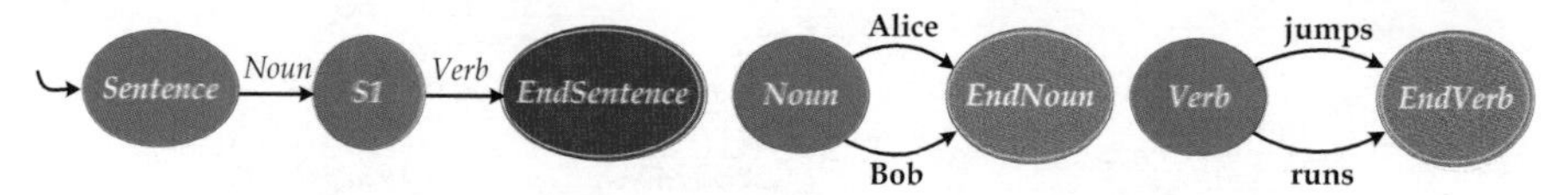

Figure 2.3. Recursive transition network with subnetworks.

Suppose we replace the *Noun* subnetwork with the more interesting version shown in Figure 2.4.This subnetwork includes an edge from *Noun* to *N1* labeled *Noun*. Following this edge involves following a path through the *Noun* subnetwork. Starting from *Noun*, we can generate complex phrases like "Alice and Bob" or "Alice and Bob and Alice" (find the two different paths through the network that generate this phrase).

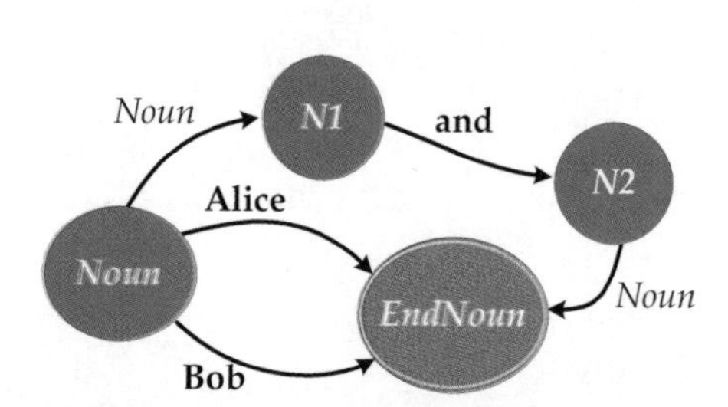

Figure 2.4. Alternate *Noun* subnetwork.

To keep track of paths through RTNs without subnetworks, a single marker suffices. We can start with the marker on the start node, and move it along the path through each node to the final node. Keeping track of paths on an RTN with subnetworks is more complicated. We need to keep track of where we are in the current network, and also where to continue to when a final node of the current subnetwork is reached. Since we can enter subnetworks within subnetworks, we need a way to keep track of arbitrarily many jump points.

stack

A *stack* is a useful way to keep track of the subnetworks. We can think of a stack like a stack of trays in a cafeteria. At any point in time, only the top tray on the stack can be reached. We can *pop* the top tray off the stack, after which the next tray is now on top. We can *push* a new tray on top of the stack, which makes the old top of the stack now one below the top.

We use a stack of nodes to keep track of the subnetworks as they are entered. The top of the stack represents the next node to process. At each step, we pop the node off the stack and follow a transition from that node.

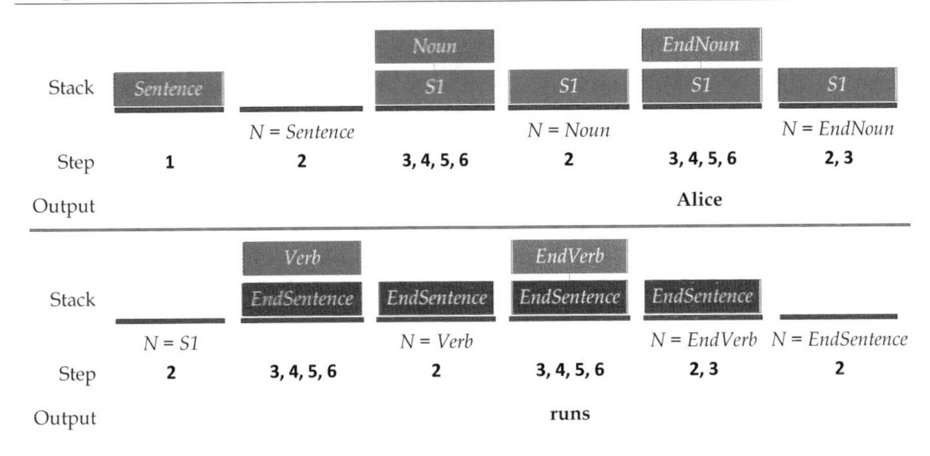

Figure 2.5. RTN generating "Alice runs".

Using a stack, we can derive a path through an RTN using this procedure:

1. Initially, push the starting node on the stack.
2. If the stack is empty, **stop**. Otherwise, pop a node, N, off the stack.
3. If the popped node, N, is a final node return to step 2.[2]
4. Select an edge from the RTN that starts from node N. Use D to denote the destination of that edge, and s to denote the output symbol on the edge.
5. Push D on the stack.
6. If s is a subnetwork, push the node s on the stack. Otherwise, output s, which is a terminal.
7. Go back to step 2.

Consider generating the string "Alice runs" using the RTN in Figure 2.3. We start following step 1 by pushing *Sentence* on the stack. In step 2, we pop the stack, so the current node, N, is *Sentence*. Since *Sentence* is not a final node, we do nothing for step 3. In step 4, we follow an edge starting from *Sentence*. There is only one edge to choose and it leads to the node labeled *S1*. In step 5, we push *S1* on the stack. The edge we followed is labeled with the node *Noun*, so we push *Noun* on the stack. The stack now contains two items: [*Noun, S1*]. Since *Noun* is on top, this means we will first traverse the *Noun* subnetwork, and then continue from *S1*.

As directed by step 7, we go back to step 2 and continue by popping the top node, *Noun*, off the stack. It is not a final node, so we continue to step 4, and select the edge labeled "Alice" from *Noun* to *EndNoun*. We push *EndNoun* on the stack, which now contains: [*EndNoun, S1*]. The label on the edge is the terminal, "Alice", so we output "Alice" following step 6. We continue in the same manner, following the steps in the procedure as we keep track of a path through the network. The full processing steps are shown in Figure 2.5.

Exercise 2.8. Show the sequence of stacks used in generating the string "Alice and Bob and Alice runs" using the network in Figure 2.3 with the alternate *Noun* subnetwork from Figure 2.4.

[2]For simplicity, this procedure assumes we always stop when a final node is reached. RTNs can have edges out of final nodes (as in Figure 2.2) where it is possible to either stop or continue from a final node.

Exercise 2.9. Identify a string that cannot be produced using the RTN from Figure 2.3 with the alternate *Noun* subnetwork from Figure 2.4 without the stack growing to contain five elements.

Exercise 2.10. The procedure given for traversing RTNs assumes that a subnetwork path always stops when a final node is reached. Hence, it cannot follow all possible paths for an RTN where there are edges out of a final node. Describe a procedure that can follow all possible paths, even for RTNs that include edges from final nodes.

2.4 Replacement Grammars

Another way to define a language is to use a grammar. This is the most common way languages are defined by computer scientists today, and the way we will use for the rest of this book.

grammar

A *grammar* is a set of rules for generating all strings in the language. We use the *Backus-Naur Form* (BNF) notation to define a grammar. BNF grammars are exactly as powerful as recursive transition networks (Exploration 2.1 explains what this means and why it is the case), but easier to write down.

John Backus

BNF was invented by John Backus in the late 1950s. Backus led efforts at IBM to define and implement Fortran, the first widely used programming language. Fortran enabled computer programs to be written in a language more like familiar algebraic formulas than low-level machine instructions, enabling programs to be written more quickly. In defining the Fortran language, Backus and his team used ad hoc English descriptions to define the language. These ad hoc descriptions were often misinterpreted, motivating the need for a more precise way of defining a language.

Rules in a Backus-Naur Form grammar have the form:

$$nonterminal ::\Rightarrow\ replacement$$

I flunked out every year. I never studied. I hated studying. I was just goofing around. It had the delightful consequence that every year I went to summer school in New Hampshire where I spent the summer sailing and having a nice time.
John Backus

The left side of a rule is always a single symbol, known as a *nonterminal* since it can never appear in the final generated string. The right side of a rule contains one or more symbols. These symbols may include nonterminals, which will be replaced using replacement rules before generating the final string. They may also be *terminals*, which are output symbols that never appear as the left side of a rule. When we describe grammars, we use *italics* to represent nonterminal symbols, and **bold** to represent terminal symbols. The terminals are the primitives in the language; the grammar rules are its means of combination.

We can generate a string in the language described by a replacement grammar by starting from a designated start symbol (e.g., *sentence*), and at each step selecting a nonterminal in the working string, and replacing it with the right side of a replacement rule whose left side matches the nonterminal. Wherever we find a nonterminal on the left side of a rule, we can replace it with what appears on the right side of any rule where that nonterminal matches the left side. A string is generated once there are no nonterminals remaining.

Here is an example BNF grammar (that describes the same language as the RTN in Figure 2.1):

1.	*Sentence*	::⇒	*Noun Verb*
2.	*Noun*	::⇒	**Alice**
3.	*Noun*	::⇒	**Bob**
4.	*Verb*	::⇒	**jumps**
5.	*Verb*	::⇒	**runs**

Starting from *Sentence*, the grammar can generate four sentences: "Alice jumps", "Alice runs", "Bob jumps", and "Bob runs".

A *derivation* shows how a grammar generates a given string. Here is the derivation of "Alice runs":

derivation

Sentence	::⇒*Noun Verb*	using Rule 1
	::⇒**Alice** *Verb*	replacing *Noun* using Rule 2
	::⇒**Alice runs**	replacing *Verb* using Rule 5

We can represent a grammar derivation as a tree, where the root of the tree is the starting nonterminal (*Sentence* in this case), and the leaves of the tree are the terminals that form the derived sentence. Such a tree is known as a *parse tree*. Here is the parse tree for the derivation of "Alice runs":

parse tree

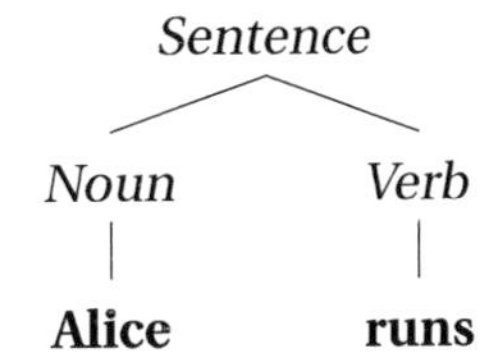

BNF grammars can be more compact than just listing strings in the language since a grammar can have many replacements for each nonterminal. For example, adding the rule, *Noun* ::⇒ **Colleen**, to the grammar adds two new strings ("Colleen runs" and "Colleen jumps") to the language.

Recursive Grammars. The real power of BNF as a compact notation for describing languages, though, comes once we start adding recursive rules to our grammar. A grammar is recursive if the grammar contains a nonterminal that can produce a production that contains itself.

Suppose we add the rule,

Sentence ::⇒ *Sentence* **and** *Sentence*

to our example grammar. Now, how many sentences can we generate?

Infinitely many! This grammar describes the same language as the RTN in Figure 2.2. It can generate "Alice runs and Bob jumps" and "Alice runs and Bob jumps and Alice runs" and sentences with any number of repetitions of "Alice runs". This is very powerful: by using recursive rules a compact grammar can be used to define a language containing infinitely many strings.

Example 2.1: Whole Numbers

This grammar defines the language of the whole numbers (0, 1, ...) with leading zeros allowed:

Number	::⇒	*Digit MoreDigits*			
MoreDigits	::⇒		*Digit*	::⇒	**4**
MoreDigits	::⇒	*Number*	*Digit*	::⇒	**5**
Digit	::⇒	**0**	*Digit*	::⇒	**6**
Digit	::⇒	**1**	*Digit*	::⇒	**7**
Digit	::⇒	**2**	*Digit*	::⇒	**8**
Digit	::⇒	**3**	*Digit*	::⇒	**9**

Here is the parse tree for a derivation of **37** from *Number*:

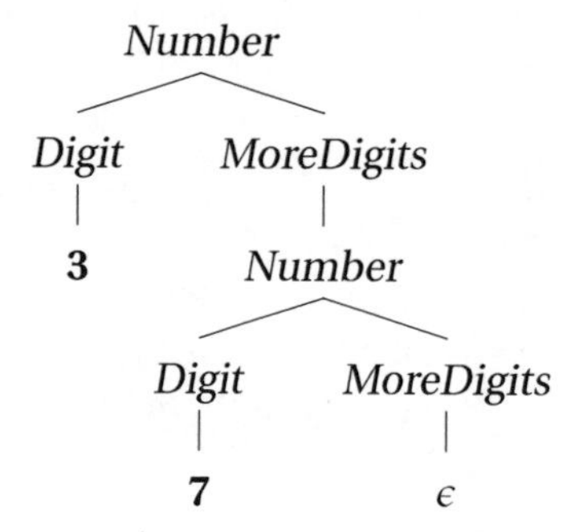

Circular vs. Recursive Definitions. The second rule means we can replace *MoreDigits* with nothing. This is sometimes written as ϵ to make it clear that the replacement is empty: *MoreDigits* ::⇒ ϵ.

This is a very important rule in the grammar—without it *no* strings could be generated; with it *infinitely* many strings can be generated. The key is that we can only produce a string when all nonterminals in the string have been replaced with terminals. Without the *MoreDigits* ::⇒ ϵ rule, the only rule we would have with *MoreDigits* on the left side is the third rule: *MoreDigits* ::⇒ *Number*.

The only rule we have with *Number* on the left side is the first rule, which replaces *Number* with *Digit MoreDigits*. Every time we follow this rule, we replace *MoreDigits* with *Digit MoreDigits*. We can produce as many *Digits* as we want, but without the *MoreDigits* ::⇒ ϵ rule we can never stop.

base case

This is the difference between a *circular* definition, and a *recursive* definition. Without the stopping rule, *MoreDigits* would be defined in a circular way. There is no way to start with *MoreDigits* and generate a production that does not contain *MoreDigits* (or a nonterminal that eventually must produce *MoreDigits*). With the *MoreDigits* ::⇒ ϵ rule, however, we have a way to produce something terminal from *MoreDigits*. This is known as a *base case* — a rule that turns an otherwise circular definition into a meaningful, recursive definition.

Condensed Notation. It is common to have many grammar rules with the same left side nonterminal. For example, the whole numbers grammar has ten rules with *Digit* on the left side to produce the ten terminal digits. Each of these is an alternative rule that can be used when the production string contains the nonterminal *Digit*. A compact notation for these types of rules is to use the vertical bar (|) to separate alternative replacements. For example, we could write the ten *Digit* rules compactly as:

Digit ::⇒ **0** | **1** | **2** | **3** | **4** | **5** | **6** | **7** | **8** | **9**

Exercise 2.11. Suppose we replaced the first rule (*Number* ::⇒ *Digit MoreDigits*) in the whole numbers grammar with: *Number* ::⇒ *MoreDigits Digit*.

a. How does this change the parse tree for the derivation of **37**? Draw the parse tree that results from the new grammar.

b. Does this change the language? Either show some string that is in the language defined by the modified grammar but not in the original language (or vice versa), or argue that both grammars generate the same strings.

Exercise 2.12. The grammar for whole numbers we defined allows strings with non-standard leading zeros such as "000" and "00005". Devise a grammar that produces all whole numbers (including "0"), but no strings with unnecessary leading zeros.

Exercise 2.13. Define a BNF grammar that describes the language of decimal numbers (the language should include 3.14159, 0.423, and 1120 but not 1.2.3).

Exercise 2.14. The BNF grammar below (extracted from Paul Mockapetris, *Domain Names - Implementation and Specification*, IETF RFC 1035) describes the language of domain names on the Internet.

Domain ::⇒ *SubDomainList*
SubDomainList ::⇒ *Label* | *SubDomainList* **.** *Label*
Label ::⇒ *Letter MoreLetters*
MoreLetters ::⇒ *LetterHyphens LetterDigit* | ϵ
LetterHyphens ::⇒ *LDHyphen* | *LDHyphen LetterHyphens* | ϵ
LDHyphen ::⇒ *LetterDigit* | **-**
LetterDigit ::⇒ *Letter* | *Digit*
Letter ::⇒ **A** | **B** | ... | **Z** | **a** | **b** | ... | **z**
Digit ::⇒ **0** | **1** | **2** | **3** | **4** | **5** | **6** | **7** | **8** | **9**

a. Show a derivation for **www.virginia.edu** in the grammar.

b. According to the grammar, which of the following are valid domain names: (1) **tj**, (2) **a.-b.c**, (3) **a-a.b-b.c-c**, (4) **a.g.r.e.a.t.d.o.m.a.i.n-**.

Exploration 2.1: Power of Language Systems

Section 2.4 claimed that recursive transition networks and BNF grammars are equally powerful. What does it mean to say two systems are equally powerful?

A language description mechanism is used to define a set of strings comprising a language. Hence, the power of a language description mechanism is determined by the set of languages it can define.

One approach to measure the power of language description mechanism would be to count the number of languages that it can define. Even the simplest mechanisms can define infinitely many languages, however, so just counting the number of languages does not distinguish well between the different language description mechanisms. Both RTNs and BNFs can describe infinitely many different languages. We can always add a new edge to an RTN to increase the number of strings in the language, or add a new replacement rule to a BNF that replaces a nonterminal with a new terminal symbol.

Instead, we need to consider the set of languages that each mechanism can define. A system A is more powerful that another system B if we can use A to define every language that can be defined by B, and there is some language L that can be defined using A that cannot be defined using B. This matches our intuitive interpretation of *more powerful* — A is more powerful than B if it can do everything B can do and more.

The diagrams in Figure 2.6 show three possible scenarios. In the leftmost picture, the set of languages that can be defined by B is a proper subset of the set of languages that can be defined by A. Hence, A is more powerful than B. In the center picture, the sets are equal. This means every language that can be defined by A can also be defined by B, and every language that can be defined by B can also be defined by A, and the systems are equally powerful. In the rightmost picture, there are some elements of A that are not elements of B, but there are also some elements of B that are not elements of A. This means we cannot say either one is more powerful; A can do some things B cannot do, and B can do some things A cannot do.

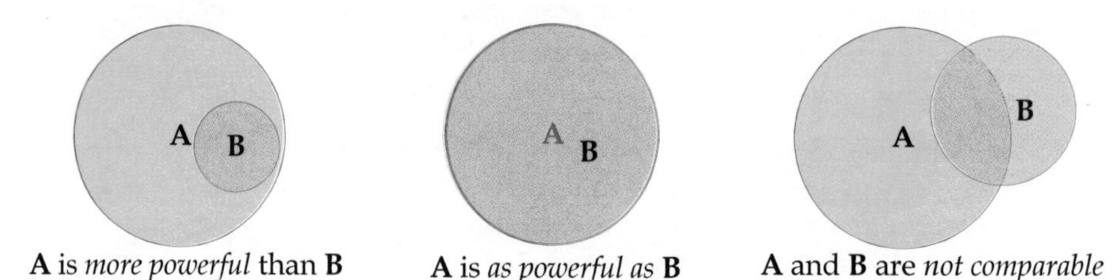

Figure 2.6. System power relationships.

To determine the relationship between RTNs and BNFs we need to understand if there are languages that can be defined by a BNF that cannot be defined by a RTN and if there are languages that can be defined by a RTN that cannot be defined by an BNF. We will show only the first part of the proof here, and leave the second part as an exercise.

For the first part, we prove that there are no languages that can be defined by a BNF that cannot be defined by an RTN. Equivalently, *every* language that can be defined by a BNF grammar has a corresponding RTN. Since there are infinitely many languages that can be defined by BNF grammars, we cannot prove this by enumerating each language and showing its corresponding RTN. Instead, we use a proof technique commonly used in computer science: *proof by construction*. We show an algorithm that given any BNF grammar constructs an RTN that defines the same language as the input BNF grammar.

proof by construction

Our strategy is to construct a subnetwork corresponding to each nonterminal. For each rule where the nonterminal is on the left side, the right hand side is converted to a path through that node's subnetwork.

Before presenting the general construction algorithm, we illustrate the approach with the example BNF grammar from Example 2.1:

Number	$::\Rightarrow$	*Digit MoreDigits*
MoreDigits	$::\Rightarrow$	ϵ
MoreDigits	$::\Rightarrow$	*Number*
Digit	$::\Rightarrow$	**0** | **1** | **2** | **3** | **4** | **5** | **6** | **7** | **8** | **9**

The grammar has three nonterminals: *Number*, *Digit*, and *MoreDigits*. For each nonterminal, we construct a subnetwork by first creating two nodes corresponding to the start and end of the subnetwork for the nonterminal. We make *StartNumber* the start node for the RTN since *Number* is the starting nonterminal for the grammar.

Next, we need to add edges to the RTN corresponding to the production rules in the grammar. The first rule indicates that *Number* can be replaced by *Digit MoreDigits*. To make the corresponding RTN, we need to introduce an intermediate node since each RTN edge can only contain one label. We need to traverse two edges, with labels *StartDigit* and *StartMoreDigits* between the *StartNumber* and *EndNumber* nodes. The resulting partial RTN is shown in Figure 2.7.

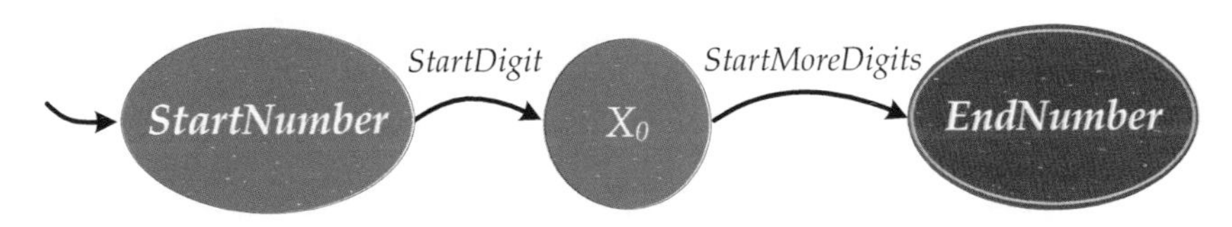

Figure 2.7. Converting the *Number* **productions to an RTN.**

For the *MoreDigits* nonterminal there are two productions. The first means *MoreDigits* can be replaced with nothing. In an RTN, we cannot have edges with unlabeled outputs. So, the equivalent of outputting nothing is to turn *StartMoreDigits* into a final node. The second production replaces *MoreDigits* with *Number*. We do this in the RTN by adding an edge between *StartMoreDigits* and *EndMoreDigits* labeled with *Number*, as shown in Figure 2.8.

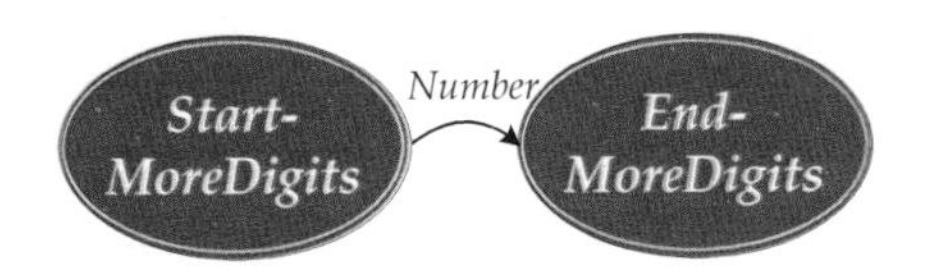

Figure 2.8. Converting the *MoreDigits* **productions to an RTN.**

Finally, we convert the ten *Digit* productions. For each rule, we add an edge between *StartDigit* and *EndDigit* labeled with the digit terminal, as shown in Figure 2.9.

This example illustrates that it is possible to convert a particular grammar to an RTN. For a general proof, we present a general an algorithm that can be used to do the same conversion for any BNF:

1. For each nonterminal *X* in the grammar, construct two nodes, *StartX* and

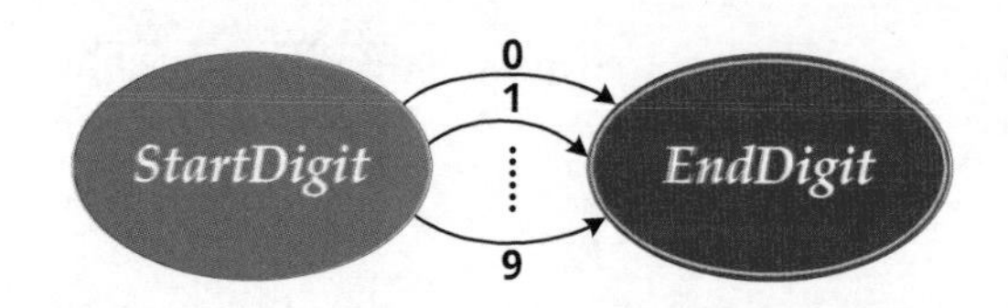

Figure 2.9. Converting the *Digit* productions to an RTN.

EndX, where *EndX* is a final node. Make the node *StartS* the start node of the RTN, where *S* is the start nonterminal of the grammar.

2. For each rule in the grammar, add a corresponding path through the RTN. All BNF rules have the form X ::⇒ *replacement* where *X* is a nonterminal in the grammar and *replacement* is a sequence of zero or more terminals and nonterminals: $[R_0, R_1, \ldots, R_n]$.

   (a) If the replacement is empty, make *StartX* a final node.

   (b) If the replacement has just one element, R_0, add an edge from *StartX* to *EndX* with edge label R_0.

   (c) Otherwise:

      i. Add an edge from *StartX* to a new node labeled $X_{i,0}$ (where *i* identifies the grammar rule), with edge label R_0.

      ii. For each remaining element R_j in the replacement add an edge from $X_{i,j-1}$ to a new node labeled $X_{i,j}$ with edge label R_j. (For example, for element R_1, a new node $X_{i,1}$ is added, and an edge from $X_{i,0}$ to $X_{i,1}$ with edge label R_1.)

      iii. Add an edge from $X_{i,n-1}$ to *EndX* with edge label R_n.

Following this procedure, we can convert any BNF grammar into an RTN that defines the same language. Hence, we have proved that RTNs are at least as powerful as BNF grammars.

To complete the proof that BNF grammars and RTNs are equally powerful ways of defining languages, we also need to show that a BNF can define every language that can be defined using an RTN. This part of the proof can be done using a similar strategy in reverse: by showing a procedure that can be used to construct a BNF equivalent to any input RTN. We leave the details as an exercise for especially ambitious readers.

Exercise 2.15. Produce an RTN that defines the same languages as the BNF grammar from Exercise 2.14.

Exercise 2.16. [★] Prove that BNF grammars are as powerful as RTNs by devising a procedure that can construct a BNF grammar that defines the same language as any input RTN.

2.5 Summary

Languages define a set of surface forms and associated meanings. Since useful language must be able to express infinitely many things, we need tools for defining infinite sets of surface forms using compact and precise notations. The tool we will use for the remainder of this book is the BNF replacement grammar which precisely defines a language using replacement rules. This system can describe infinite languages with small representations because of the power of recursive rules. In the next chapter, we introduce the Scheme programming language that we will use to describe procedures.

3 Programming

The Analytical Engine has no pretensions whatever to originate any thing. It can do whatever we know how to order it to perform. It can follow analysis; but it has no power of anticipating any analytical relations or truths. Its province is to assist us in making available what we are already acquainted with.
Augusta Ada Countess of Lovelace, in *Notes on the Analytical Engine*, 1843

What distinguishes a computer from other machines is its *programmability*. Without a program, a computer is an overpriced door stopper. With the right program, though, a computer can be a tool for communicating across the continent, discovering a new molecule that can cure cancer, composing a symphony, or managing the logistics of a retail empire.

Programming is the act of writing instructions that make the computer do something useful. It is an intensely creative activity, involving aspects of art, engineering, and science. Good programs are written to be executed efficiently by computers, but also to be read and understood by humans. The best programs are delightful in ways similar to the best architecture, elegant in both form and function.

Golden Gate Bridge

The ideal programmer would have the vision of Isaac Newton, the intellect of Albert Einstein, the creativity of Miles Davis, the aesthetic sense of Maya Lin, the wisdom of Benjamin Franklin, the literary talent of William Shakespeare, the oratorical skills of Martin Luther King, the audacity of John Roebling, and the self-confidence of Grace Hopper.

Fortunately, it is not necessary to possess all of those rare qualities to be a good programmer! Indeed, anyone who is able to master the intellectual challenge of learning a language (which, presumably, anyone who has gotten this far has done at least for English) can become a good programmer. Since programming is a new way of thinking, many people find it challenging and even frustrating at first. Because the computer does exactly what it is told, a small mistake in a program may prevent it from working as intended. With a bit of patience and persistence, however, the tedious parts of programming become easier, and you will be able to focus your energies on the fun and creative problem solving parts.

In the previous chapter, we explored the components of language and mechanisms for defining languages. In this chapter, we explain why natural languages are not a satisfactory way for defining procedures and introduce a language for programming computers and how it can be used to define procedures.

3.1 Problems with Natural Languages

Natural languages, such as English, work adequately (most, but certainly not all, of the time) for human-human communication, but are not well-suited for human-computer or computer-computer communication. Why can't we use natural languages to program computers?

Next, we survey several of the reasons for this. We use specifics from English, although all natural languages suffer from these problems to varying degrees.

Complexity. Although English may seem simple to you now, it took many years of intense effort (most of it subconscious) for you to learn it. Despite using it for most of their waking hours for many years, native English speakers know a small fraction of the entire language. The Oxford English Dictionary contains 615,000 words, of which a typical native English speaker knows about 40,000.

Ambiguity. Not only do natural languages have huge numbers of words, most words have many different meanings. Understanding the intended meaning of an utterance requires knowing the context, and sometimes pure guesswork.

For example, what does it mean to be paid *biweekly*? According to the American Heritage Dictionary[1], *biweekly* has two definitions:

1. *Happening every two weeks.*
2. *Happening twice a week; semiweekly.*

Merriam-Webster's Dictionary[2] takes the opposite approach:

1. *occurring twice a week*
2. *occurring every two weeks : fortnightly*

So, depending on which definition is intended, someone who is paid biweekly could either be paid once or four times every two weeks! The behavior of a payroll management program better not depend on how biweekly is interpreted.

Even if we can agree on the definition of every word, the meaning of a sentence is often ambiguous. This particularly difficult example is taken from the instructions with a shipment of ballistic missiles from the British Admiralty:[3]

> *It is necessary for technical reasons that these warheads be stored upside down, that is, with the top at the bottom and the bottom at the top. In order that there be no doubt as to which is the bottom and which is the top, for storage purposes, it will be seen that the bottom of each warhead has been labeled 'TOP'.*

Irregularity. Because natural languages evolve over time as different cultures interact and speakers misspeak and listeners mishear, natural languages end up a morass of irregularity. Nearly all grammar rules have exceptions. For example, English has a rule that we can make a word plural by appending an *s*. The new

[1] American Heritage, *Dictionary of the English Language* (Fourth Edition), Houghton Mifflin Company, 2007 (http://www.answers.com/biweekly).

[2] *Merriam-Webster Online*, Merriam-Webster, 2008 (http://www.merriam-webster.com/dictionary/biweekly).

[3] Carl C. Gaither and Alma E. Cavazos-Gaither, *Practically Speaking: A Dictionary of Quotations on Engineering, Technology and Architecture*, Taylor & Francis, 1998.

word means "more than one of the original word's meaning". This rule works for most words: *word* ↦ *words*, *language* ↦ *languages*, *person* ↦ *persons*.[4]

It does not work for *all* words, however. The plural of *goose* is *geese* (and *gooses* is not an English word), the plural of *deer* is *deer* (and *deers* is not an English word), and the plural of *beer* is controversial (and may depend on whether you speak American English or Canadian English).

These irregularities can be charming for a natural language, but they are a constant source of difficulty for non-native speakers attempting to learn a language. There is no sure way to predict when the rule can be applied, and it is necessary to memorize each of the irregular forms.

Uneconomic. It requires a lot of space to express a complex idea in a natural language. Many superfluous words are needed for grammatical correctness, even though they do not contribute to the desired meaning. Since natural languages evolved for everyday communication, they are not well suited to describing the precise steps and decisions needed in a computer program.

I have made this letter longer than usual, only because I have not had the time to make it shorter.
Blaise Pascal, 1657

As an example, consider a procedure for finding the maximum of two numbers. In English, we could describe it like this:

> *To find the maximum of two numbers, compare them. If the first number is greater than the second number, the maximum is the first number. Otherwise, the maximum is the second number.*

Perhaps shorter descriptions are possible, but any much shorter description probably assumes the reader already knows a lot. By contrast, we can express the same steps in the Scheme programming language in very concise way (don't worry if this doesn't make sense yet—it should by the end of this chapter):

```
(define (bigger a b) (if (> a b) a b))
```

Limited means of abstraction. Natural languages provide small, fixed sets of pronouns to use as means of abstraction, and the rules for binding pronouns to meanings are often unclear. Since programming often involves using simple names to refer to complex things, we need more powerful means of abstraction than natural languages provide.

3.2 Programming Languages

For programming computers, we want simple, unambiguous, regular, and economical languages with powerful means of abstraction. A *programming language* is a language that is designed to be read and written by humans to create programs that can be executed by computers.

programming language

Programming languages come in many flavors. It is difficult to simultaneously satisfy all desired properties since simplicity is often at odds with economy. Every feature that is added to a language to increase its expressiveness incurs a cost in reducing simplicity and regularity. For the first two parts of this book, we use the Scheme programming language which was designed primarily for simplicity. For the later parts of the book, we use the Python programming language, which provides more expressiveness but at the cost of some added complexity.

[4] Or is it *people*? What is the singular of *people*? What about *peeps*? Can you only have one *peep*?

Another reason there are many different programming languages is that they are at different *levels of abstraction*. Some languages provide programmers with detailed control over machine resources, such as selecting a particular location in memory where a value is stored. Other languages hide most of the details of the machine operation from the programmer, allowing them to focus on higher-level actions.

Ultimately, we want a program the computer can execute. This means at the lowest level we need languages the computer can understand directly. At this level, the program is just a sequence of bits encoding machine instructions. Code at this level is not easy for humans to understand or write, but it is easy for a processor to execute quickly. The machine code encodes instructions that direct the processor to take simple actions like moving data from one place to another, performing simple arithmetic, and jumping around to find the next instruction to execute.

Grace Hopper
Image courtesy Computer History Museum (1952)

For example, the bit sequence 1110101111111110 encodes an instruction in the Intel x86 instruction set (used on most PCs) that instructs the processor to jump backwards two locations. Since the instruction itself requires two locations of space, jumping back two locations actually jumps back to the beginning of this instruction. Hence, the processor gets stuck running forever without making any progress.

The computer's processor is designed to execute very simple instructions like jumping, adding two small numbers, or comparing two values. This means each instruction can be executed very quickly. A typical modern processor can execute *billions* of instructions in a second.[5]

Until the early 1950s, all programming was done at the level of simple instructions. The problem with instructions at this level is that they are not easy for humans to write and understand, and you need many simple instructions before you have a useful program.

compiler

A *compiler* is a computer program that generates other programs. It translates an input program written in a *high-level language* that is easier for humans to create into a program in a machine-level language that can be executed by the computer. Admiral Grace Hopper developed the first compilers in the 1950s.

interpreter

An alternative to a compiler is an interpreter. An *interpreter* is a tool that translates between a higher-level language and a lower-level language, but where a compiler translates an entire program at once and produces a machine language program that can be executed directly, an interpreter interprets the program a small piece at a time while it is running. This has the advantage that we do not have to run a separate tool to compile a program before running it; we can simply enter our program into the interpreter and run it right away. This makes it easy to make small changes to a program and try it again, and to observe the state of our program as it is running.

Nobody believed that I had a running compiler and nobody would touch it. They told me computers could only do arithmetic.
Grace Hopper

One disadvantage of using an interpreter instead of a compiler is that because the translation is happening while the program is running, the program executes slower than a compiled program. Another advantage of compilers over

[5] A "2GHz processor" executes 2 billion cycles per second. This does not map directly to the number of instructions it can execute in a second, though, since some instructions take several cycles to execute.

interpreters is that since the compiler translates the entire program it can also analyze the program for consistency and detect certain types of programming mistakes automatically instead of encountering them when the program is running (or worse, not detecting them at all and producing unintended results). This is especially important when writing critical programs such as flight control software — we want to detect as many problems as possible in the flight control software before the plane is flying!

Since we are more concerned with interactive exploration than with performance and detecting errors early, we use an interpreter instead of a compiler.

3.3 Scheme

The programming system we use for the first part of this book is depicted in Figure 3.1. The input to our programming system is a program written in a programming language named *Scheme*. A Scheme interpreter interprets a Scheme program and executes it on the machine processor.

Scheme was developed at MIT in the 1970s by Guy Steele and Gerald Sussman, based on the LISP programming language that was developed by John McCarthy in the 1950s. Although many large systems have been built using Scheme, it is not widely used in industry. It is, however, a great language for learning about computing and programming. The primary advantage of using Scheme to learn about computing is its simplicity and elegance. The language is simple enough that this chapter covers nearly the entire language (we defer describing a few aspects until Chapter 9), and by the end of this book you will know enough to implement your own Scheme interpreter. By contrast, some programming languages that are widely used in industrial programming such as C++ and Java require thousands of pages to describe, and even the world's experts in those languages do not agree on exactly what all programs mean.

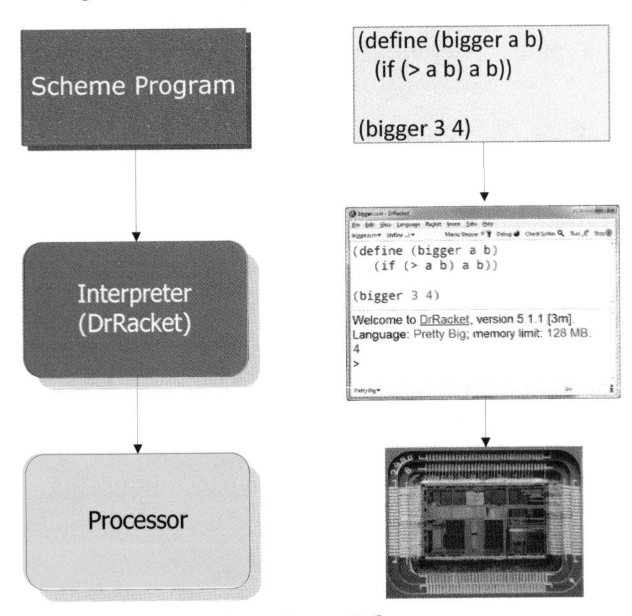

Figure 3.1. Running a Scheme program.

Although almost everything we describe should work in all Scheme interpreters, for the examples in this book we assume the DrRacket programming environment which is freely available from http://racket-lang.org/. DrRacket includes interpreters for many different languages, so you must select the desired language using the Language menu. The selected language defines the grammar and evaluation rules that will be used to interpret your program. For all the examples in this book, we use a version of the Scheme language named Pretty Big.

3.4 Expressions

A Scheme program is composed of expressions and definitions (we cover definitions in Section 3.5). An *expression* is a syntactic element that has a *value.*

expression

The act of determining the value associated with an expression is called *evaluation.* A Scheme interpreter, such as the one provided in DrRacket, is a machine for evaluating Scheme expressions. If you enter an expression into a Scheme interpreter, the interpreter evaluates the expression and displays its value.

evaluation

Expressions may be primitives. Scheme also provides means of combination for producing complex expressions from simple expressions. The next subsections describe primitive expressions and application expressions. Section 3.6 describes expressions for making procedures and Section 3.7 describes expressions that can be used to make decisions.

3.4.1 Primitives

An expression can be replaced with a primitive:

Expression ::⇒ *PrimitiveExpression*

As with natural languages, primitives are the smallest units of meaning. Hence, the value of a primitive is its pre-defined meaning.

Scheme provides many different primitives. Three useful types of primitives are described next: numbers, Booleans, and primitive procedures.

Numbers. Numbers represent numerical values. Scheme provides all the kinds of numbers you are familiar with including whole numbers, negative numbers, decimals, and rational numbers.

Example numbers include:

```
150       0     −12
3.14159   3/4   99999999999999999999
```

Numbers evaluate to their value. For example, the value of the primitive expression 1120 is 1120.

Booleans. Booleans represent truth values. There are two primitives for representing true and false:

PrimitiveExpression ::⇒ *true* | *false*

The meaning of *true* is true, and the meaning of *false* is false. In the DrRacket interpreter, #t and #f are used to represent the primitive truth values. So, the value *true* appears as #t in the interactions window.

Symbol	Description	Inputs	Output
+	add	zero or more numbers	sum of the input numbers (0 if there are no inputs)
*	multiply	zero or more numbers	product of the input numbers (1 if there are no inputs)
−	subtract	two numbers	the value of the first number minus the value the second number
/	divide	two numbers	the value of the first number divided by the value of the second number
zero?	is zero?	one number	true if the input value is 0, otherwise false
=	is equal to?	two numbers	true if the input values have the same value, otherwise false
<	is less than?	two numbers	true if the first input value has lesser value than the second input value, otherwise false
>	is greater than?	two numbers	true if the first input value has greater value than the second input value, otherwise false
<=	is less than or equal to?	two numbers	true if the first input value is not greater than the second input value, otherwise false
>=	is greater than or equal to?	two numbers	true if the first input value is not less than the second input value, otherwise false

Table 3.1. Selected Scheme Primitive Procedures.
All of these primitive procedures operate on numbers. The first four are the basic arithmetic operators; the rest are comparison procedures. Some of these procedures are defined for more inputs than just the ones shown here (e.g., the subtract procedure also works on one number, producing its negation).

Primitive Procedures. Scheme provides primitive procedures corresponding to many common functions. Mathematically, a *function* is a mapping from inputs to outputs. For each valid input to the function, there is exactly one associated output. For example, + is a procedure that takes zero or more inputs, each of which must be a number. Its output is the sum of the values of the inputs. Table 3.1 describes some primitive procedures for performing arithmetic and comparisons on numbers.

function

3.4.2 Application Expressions

Most of the actual work done by a Scheme program is done by *application expressions* that apply procedures to operands. The expression (+ 1 2) is an *ApplicationExpression*, consisting of three subexpressions. Although this example is probably simple enough that you can probably guess that it evaluates to 3, we will show in detail how it is evaluated by breaking down into its subexpressions using the grammar rules. The same process will allow us to understand how *any* expression is evaluated.

The grammar rule for application is:

$$\begin{aligned} \textit{Expression} &::\Rightarrow \textit{ApplicationExpression} \\ \textit{ApplicationExpression} &::\Rightarrow (\textit{Expression MoreExpressions}) \\ \textit{MoreExpressions} &::\Rightarrow \epsilon \mid \textit{Expression MoreExpressions} \end{aligned}$$

This rule produces a list of one or more expressions surrounded by parentheses. The value of the first expression should be a procedure; the remaining expressions are the inputs to the procedure known as *operands*. Another name for operands is *arguments*.

operands
arguments

Here is a parse tree for the expression (+ 1 2):

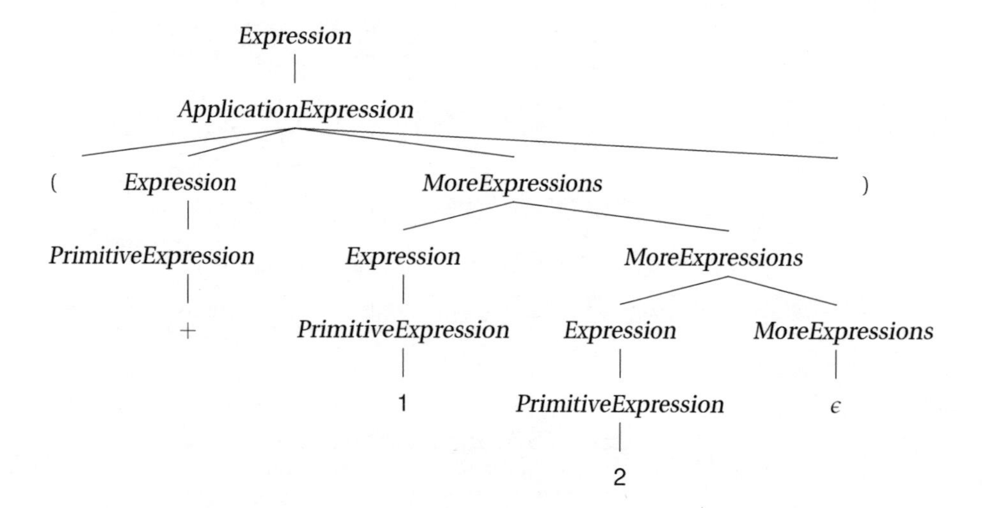

Following the grammar rules, we replace *Expression* with *ApplicationExpression* at the top of the parse tree. Then, we replace *ApplicationExpression* with (*Expression MoreExpressions*). The *Expression* term is replaced *PrimitiveExpression*, and finally, the primitive addition procedure +. This is the first subexpression of the application, so it is the procedure to be applied. The *MoreExpressions* term produces the two operand expressions: 1 and 2, both of which are primitives that evaluate to their own values. The application expression is evaluated by applying the value of the first expression (the primitive procedure +) to the inputs given by the values of the other expressions. Following the meaning of the primitive procedure, (+ 1 2) evaluates to 3 as expected.

The *Expression* nonterminals in the application expression can be replaced with anything that appears on the right side of an expression rule, including an *ApplicationExpression*.

We can build up complex expressions like (+ (∗ 10 10) (+ 25 25)). Its parse tree is:

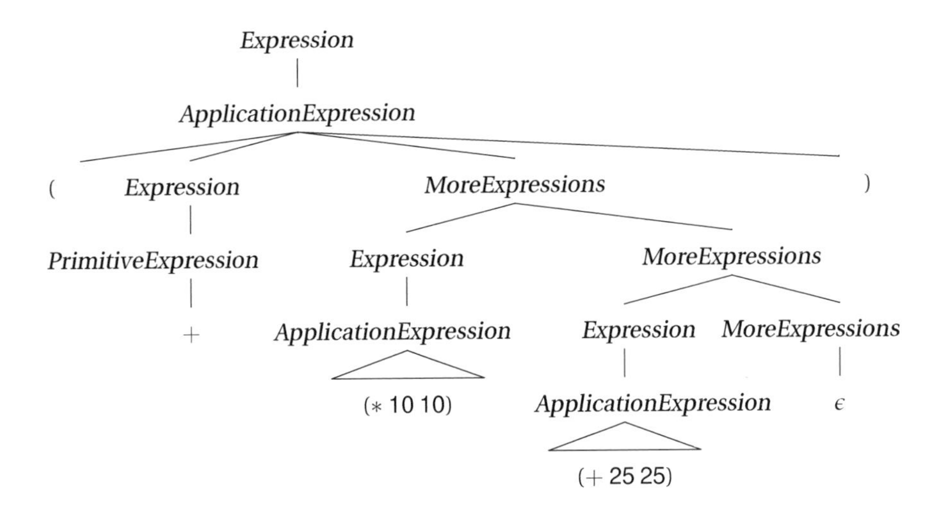

This tree is similar to the previous tree, except instead of the subexpressions of the first application expression being simple primitive expressions, they are now application expressions. (Instead of showing the complete parse tree for the nested application expressions, we use triangles.)

To evaluate the output application, we need to evaluate all the subexpressions. The first subexpression, +, evaluates to the primitive procedure. The second subexpression, (* 10 10), evaluates to 100, and the third expression, (+ 25 25), evaluates to 50. Now, we can evaluate the original expression using the values for its three component subexpressions: (+ 100 50) evaluates to 150.

Exercise 3.1. Draw a parse tree for the Scheme expression (+ 100 (* 5 (+ 5 5))) and show how it is evaluated.

Exercise 3.2. Predict how each of the following Scheme expressions is evaluated. After making your prediction, try evaluating the expression in DrRacket. If the result is different from your prediction, explain why the Scheme interpreter evaluates the expression as it does.

a. 1120

b. (+ 1120)

c. (+ (+ 10 20) (* 2 0))

d. (= (+ 10 20) (* 15 (+ 5 5)))

e. +

f. (+ + <)

Exercise 3.3. For each question, construct a Scheme expression and evaluate it in DrRacket.

a. How many seconds are there in a year?

b. For how many seconds have you been alive?

c. For what fraction of your life have you been in school?

Exercise 3.4. Construct a Scheme expression to calculate the distance in inches that light travels during the time it takes the processor in your computer to execute one cycle. (A meter is defined as the distance light travels in $1/299792458^{th}$ of a second in a vacuum. Hence, light travels at $299,792,458$ meters per second. Your processor speed is probably given in *gigahertz* (GHz), which are 1,000,000,000 hertz. One hertz means once per second, so 1 GHz means the processor executes 1,000,000,000 cycles per second. On a Windows machine, you can find the speed of your processor by opening the Control Panel (select it from the Start menu) and selecting System. Note that Scheme performs calculations exactly, so the result will be displayed as a fraction. To see a more useful answer, use (*exact->inexact Expression*) to convert the value of the expression to a decimal representation.)

3.5 Definitions

Scheme provides a simple, yet powerful, mechanism for abstraction. A definition introduces a new name and gives it a value:

Definition ::⇒ (**define** ***Name*** *Expression*)

After a definition, the ***Name*** in the definition is now associated with the value of the expression in the definition. A definition is not an expression since it does not evaluate to a value.

A name can be any sequence of letters, digits, and special characters (such as −, >, ?, and !) that starts with a letter or special character. Examples of valid names include *a, Ada, Augusta-Ada, gold49, !yuck,* and *yikes!\%@\#*. We don't recommend using some of these names in your programs, however! A good programmer will pick names that are easy to read, pronounce, and remember, and that are not easily confused with other names.

After a name has been bound to a value by a definition, that name may be used in an expression:

Expression ::⇒ *NameExpression*
NameExpression ::⇒ ***Name***

The value of a *NameExpression* is the value associated with the ***Name***. (Alert readers should be worried that we need a more precise definition of the meaning of definitions to know what it means for a value to be associated with a name. This informal notion will serve us well for now, but we will need a more precise explanation of the meaning of a definition in Chapter 9.)

Below we define *speed-of-light* to be the speed of light in meters per second, define *seconds-per-hour* to be the number of seconds in an hour, and use them to calculate the speed of light in kilometers per hour:

```
> (define speed-of-light 299792458)
> speed-of-light
299792458
> (define seconds-per-hour (* 60 60))
> (/ (* speed-of-light seconds-per-hour) 1000)
1079252848 4/5
```

3.6 Procedures

In Chapter 1 we defined a procedure as a description of a process. Scheme provides a way to define procedures that take inputs, carry out a sequence of actions, and produce an output. Section 3.4.1 introduced some of Scheme's primitive procedures. To construct complex programs, however, we need to be able to create our own procedures.

Procedures are similar to mathematical functions in that they provide a mapping between inputs and outputs, but they differ from mathematical functions in two important ways:

State. In addition to producing an output, a procedure may access and modify state. This means that even when the same procedure is applied to the same inputs, the output produced may vary. Because mathematical functions do not have external state, when the same function is applied to the same inputs it always produces the same result. State makes procedures much harder to reason about. We will ignore this issue until Chapter 9, and focus until then only on procedures that do not involve any state.

Resources. Unlike an ideal mathematical function, which provides an instantaneous and free mapping between inputs and outputs, a procedure requires resources to execute before the output is produced. The most important resources are *space* (memory) and *time*. A procedure may need space to keep track of intermediate results while it is executing. Each step of a procedure requires some time to execute. Predicting how long a procedure will take to execute and finding the fastest procedure possible for solving some problem are core problems in computer science. We consider this throughout this book, and in particular in Chapter 7.

For the rest of this chapter, we view procedures as idealized mathematical functions: we consider only procedures that involve no state and do not worry about the resources required to execute our procedures.

3.6.1 Making Procedures

Scheme provides a general mechanism for making a procedure:

Expression ::⇒ *ProcedureExpression*
ProcedureExpression ::⇒ (**lambda** (*Parameters*) *Expression*)
Parameters ::⇒ ϵ | ***Name*** *Parameters*

Evaluating a *ProcedureExpression* produces a procedure that takes as inputs the *Parameters* following the **lambda**. The **lambda** special form means "make a procedure". The body of the resulting procedure is the *Expression*, which is not evaluated until the procedure is applied.

A *ProcedureExpression* can replace an *Expression*. This means anywhere an *Expression* is used we can create a new procedure. This is very powerful since it means we can use procedures as inputs to other procedures and create procedures that return new procedures as their output!

Here are some example procedures:

(**lambda** (x) ($*$ x x))
Procedure that takes one input, and produces the square of the input value

as its output.

(lambda (*a b*) (+ *a b*))
Procedure that takes two inputs, and produces the sum of the input values as its output.

(lambda () 0)
Procedure that takes no inputs, and produces 0 as its output. The result of applying this procedure to any argument is always 0.

(lambda (*a*) **(lambda** (*b*) (+ *a b*)))
Procedure that takes one input (*a*), and produces as its output a procedure that takes one input and produces the sum of *a* and that input as its output. This is an example of a *higher-order procedure*. Higher-order procedures produce procedures as their output or take procedures as their arguments. This can be confusing, but is also very powerful.

higher-order procedure

3.6.2 Substitution Model of Evaluation

For a procedure to be useful, we need to apply it. In Section 3.4.2, we saw the syntax and evaluation rule for an *ApplicationExpression* when the procedure to be applied is a primitive procedure. The syntax for applying a constructed procedure is identical to the syntax for applying a primitive procedure:

Expression ::⇒ *ApplicationExpression*
ApplicationExpression ::⇒ (*Expression MoreExpressions*)
MoreExpressions ::⇒ ϵ | *Expression MoreExpressions*

To understand how constructed procedures are evaluated, we need a new evaluation rule. In this case, the first *Expression* evaluates to a procedure that was created using a *ProcedureExpression*, so the *ApplicationExpression* becomes:

ApplicationExpression ::⇒
((**lambda** (*Parameters*) *Expression*) *MoreExpressions*)

(The underlined part is the replacement for the *ProcedureExpression*.)

To evaluate the application, first evaluate the *MoreExpressions* in the application expression. These expressions are known as the *operands* of the application. The resulting values are the inputs to the procedure. There must be exactly one expression in the *MoreExpressions* corresponding to each name in the parameters list. Next, associate the names in the *Parameters* list with the corresponding operand values. Finally, evaluate the expression that is the body of the procedure. Whenever any parameter name is used inside the body expression, the name evaluates to the value of the corresponding input that is associated with that name.

Example 3.1: Square

Consider evaluating the following expression:

((**lambda** (*x*) (∗ *x x*)) 2)

It is an *ApplicationExpression* where the first subexpression is the *ProcedureExpression*, (**lambda** (*x*) (∗ *x x*)). To evaluate the application, we evaluate all the subexpressions and apply the value of the first subexpression to the values of the remaining subexpressions. The first subexpression evaluates to a procedure that takes one parameter named *x* and has the expression body (∗ *x x*). There is one operand expression, the primitive 2, that evaluates to 2.

To evaluate the application we bind the first parameter, *x*, to the value of the first operand, 2, and evaluate the procedure body, (∗ *x x*). After substituting the parameter values, we have (∗ 2 2). This is an application of the primitive multiplication procedure. Evaluating the application results in the value 4.

The procedure in our example, (**lambda** (*x*) (∗ *x x*)), is a procedure that takes a number as input and as output produces the square of that number. We can use the definition mechanism (from Section 3.5) to give this procedure a name so we can reuse it:

```
(define square (lambda (x) (* x x)))
```

This defines the name *square* as the procedure. After this, we can apply *square* to any number:

```
> (square 2)
4
> (square 1/4)
1/16
> (square (square 2))
16
```

Example 3.2: Make adder

The expression

```
((lambda (a)
   (lambda (b) (+ a b)))
 3)
```

evaluates to a procedure that adds 3 to its input. Applying that procedure to 4,

```
(((lambda (a) (lambda (b) (+ a b))) 3)
 4)
```

evaluates to 7. By using **define**, we can give these procedures sensible names:

```
(define make-adder
  (lambda (a)
    (lambda (b) (+ a b))))
```

Then, (**define** *add-three* (*make-adder* 3)) defines *add-three* as a procedure that takes one parameter and outputs the value of that parameter plus 3.

Abbreviated Procedure Definitions. Since we commonly define new procedures, Scheme provides a condensed notation for defining a procedure[6]:

[6]The condensed notation also includes a begin expression, which is a special form. We will not need the begin expression until we start dealing with procedures that have side effects. We describe the **begin** special form in Chapter 9.

Definition ::⇒ (**define** (***Name*** *Parameters*) *Expression*)

This incorporates the **lambda** invisibly into the definition, but means exactly the same thing. For example,

(**define** *square* (**lambda** (*x*) (∗ *x x*)))

can be written equivalently as:

(**define** (*square x*) (∗ *x x*))

Exercise 3.5. Define a procedure, *cube*, that takes one number as input and produces as output the cube of that number.

Exercise 3.6. Define a procedure, *compute-cost*, that takes as input two numbers, the first represents that price of an item, and the second represents the sales tax rate. The output should be the total cost, which is computed as the price of the item plus the sales tax on the item, which is its price times the sales tax rate. For example, (*compute-cost* 13 0.05) should evaluate to 13.65.

3.7 Decisions

To make more useful procedures, we need the actions taken to depend on the input values. For example, we may want a procedure that takes two numbers as inputs and evaluates to the greater of the two inputs. To define such a procedure we need a way of making a decision. The *IfExpression* expression provides a way of using the result of one expression to select which of two possible expressions to evaluate:

Expression ::⇒ *IfExpression*
IfExpression ::⇒ (**if** $Expression_{\text{Predicate}}$
$Expression_{\text{Consequent}}$
$Expression_{\text{Alternate}}$)

The *IfExpression* replacement has three *Expression* terms. For clarity, we give each of them names as denoted by the Predicate, Consequent, and Alternate subscripts. To evaluate an *IfExpression*, first evaluate the predicate expression, $Expression_{\text{Predicate}}$. If it evaluates to any non-false value, the value of the *IfExpression* is the value of $Expression_{\text{Consequent}}$, the consequent expression, and the alternate expression is not evaluated at all. If the predicate expression evaluates to false, the value of the *IfExpression* is the value of $Expression_{\text{Alternate}}$, the alternate expression, and the consequent expression is not evaluated at all.

The predicate expression determines which of the two following expressions is evaluated to produce the value of the *IfExpression*. If the value of the predicate is *anything* other than false, the consequent expression is used. For example, if the predicate evaluates to true, to a number, or to a procedure the consequent expression is evaluated.

special form

The if expression is a *special form*. This means that although it looks syntactically identical to an application (that is, it could be an application of a procedure named **if**), it is not evaluated as a normal application would be. Instead, we have a special evaluation rule for if expressions. The reason a special evaluation rule is needed is because we do not want all the subexpressions to be evaluated. With the normal application rule, all the subexpressions are evaluated first, and then the procedure resulting from the first subexpression is applied to the values resulting from the others. With the if special form evaluation rule, the predicate expression is always evaluated first and only one of the following subexpressions is evaluated depending on the result of evaluating the predicate expression.

This means an if expression can evaluate to a value even if evaluating one of its subexpressions would produce an error. For example,

```
(if (> 3 4) (* + +) 7)
```

evaluates to 7 even though evaluating the subexpression (* + +) would produce an error. Because of the special evaluation rule for if expressions, the consequent expression is never evaluated.

Example 3.3: Bigger

Now that we have procedures, decisions, and definitions, we can understand the *bigger* procedure from the beginning of the chapter. The definition,

```
(define (bigger a b) (if (> a b) a b))
```

is a condensed procedure definition. It is equivalent to:

```
(define bigger (lambda (a b) (if (> a b) a b)))
```

This defines the name *bigger* as the value of evaluating the procedure expression (**lambda** (*a b*) (**if** (> *a b*) *a b*)). This is a procedure that takes two inputs, named *a* and *b*. Its body is an if expression with predicate expression (> *a b*). The predicate expression compares the value that is bound to the first parameter, *a*, with the value that is bound to the second parameter, *b*, and evaluates to true if the value of the first parameter is greater, and false otherwise. According to the evaluation rule for an if expression, when the predicate evaluates to any non-false value (in this case, true), the value of the if expression is the value of the consequent expression, *a*. When the predicate evaluates to false, the value of the if expression is the value of the alternate expression, *b*. Hence, our *bigger* procedure takes two numbers as inputs and produces as output the greater of the two inputs.

Exercise 3.7. Follow the evaluation rules to evaluate the Scheme expression:

```
(bigger 3 4)
```

where *bigger* is the procedure defined above. (It is very tedious to follow all of the steps (that's why we normally rely on computers to do it!), but worth doing once to make sure you understand the evaluation rules.)

Exercise 3.8. Define a procedure, *xor*, that implements the logical exclusive-or operation. The *xor* function takes two inputs, and outputs true if exactly one of those outputs has a true value. Otherwise, it outputs false. For example, (*xor true true*) should evaluate to false and (*xor* (< 3 5) (= 8 8)) should evaluate to true.

Exercise 3.9. Define a procedure, *absvalue*, that takes a number as input and produces the absolute value of that number as its output. For example, (*absvalue* 3) should evaluate to 3 and (*absvalue* −150) should evaluate to 150.

Exercise 3.10. Define a procedure, *bigger-magnitude*, that takes two inputs, and outputs the value of the input with the greater magnitude (that is, absolute distance from zero). For example, (*bigger-magnitude* 5 −7) should evaluate to −7, and (*bigger-magnitude* 9 −3) should evaluate to 9.

Exercise 3.11. Define a procedure, *biggest*, that takes three inputs, and produces as output the maximum value of the three inputs. For example, (*biggest* 5 7 3) should evaluate to 7. Find at least two different ways to define *biggest*, one using *bigger*, and one without using it.

3.8 Evaluation Rules

Here we summarize the grammar rules and evaluation rules. Since each grammar rule has an associated evaluation rule, we can determine the meaning of any grammatical Scheme fragment by combining the evaluation rules corresponding to the grammar rules followed to derive that fragment.

Program ::⇒ ϵ | *ProgramElement Program*
ProgramElement ::⇒ *Expression* | *Definition*

A program is a sequence of expressions and definitions.

Definition ::⇒ (**define** ***Name*** *Expression*)

A definition evaluates the expression, and associates the value of the expression with the name.

Definition ::⇒ (**define** (***Name*** *Parameters*) *Expression*)

Abbreviation for
(**define** ***Name*** (**lambda** *Parameters*) *Expression*)

Expression ::⇒ *PrimitiveExpression* | *NameExpression*
| *ApplicationExpression*
| *ProcedureExpression* | *IfExpression*

The value of the expression is the value of the replacement expression.

PrimitiveExpression ::⇒ ***Number*** | *true* | *false* | *primitive procedure*

Evaluation Rule 1: Primitives. A primitive expression evaluates to its pre-defined value.

NameExpression ::⇒ ***Name***

Evaluation Rule 2: Names. A name evaluates to the value associated with that name.

ApplicationExpression ::⇒ (*Expression MoreExpressions*)

Evaluation Rule 3: Application. To evaluate an application expression:

a. **Evaluate** all the subexpressions;
b. Then, **apply** the value of the first subexpression to the values of the remaining subexpressions.

MoreExpressions ::⇒ ϵ | *Expression MoreExpressions*
ProcedureExpression ::⇒ (**lambda** (*Parameters*) *Expression*)
Parameters ::⇒ ϵ | ***Name*** *Parameters*

Evaluation Rule 4: Lambda. Lambda expressions evaluate to a procedure that takes the given parameters and has the expression as its body.

IfExpression ::⇒ (**if** $\mathit{Expression}_{\text{Predicate}}$
$\mathit{Expression}_{\text{Consequent}}$
$\mathit{Expression}_{\text{Alternate}}$)

Evaluation Rule 5: If. To evaluate an if expression, (a) evaluate the predicate expression; then, (b) if the value of the predicate expression is a false value then the value of the if expression is the value of the alternate expression; otherwise, the value of the if expression is the value of the consequent expression.

The evaluation rule for an application (Rule 3b) uses **apply** to perform the application. Apply is defined by the two application rules:

Application Rule 1: Primitives.
To apply a primitive procedure, just do it.

Application Rule 2: Constructed Procedures.
To apply a constructed procedure, **evaluate** the body of the procedure with each parameter name bound to the corresponding input expression value.

Application Rule 2 uses the evaluation rules to **evaluate** the expression. Thus, the evaluation rules are defined using the application rules, which are defined using the evaluation rules! This appears to be a circular definition, but as with the grammar examples, it has a base case. Some expressions evaluate without using the application rules (e.g., primitive expressions, name expressions), and some applications can be performed without using the evaluation rules (when the procedure to apply is a primitive). Hence, the process of evaluating an expression will sometimes finish and when it does we end with the value of the expression.[7]

[7]This does not guarantee that evaluation *always* finishes, however! The next chapter includes some examples where evaluation never finishes.

3.9 Summary

At this point, we have covered enough of Scheme to write useful programs (even if the programs we have seen so far seem rather dull). In fact (as we show in Chapter 12), we have covered enough to express *every* possible computation! We just need to combine these constructs in more complex ways to perform more interesting computations. The next chapter (and much of the rest of this book), focuses on ways to combine the constructs for making procedures, making decisions, and applying procedures in more powerful ways.

4

Problems and Procedures

A great discovery solves a great problem, but there is a grain of discovery in the solution of any problem. Your problem may be modest, but if it challenges your curiosity and brings into play your inventive faculties, and if you solve it by your own means, you may experience the tension and enjoy the triumph of discovery.
George Pólya, *How to Solve It*

Computers are tools for performing computations to solve problems. In this chapter, we consider what it means to solve a problem and explore some strategies for constructing procedures that solve problems.

4.1 Solving Problems

Traditionally, a problem is an obstacle to overcome or some question to answer. Once the question is answered or the obstacle circumvented, the problem is solved and we can declare victory and move on to the next one.

When we talk about writing programs to solve problems, though, we have a larger goal. We don't just want to solve *one* instance of a problem, we want an algorithm that can solve *all* instances of a problem. A *problem* is defined by its inputs and the desired property of the output. Recall from Chapter 1, that a procedure is a precise description of a process and a procedure is guaranteed to always finish is called an *algorithm*. The name algorithm is a Latinization of the name of the Persian mathematician and scientist, Muhammad ibn Mūsā al-Khwārizmī, who published a book in 825 on calculation with Hindu numerals. Although the name algorithm was adopted after al-Khwārizmī's book, algorithms go back much further than that. The ancient Babylonians had algorithms for finding square roots more than 3500 years ago (see Exploration 4.1).

problem

For example, we don't just want to find the best route between New York and Washington, we want an algorithm that takes as inputs the map, start location, and end location, and outputs the best route. There are infinitely many possible inputs that each specify different instances of the problem; a general solution to the problem is a procedure that finds the best route for all possible inputs.[1]

To define a procedure that can solve a problem, we need to define a procedure that takes inputs describing the problem instance and produces a different information process depending on the actual values of its inputs. A procedure

[1]Actually finding a general algorithm that does without needing to essentially try all possible routes is a challenging and interesting problem, for which no efficient solution is known. Finding one (or proving no fast algorithm exists) would resolve the most important open problem in computer science!

takes zero or more inputs, and produces one output or no outputs[2], as shown in Figure 4.1.

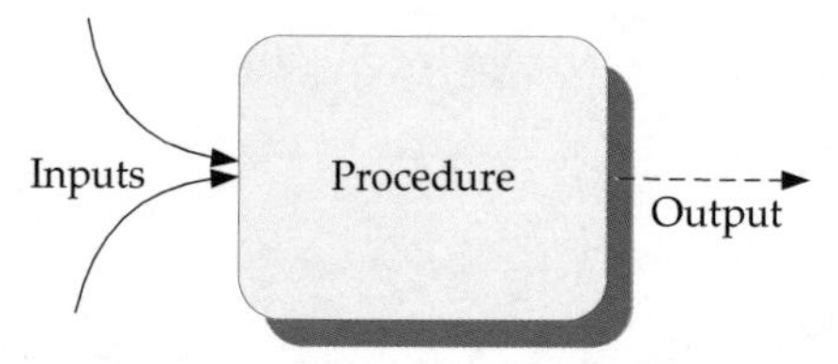

Figure 4.1. A procedure maps inputs to an output.

Our goal in solving a problem is to devise a procedure that takes inputs that define a problem instance, and produces as output the solution to that problem instance. The procedure should be an algorithm — this means every application of the procedure must eventually finish evaluating and produce an output value.

There is no magic wand for solving problems. But, most problem solving involves breaking problems you do not yet know how to solve into simpler and simpler problems until you find problems simple enough that you already know how to solve them. The creative challenge is to find the simpler subproblems that can be combined to solve the original problem. This approach of solving problems by breaking them into simpler parts is known as *divide-and-conquer*.

divide-and-conquer

The following sections describe a two key forms of divide-and-conquer problem solving: composition and recursive problem solving. We will use these same problem-solving techniques in different forms throughout this book.

4.2 Composing Procedures

One way to divide a problem is to split it into steps where the output of the first step is the input to the second step, and the output of the second step is the solution to the problem. Each step can be defined by one procedure, and the two procedures can be combined to create one procedure that solves the problem.

Figure 4.2 shows a composition of two functions, f and g. The output of f is used as the input to g.

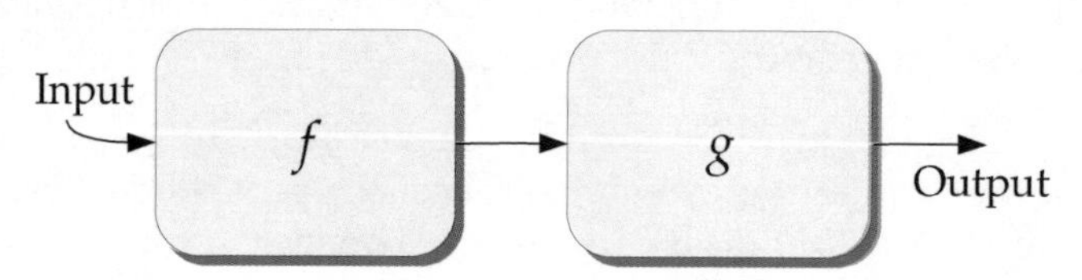

Figure 4.2. Composition.

We can express this composition with the Scheme expression $(g\ (f\ x))$ where x is the input. The written order appears to be reversed from the picture in Figure 4.2. This is because we apply a procedure to the values of its subexpressions:

[2]Although procedures can produce more than one output, we limit our discussion here to procedures that produce no more than one output. In the next chapter, we introduce ways to construct complex data, so any number of output values can be packaged into a single output.

the values of the inner subexpressions must be computed first, and then used as the inputs to the outer applications. So, the inner subexpression (*f x*) is evaluated first since the evaluation rule for the outer application expression is to first evaluate all the subexpressions.

To define a procedure that implements the composed procedure we make *x* a parameter:

```
(define fog (lambda (x) (g (f x))))
```

This defines *fog* as a procedure that takes one input and produces as output the composition of *f* and *g* applied to the input parameter. This works for any two procedures that both take a single input parameter.

We can compose the *square* and *cube* procedures from Chapter 3:

```
(define sixth-power (lambda (x) (cube (square x))))
```

Then, (*sixth-power* 2) evaluates to 64.

4.2.1 Procedures as Inputs and Outputs

All the procedure inputs and outputs we have seen so far have been numbers. The subexpressions of an application can be any expression including a procedure. A *higher-order procedure* is a procedure that takes other procedures as inputs or that produces a procedure as its output. Higher-order procedures give us the ability to write procedures that behave differently based on the procedures that are passed in as inputs.

higher-order procedure

We can create a generic composition procedure by making *f* and *g* parameters:

```
(define fog (lambda (f g x) (g (f x))))
```

The *fog* procedure takes three parameters. The first two are both procedures that take one input. The third parameter is a value that can be the input to the first procedure.

For example, (*fog square cube* 2) evaluates to 64, and (*fog* (**lambda** (*x*) (+ *x* 1)) *square* 2) evaluates to 9. In the second example, the first parameter is the procedure produced by the lambda expression (**lambda** (*x*) (+ *x* 1)). This procedure takes a number as input and produces as output that number plus one. We use a definition to name this procedure *inc* (short for increment):

```
(define inc (lambda (x) (+ x 1)))
```

A more useful composition procedure would separate the input value, *x*, from the composition. The *fcompose* procedure takes two procedures as inputs and produces as output a procedure that is their composition:[3]

```
(define fcompose
    (lambda (f g) (lambda (x) (g (f x)))))
```

The body of the *fcompose* procedure is a lambda expression that makes a procedure. Hence, the result of applying *fcompose* to two procedures is not a simple value, but a procedure. The resulting procedure can then be applied to a value.

[3] We name our composition procedure *fcompose* to avoid collision with the built-in *compose* procedure that behaves similarly.

Here are some examples using *fcompose*:

```
> (fcompose inc inc)
#<procedure>
> ((fcompose inc inc) 1)
3
> ((fcompose inc square) 2)
9
> ((fcompose square inc) 2)
5
```

Exercise 4.1. For each expression, give the value to which the expression evaluates. Assume *fcompose* and *inc* are defined as above.

a. ((*fcompose square square*) 3)

b. (*fcompose* (**lambda** (*x*) (* *x* 2)) (**lambda** (*x*) (/ *x* 2)))

c. ((*fcompose* (**lambda** (*x*) (* *x* 2)) (**lambda** (*x*) (/ *x* 2))) 1120)

d. ((*fcompose* (*fcompose inc inc*) *inc*) 2)

Exercise 4.2. Suppose we define *self-compose* as a procedure that composes a procedure with itself:

```
(define (self-compose f) (fcompose f f))
```

Explain how (((*fcompose self-compose self-compose*) *inc*) 1) is evaluated.

Exercise 4.3. Define a procedure *fcompose3* that takes three procedures as input, and produces as output a procedure that is the composition of the three input procedures. For example, ((*fcompose3 abs inc square*) −5) should evaluate to 36. Define *fcompose3* two different ways: once without using *fcompose*, and once using *fcompose*.

Exercise 4.4. The *fcompose* procedure only works when both input procedures take one input. Define a *f2compose* procedure that composes two procedures where the first procedure takes two inputs, and the second procedure takes one input. For example, ((*f2compose* + *abs*) 3 −5) should evaluate to 2.

4.3 Recursive Problem Solving

In the previous section, we used functional composition to break a problem into two procedures that can be composed to produce the desired output. A particularly useful variation on this is when we can break a problem into a smaller version of the original problem.

The goal is to be able to feed the output of one application of the procedure back into the same procedure as its input for the next application, as shown in Figure 4.3.

Here's a corresponding Scheme procedure:

```
(define f (lambda (n) (f n)))
```

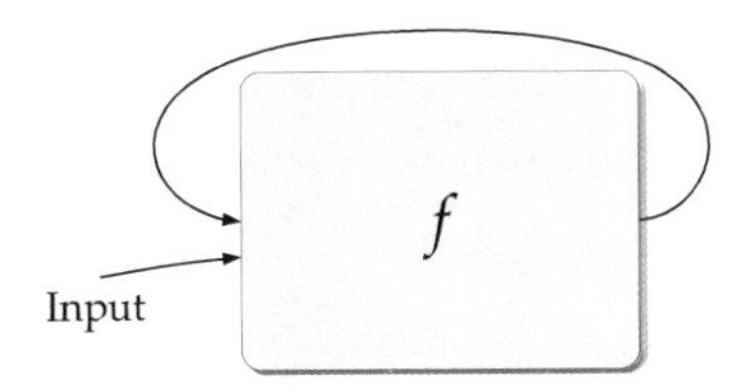

Figure 4.3. Circular Composition.

Of course, this doesn't work very well![4] Every application of f results in another application of f to evaluate. This never stops — no output is ever produced and the interpreter will keep evaluating applications of f until it is stopped or runs out of memory.

We need a way to make progress and eventually stop, instead of going around in circles. To make progress, each subsequent application should have a *smaller* input. Then, the applications stop when the input to the procedure is simple enough that the output is already known. The stopping condition is called the *base case*, similarly to the grammar rules in Section 2.4. In our grammar examples, the base case involved replacing the nonterminal with nothing (e.g., *MoreDigits* ::⇒ ϵ) or with a terminal (e.g., *Noun* ::⇒ **Alice**). In recursive procedures, the base case will provide a solution for some input for which the problem is so simple we already know the answer. When the input is a number, this is often (but not necessarily) when the input is 0 or 1.

base case

To define a recursive procedure, we use an if expression to test if the input matches the base case input. If it does, the consequent expression is the known answer for the base case. Otherwise, the recursive case applies the procedure again but with a smaller input. That application needs to make progress towards reaching the base case. This means, the input has to change in a way that gets closer to the base case input. If the base case is for 0, and the original input is a positive number, one way to get closer to the base case input is to subtract 1 from the input value with each recursive application.

This evaluation spiral is depicted in Figure 4.4. With each subsequent recursive call, the input gets smaller, eventually reaching the base case. For the base case application, a result is returned to the previous application. This is passed back up the spiral to produce the final output. Keeping track of where we are in a recursive evaluation is similar to keeping track of the subnetworks in an RTN traversal. The evaluator needs to keep track of where to return after each recursive evaluation completes, similarly to how we needed to keep track of the stack of subnetworks to know how to proceed in an RTN traversal.

Here is the corresponding procedure:

```
(define g
  (lambda (n)
    (if (= n 0) 1 (g (− n 1)))))
```

Unlike the earlier circular f procedure, if we apply g to any non-negative integer it will eventually produce an output. For example, consider evaluating (g 2).

[4]Curious readers should try entering this definition into a Scheme interpreter and evaluating (f 0). If you get tired of waiting for an output, in DrRacket you can click the **Stop** button in the upper right corner to interrupt the evaluation.

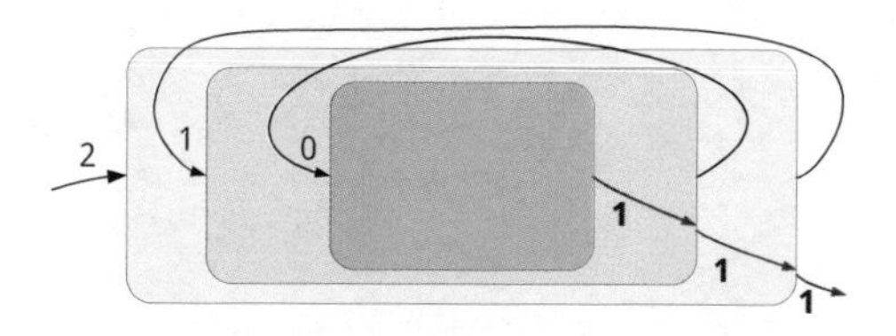

Figure 4.4. Recursive Composition.

When we evaluate the first application, the value of the parameter n is 2, so the predicate expression $(= n\ 0)$ evaluates to false and the value of the procedure body is the value of the alternate expression, $(g\ (- n\ 1))$. The subexpression, $(- n\ 1)$ evaluates to 1, so the result is the result of applying g to 1. As with the previous application, this leads to the application, $(g\ (- n\ 1))$, but this time the value of n is 1, so $(- n\ 1)$ evaluates to 0. The next application leads to the application, $(g\ 0)$. This time, the predicate expression evaluates to true and we have reached the base case. The consequent expression is just 1, so no further applications of g are performed and this is the result of the application $(g\ 0)$. This is returned as the result of the $(g\ 1)$ application in the previous recursive call, and then as the output of the original $(g\ 2)$ application.

We can think of the recursive evaluation as winding until the base case is reached, and then unwinding the outputs back to the original application. For this procedure, the output is not very interesting: no matter what positive number we apply g to, the eventual result is 1. To solve interesting problems with recursive procedures, we need to accumulate results as the recursive applications wind or unwind. Examples 4.1 and 4.2 illustrate recursive procedures that accumulate the result during the unwinding process. Example 4.3 illustrates a recursive procedure that accumulates the result during the winding process.

Example 4.1: Factorial

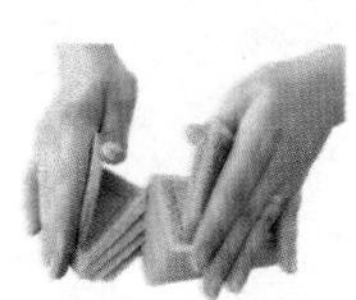

How many different arrangements are there of a deck of 52 playing cards?

The top card in the deck can be any of the 52 cards, so there are 52 possible choices for the top card. The second card can be any of the cards except for the card that is the top card, so there are 51 possible choices for the second card. The third card can be any of the 50 remaining cards, and so on, until the last card for which there is only one choice remaining.

$$52 * 51 * 50 * \cdots * 2 * 1$$

factorial

This is known as the *factorial* function (denoted in mathematics using the exclamation point, e.g., 52!). It can be defined recursively:

$$0! = 1$$
$$n! = n * (n-1)! \text{ for all } n > 0$$

The mathematical definition of factorial is recursive, so it is natural that we can define a recursive procedure that computes factorials:

```
(define (factorial n)
  (if (= n 0)
      1
      (* n (factorial (- n 1)))))
```

Evaluating (*factorial* 52) produces the number of arrangements of a 52-card deck: a sixty-eight digit number starting with an 8.

The *factorial* procedure has structure very similar to our earlier definition of the useless recursive *g* procedure. The only difference is the alternative expression for the if expression: in *g* we used (*g* (− *n* 1)); in *factorial* we added the outer application of $*$: ($*$ *n* (*factorial* (− *n* 1))). Instead of just evaluating to the result of the recursive application, we are now combining the output of the recursive evaluation with the input *n* using a multiplication application.

Exercise 4.5. How many different ways are there of choosing an unordered 5-card hand from a 52-card deck?

This is an instance of the "n choose k" problem (also known as the binomial coefficient): how many different ways are there to choose a set of k items from n items. There are n ways to choose the first item, $n-1$ ways to choose the second, ..., and $n-k+1$ ways to choose the kth item. But, since the order does not matter, some of these ways are equivalent. The number of possible ways to order the k items is $k!$, so we can compute the number of ways to choose k items from a set of n items as:

$$\frac{n * (n-1) * \cdots * (n-k+1)}{k!} = \frac{n!}{(n-k)!k!}$$

a. Define a procedure *choose* that takes two inputs, n (the size of the item set) and k (the number of items to choose), and outputs the number of possible ways to choose k items from n.

b. Compute the number of possible 5-card hands that can be dealt from a 52-card deck.

c. [⋆] Compute the likelihood of being dealt a flush (5 cards all of the same suit). In a standard 52-card deck, there are 13 cards of each of the four suits. Hint: divide the number of possible flush hands by the number of possible hands.

Exercise 4.6. Reputedly, when Karl Gauss was in elementary school his teacher assigned the class the task of summing the integers from 1 to 100 (e.g., $1+2+3+\cdots+100$) to keep them busy. Being the (future) "Prince of Mathematics", Gauss developed the formula for calculating this sum, that is now known as the *Gauss sum*. Had he been a computer scientist, however, and had access to a Scheme interpreter in the late 1700s, he might have instead defined a recursive procedure to solve the problem. Define a recursive procedure, *gauss-sum*, that takes a number n as its input parameter, and evaluates to the sum of the integers from 1 to n as its output. For example, (*gauss-sum* 100) should evaluate to 5050.

Karl Gauss

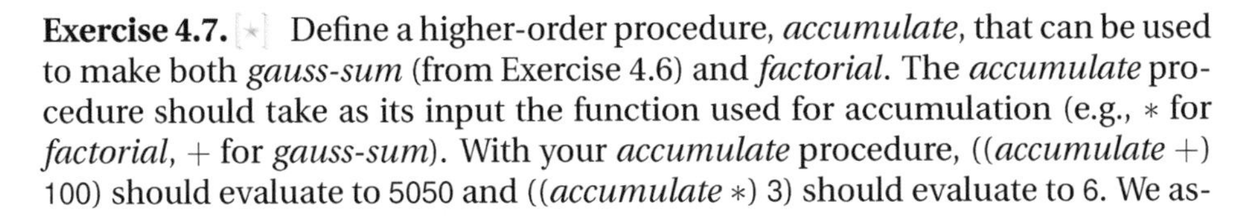

Exercise 4.7. [⋆] Define a higher-order procedure, *accumulate*, that can be used to make both *gauss-sum* (from Exercise 4.6) and *factorial*. The *accumulate* procedure should take as its input the function used for accumulation (e.g., $*$ for *factorial*, $+$ for *gauss-sum*). With your *accumulate* procedure, ((*accumulate* $+$) 100) should evaluate to 5050 and ((*accumulate* $*$) 3) should evaluate to 6. We as-

sume the result of the base case is 1 (although a more general procedure could take that as a parameter).

Hint: since your procedure should produce a procedure as its output, it could start like this:

```
(define (accumulate f)
  (lambda (n)
    (if (= n 1) 1
      ...
```

Example 4.2: Find Maximum

Consider the problem of defining a procedure that takes as its input a procedure, a low value, and a high value, and outputs the maximum value the input procedure produces when applied to an integer value between the low value and high value input. We name the inputs *f*, *low*, and *high*. To find the maximum, the *find-maximum* procedure should evaluate the input procedure *f* at every integer value between the *low* and *high*, and output the greatest value found.

Here are a few examples:

```
> (find-maximum (lambda (x) x) 1 20)
20
> (find-maximum (lambda (x) (− 10 x)) 1 20)
9
> (find-maximum (lambda (x) (* x (− 10 x))) 1 20)
25
```

To define the procedure, think about how to combine results from simpler problems to find the result. For the base case, we need a case so simple we already know the answer. Consider the case when *low* and *high* are equal. Then, there is only one value to use, and we know the value of the maximum is (*f low*). So, the base case is (**if** (= *low high*) (*f low*) ...).

How do we make progress towards the base case? Suppose the value of *high* is equal to the value of *low* plus 1. Then, the maximum value is either the value of (*f low*) or the value of (*f* (+ *low* 1)). We could select it using the *bigger* procedure (from Example 3.3): (*bigger* (*f low*) (*f* (+ *low* 1))). We can extend this to the case where *high* is equal to *low* plus 2:

```
(bigger (f low) (bigger (f (+ low 1)) (f (+ low 2))))
```

The second operand for the outer *bigger* evaluation is the maximum value of the input procedure between the low value plus one and the high value input. If we name the procedure we are defining *find-maximum*, then this second operand is the result of (*find-maximum f* (+ *low* 1) *high*). This works whether *high* is equal to (+ *low* 1), or (+ *low* 2), or any other value greater than *high*.

Putting things together, we have our recursive definition of *find-maximum*:

```
(define (find-maximum f low high)
  (if (= low high)
    (f low)
    (bigger (f low) (find-maximum f (+ low 1) high))))
```

Exercise 4.8. To find the maximum of a function that takes a real number as its input, we need to evaluate at all numbers in the range, not just the integers. There are infinitely many numbers between any two numbers, however, so this is impossible. We can approximate this, however, by evaluating the function at many numbers in the range.

Define a procedure *find-maximum-epsilon* that takes as input a function f, a low range value *low*, a high range value *high*, and an increment *epsilon*, and produces as output the maximum value of f in the range between *low* and *high* at interval *epsilon*. As the value of *epsilon* decreases, *find-maximum-epsilon* should evaluate to a value that approaches the actual maximum value.

For example,

(*find-maximum-epsilon* (**lambda** (x) ($*$ x ($-$ 5.5 x))) 1 10 1)

evaluates to 7.5. And,

(*find-maximum-epsilon* (**lambda** (x) ($*$ x ($-$ 5.5 x))) 1 10 0.01)

evaluates to 7.5625.

Exercise 4.9. [⋆] The *find-maximum* procedure we defined evaluates to the maximum value of the input function in the range, but does not provide the input value that produces that maximum output value. Define a procedure that finds the input in the range that produces the maximum output value. For example, (*find-maximum-input inc* 1 10) should evaluate to 10 and (*find-maximum-input* (**lambda** (x) ($*$ x ($-$ 5.5 x))) 1 10) should evaluate to 3.

Exercise 4.10. [⋆] Define a *find-area* procedure that takes as input a function f, a low range value *low*, a high range value *high*, and an increment *epsilon*, and produces as output an estimate for the area under the curve produced by the function f between *low* and *high* using the *epsilon* value to determine how many regions to evaluate.

Example 4.3: Euclid's Algorithm

In Book 7 of the *Elements*, Euclid describes an algorithm for finding the greatest common divisor of two non-zero integers. The greatest common divisor is the greatest integer that divides both of the input numbers without leaving any remainder. For example, the greatest common divisor of 150 and 200 is 50 since (/ 150 50) evaluates to 3 and (/ 200 50) evaluates to 4, and there is no number greater than 50 that can evenly divide both 150 and 200.

The *modulo* primitive procedure takes two integers as its inputs and evaluates to the remainder when the first input is divided by the second input. For example, (*modulo* 6 3) evaluates to 0 and (*modulo* 7 3) evaluates to 1.

Euclid's algorithm stems from two properties of integers:

1. If (*modulo a b*) evaluates to 0 then b is the greatest common divisor of a and b.
2. If (*modulo a b*) evaluates to a non-zero integer r, the greatest common divisor of a and b is the greatest common divisor of b and r.

We can define a recursive procedure for finding the greatest common divisor closely following Euclid's algorithm[5]:

```
(define (gcd-euclid a b)
  (if (= (modulo a b) 0) b (gcd-euclid b (modulo a b))))
```

The structure of the definition is similar to the *factorial* definition: the procedure body is an if expression and the predicate tests for the base case. For the *gcd-euclid* procedure, the base case corresponds to the first property above. It occurs when *b* divides *a* evenly, and the consequent expression is *b*. The alternate expression, (*gcd-euclid b* (*modulo a b*)), is the recursive application.

The *gcd-euclid* procedure differs from the *factorial* definition in that there is no outer application expression in the recursive call. We do not need to combine the result of the recursive application with some other value as was done in the *factorial* definition, the result of the recursive application is the final result. Unlike the *factorial* and *find-maximum* examples, the *gcd-euclid* procedure produces the result in the base case, and no further computation is necessary to produce the final result. When no further evaluation is necessary to get from the result of the recursive application to the final result, a recursive definition is said to be *tail recursive*. Tail recursive procedures have the advantage that they can be evaluated without needing to keep track of the stack of previous recursive calls. Since the final call produces the final result, there is no need for the interpreter to unwind the recursive calls to produce the answer.

tail recursive

Exercise 4.11. Show the structure of the *gcd-euclid* applications in evaluating (*gcd-euclid* 6 9).

Exercise 4.12. [★] Provide a convincing argument why the evaluation of (*gcd-euclid a b*) will always finish when the inputs are both positive integers.

Exercise 4.13. Provide an alternate definition of *factorial* that is tail recursive. To be tail recursive, the expression containing the recursive application cannot be part of another application expression. (Hint: define a *factorial-helper* procedure that takes an extra parameter, and then define *factorial* as (**define** (*factorial n*) (*factorial-helper n* 1)).)

Exercise 4.14. Provide a tail recursive definition of *find-maximum*.

Exercise 4.15. [★★] Provide a convincing argument why it is possible to transform any recursive procedure into an equivalent procedure that is tail recursive.

Exploration 4.1: Square Roots

One of the earliest known algorithms is a method for computing square roots. It is known as Heron's method after the Greek mathematician Heron of Alexandria who lived in the first century AD who described the method, although it was also known to the Babylonians many centuries earlier. Isaac Newton developed a

[5]DrRacket provides a built-in procedure *gcd* that computes the greatest common divisor. We name our procedure *gcd-euclid* to avoid a clash with the build-in procedure.

more general method for estimating functions based on their derivatives known as Netwon's method, of which Heron's method is a specialization.

Square root is a mathematical function that take a number, a, as input and outputs a value x such that $x^2 = a$. For many numbers (including 2), the square root is irrational, so the best we can hope for with is a good approximation. We define a procedure *find-sqrt* that takes the target number as input and outputs an approximation for its square root.

Heron's method works by starting with an arbitrary guess, g_0. Then, with each iteration, compute a new guess (g_n is the nth guess) that is a function of the previous guess (g_{n-1}) and the target number (a):

$$g_n = \frac{g_{n-1} + \frac{a}{g_{n-1}}}{2}$$

Heron of Alexandria

As n increases g_n gets closer and closer to the square root of a.

The definition is recursive since we compute g_n as a function of g_{n-1}, so we can define a recursive procedure that computes Heron's method. First, we define a procedure for computing the next guess from the previous guess and the target:

```
(define (heron-next-guess a g) (/ (+ g (/ a g)) 2))
```

Next, we define a recursive procedure to compute the nth guess using Heron's method. It takes three inputs: the target number, a, the number of guesses to make, n, and the value of the first guess, g.

```
(define (heron-method a n g)
  (if (= n 0)
    g
    (heron-method a (- n 1) (heron-next-guess a g))))
```

To start, we need a value for the first guess. The choice doesn't really matter — the method works with any starting guess (but will reach a closer estimate quicker if the starting guess is good). We will use 1 as our starting guess. So, we can define a *find-sqrt* procedure that takes two inputs, the target number and the number of guesses to make, and outputs an approximation of the square root of the target number.

```
(define (find-sqrt a guesses)
  (heron-method a guesses 1))
```

Heron's method converges to a good estimate very quickly:

```
> (square (find-sqrt 2 0))
1
> (square (find-sqrt 2 1))
2 1/4
> (square (find-sqrt 2 2))
2 1/144
> (square (find-sqrt 2 4))
2 1/221682772224
> (exact->inexact (find-sqrt 2 5))
1.4142135623730951
```

The actual square root of 2 is 1.4142135623730950 48 . . ., so our estimate is correct to 16 digits after only five guesses.

Users of square roots don't really care about the method used to find the square root (or how many guesses are used). Instead, what is important to a square root user is how close the estimate is to the actual value. Can we change our *find-sqrt* procedure so that instead of taking the number of guesses to make as its second input it takes a minimum tolerance value?

Since we don't know the actual square root value (otherwise, of course, we could just return that), we need to measure tolerance as how close the square of the approximation is to the target number. Hence, we can stop when the square of the guess is close enough to the target value.

```
(define (close-enough? a tolerance g)
  (<= (abs (- a (square g))) tolerance))
```

The stopping condition for the recursive definition is now when the guess is close enough. Otherwise, our definitions are the same as before.

```
(define (heron-method-tolerance a tolerance g)
  (if (close-enough? a tolerance g)
      g
      (heron-method-tolerance a tolerance (heron-next-guess a g))))

(define (find-sqrt-approx a tolerance)
  (heron-method-tolerance a tolerance 1))
```

Note that the value passed in as *tolerance* does not change with each recursive call. We are making the problem smaller by making each successive guess closer to the required answer.

Here are some example interactions with *find-sqrt-approx*:

```
> (exact->inexact (square (find-sqrt-approx 2 0.01)))
2.0069444444444446
> (exact->inexact (square (find-sqrt-approx 2 0.0000001)))
2.000000000004511
```

a. How accurate is the built-in *sqrt* procedure?

b. Can you produce more accurate square roots than the built-in *sqrt* procedure?

c. Why doesn't the built-in procedure do better?

4.4 Evaluating Recursive Applications

Evaluating an application of a recursive procedure follows the evaluation rules just like any other expression evaluation. It may be confusing, however, to see that this works because of the apparent circularity of the procedure definition.

Here, we show in detail the evaluation steps for evaluating (*factorial* 2). The evaluation and application rules refer to the rules summary in Section 3.8. We first show the complete evaluation following the substitution model evaluation rules in full gory detail, and later review a subset showing the most revealing steps. Stepping through even a fairly simple evaluation using the evaluation rules is quite tedious, and not something humans should do very often (that's why we have computers!) but instructive to do once to understand exactly how an expression is evaluated.

The evaluation rule for an application expression does not specify the order in which the subexpressions are evaluated. A Scheme interpreter is free to evaluate them in any order. Here, we choose to evaluate the subexpressions in the order that is most readable. The value produced by an evaluation does not depend on the order in which the subexpressions are evaluated.[6]

In the evaluation steps, we use `typewriter` font for uninterpreted Scheme expressions and sans-serif font to show values. So, `2` represents the Scheme expression that evaluates to the number 2.

```
1  (factorial 2)                          Evaluation Rule 3(a): Application subexpressions
2  (factorial 2)                          Evaluation Rule 2: Name
3  ((lambda (n) (if (= n 0) 1 (* n (factorial (- n 1))))) 2)
                                          Evaluation Rule 4: Lambda
4  ((lambda (n) (if (= n 0) 1 (* n (factorial (- n 1))))) 2)   Evaluation Rule 1: Primitive
5  ((lambda (n) (if (= n 0) 1 (* n (factorial (- n 1))))) 2)
                                          Evaluation Rule 3(b): Application, Application Rule 2
6  (if (= 2 0) 1 (* 2 (factorial (- 2 1))))    Evaluation Rule 5(a): If predicate
7  (if (= 2 0) 1 (* 2 (factorial (- 2 1))))
                                          Evaluation Rule 3(a): Application subexpressions
8  (if (= 2 0) 1 (* 2 (factorial (- 2 1))))    Evaluation Rule 1: Primitive
9  (if (= 2 0) 1 (* 2 (factorial (- 2 1))))
                                          Evaluation Rule 3(b): Application, Application Rule 1
10 (if false 1 (* 2 (factorial (- 2 1))))  Evaluation Rule 5(b): If alternate
11 (* 2 (factorial (- 2 1)))              Evaluation Rule 3(a): Application subexpressions
12 (* 2 (factorial (- 2 1)))              Evaluation Rule 1: Primitive
13 (* 2 (factorial (- 2 1)))              Evaluation Rule 3(a): Application subexpressions
14 (* 2 (factorial (- 2 1)))              Evaluation Rule 3(a): Application subexpressions
15 (* 2 (factorial (- 2 1)))              Evaluation Rule 1: Primitive
16 (* 2 (factorial (- 2 1)))              Evaluation Rule 3(b): Application, Application Rule 1
17    (* 2 (factorial 1))                 Continue Evaluation Rule 3(a); Evaluation Rule 2: Name
18    (* 2 ((lambda (n) (if (= n 0) 1 (* n (factorial (- n 1))))) 1))
                                          Evaluation Rule 4: Lambda
19    (* 2 ((lambda (n) (if (= n 0) 1 (* n (factorial (- n 1))))) 1))
                                          Evaluation Rule 3(b): Application, Application Rule 2
20    (* 2 (if (= 1 0) 1 (* 1 (factorial (- 1 1)))))
                                          Evaluation Rule 5(a): If predicate
21    (* 2 (if (= 1 0) 1 (* 1 (factorial (- 1 1)))))
                                          Evaluation Rule 3(a): Application subexpressions
22    (* 2 (if (= 1 0) 1 (* 1 (factorial (- 1 1)))))
                                          Evaluation Rule 1: Primitives
23    (* 2 (if (= 1 0) 1 (* 1 (factorial (- 1 1)))))
                                          Evaluation Rule 3(b): Application Rule 1
24    (* 2 (if false 1 (* 1 (factorial (- 1 1)))))
                                          Evaluation Rule 5(b): If alternate
25    (* 2 (* 1 (factorial (- 1 1))))     Evaluation Rule 3(a): Application
```

[6]This is only true for the subset of Scheme we have defined so far. Once we introduce side effects and mutation, it is no longer the case, and expressions can produce different results depending on the order in which they are evaluated.

```
26     (* 2 (* 1 (factorial (- 1 1))))                    Evaluation Rule 1: Primitives
27     (* 2 (* 1 (factorial (- 1 1))))                    Evaluation Rule 3(a): Application
28     (* 2 (* 1 (factorial (- 1 1))))                    Evaluation Rule 3(a): Application
29     (* 2 (* 1 (factorial (- 1 1))))                    Evaluation Rule 1: Primitives
30     (* 2 (* 1 (factorial (- 1 1))))
                               Evaluation Rule 3(b): Application, Application Rule 1
31        (* 2 (* 1 (factorial 0)))                       Evaluation Rule 2: Name
32        (* 2 (* 1 ((lambda (n) (if (= n 0) 1 (* n (fact...  )))) 0)))
                                                          Evaluation Rule 4, Lambda
33        (* 2 (* 1 ((lambda (n) (if (= n 0) 1 (* n (factorial (- n 1))))) 0)))
                                           Evaluation Rule 3(b), Application Rule 2
34        (* 2 (* 1 (if (= 0 0) 1 (* 0 (factorial (- 0 1))))))
                                                Evaluation Rule 5(a): If predicate
35        (* 2 (* 1 (if (= 0 0) 1 (* 0 (factorial (- 0 1))))))
                              Evaluation Rule 3(a): Application subexpressions
36        (* 2 (* 1 (if (= 0 0) 1 (* 0 (factorial (- 0 1))))))
                                                    Evaluation Rule 1: Primitives
37        (* 2 (* 1 (if (= 0 0) 1 (* 0 (factorial (- 0 1))))))
                               Evaluation Rule 3(b): Application, Application Rule 1
38        (* 2 (* 1 (if true 1 (* 0 (factorial (- 0 1))))))
                                               Evaluation Rule 5(b): If consequent
39        (* 2 (* 1 1))                                  Evaluation Rule 1: Primitives
40        (* 2 (* 1 1))           Evaluation Rule 3(b): Application, Application Rule 1
41     (* 2 1)                    Evaluation Rule 3(b): Application, Application Rule 1
42  2                       Evaluation finished, no unevaluated expressions remain.
```

The key to evaluating recursive procedure applications is if special evaluation rule. If the if expression were evaluated like a regular application all subexpressions would be evaluated, and the alternative expression containing the recursive call would never finish evaluating! Since the evaluation rule for if evaluates the predicate expression first and does not evaluate the alternative expression when the predicate expression is true, the circularity in the definition ends when the predicate expression evaluates to true. This is the base case. In the example, this is the base case where (= *n* 0) evaluates to true and instead of producing another recursive call it evaluates to 1.

The Evaluation Stack. The structure of the evaluation is clearer from just the most revealing steps:

```
1   (factorial 2)
17      (* 2 (factorial 1))
31          (* 2 (* 1 (factorial 0)))
40          (* 2 (* 1 1))
41      (* 2 1)
42  2
```

Step 1 starts evaluating (*factorial* 2). The result is found in Step 42. To evaluate (*factorial* 2), we follow the evaluation rules, eventually reaching the body expression of the if expression in the factorial definition in Step 17. Evaluating this expression requires evaluating the (*factorial* 1) subexpression. At Step 17, the first evaluation is in progress, but to complete it we need the value resulting from the second recursive application.

Evaluating the second application results in the body expression, (∗ 1 (*factorial* 0)), shown for Step 31. At this point, the evaluation of (*factorial* 2) is stuck in

Evaluation Rule 3, waiting for the value of (*factorial* 1) subexpression. The evaluation of the (*factorial* 1) application leads to the (*factorial* 0) subexpression, which must be evaluated before the (*factorial* 1) evaluation can complete.

In Step 40, the (*factorial* 0) subexpression evaluation has completed and produced the value 1. Now, the (*factorial* 1) evaluation can complete, producing 1 as shown in Step 41. Once the (*factorial* 1) evaluation completes, all the subexpressions needed to evaluate the expression in Step 17 are now evaluated, and the evaluation completes in Step 42.

Each recursive application can be tracked using a stack, similarly to processing RTN subnetworks (Section 2.3). A stack has the property that the first item pushed on the stack will be the last item removed—all the items pushed on top of this one must be removed before this item can be removed. For application evaluations, the elements on the stack are expressions to evaluate. To finish evaluating the first expression, all of its component subexpressions must be evaluated. Hence, the first application evaluation started is the last one to finish.

Exercise 4.16. This exercise tests your understanding of the (*factorial* 2) evaluation.

a. In step 5, the second part of the application evaluation rule, Rule 3(b), is used. In which step does this evaluation rule complete?

b. In step 11, the first part of the application evaluation rule, Rule 3(a), is used. In which step is the following use of Rule 3(b) started?

c. In step 25, the first part of the application evaluation rule, Rule 3(a), is used. In which step is the following use of Rule 3(b) started?

d. To evaluate (*factorial* 3), how many times would Evaluation Rule 2 be used to evaluate the name *factorial*?

e. [*] To evaluate (*factorial* n) for any positive integer n, how many times would Evaluation Rule 2 be used to evaluate the name *factorial*?

Exercise 4.17. For which input values n will an evaluation of (*factorial* n) eventually reach a value? For values where the evaluation is guaranteed to finish, make a convincing argument why it must finish. For values where the evaluation would not finish, explain why.

4.5 Developing Complex Programs

To develop and use more complex procedures it will be useful to learn some helpful techniques for understanding what is going on when procedures are evaluated. It is very rare for a first version of a program to be completely correct, even for an expert programmer. Wise programmers build programs incrementally, by writing and testing small components one at a time.

The process of fixing broken programs is known as *debugging*. The key to debugging effectively is to be systematic and thoughtful. It is a good idea to take notes to keep track of what you have learned and what you have tried. Thoughtless debugging can be very frustrating, and is unlikely to lead to a correct program.

debugging

A good strategy for debugging is to:

1. Ensure you understand the intended behavior of your procedure. Think of a few representative inputs, and what the expected output should be.
2. Do experiments to observe the actual behavior of your procedure. Try your program on simple inputs first. What is the relationship between the actual outputs and the desired outputs? Does it work correctly for some inputs but not others?
3. Make changes to your procedure and retest it. If you are not sure what to do, make changes in small steps and carefully observe the impact of each change.

First actual bug
Grace Hopper's notebook, 1947

For more complex programs, follow this strategy at the level of sub-components. For example, you can try debugging at the level of one expression before trying the whole procedure. Break your program into several procedures so you can test and debug each procedure independently. The smaller the unit you test at one time, the easier it is to understand and fix problems.

DrRacket provides many useful and powerful features to aid debugging, but the most important tool for debugging is using your brain to think carefully about what your program should be doing and how its observed behavior differs from the desired behavior. Next, we describe two simple ways to observe program behavior.

4.5.1 Printing

One useful procedure built-in to DrRacket is the *display* procedure. It takes one input, and produces no output. Instead of producing an output, it prints out the value of the input (it will appear in purple in the Interactions window). We can use *display* to observe what a procedure is doing as it is evaluated.

For example, if we add a (*display n*) expression at the beginning of our *factorial* procedure we can see all the intermediate calls. To make each printed value appear on a separate line, we use the *newline* procedure. The *newline* procedure prints a new line; it takes no inputs and produces no output.

```
(define (factorial n)
  (display "Enter factorial: ") (display n) (newline)
  (if (= n 0) 1 (* n (factorial (- n 1)))))
```

Evaluating (*factorial* 2) produces:

```
Enter factorial: 2
Enter factorial: 1
Enter factorial: 0
2
```

The built-in *printf* procedure makes it easier to print out many values at once. It takes one or more inputs. The first input is a string (a sequence of characters enclosed in double quotes). The string can include special ~a markers that print out values of objects inside the string. Each ~a marker is matched with a corresponding input, and the value of that input is printed in place of the ~a in the string. Another special marker, ~n, prints out a new line inside the string.

Using *printf*, we can define our *factorial* procedure with printing as:

```
(define (factorial n)
  (printf "Enter factorial: ~a~n" n)
  (if (= n 0) 1 (* n (factorial (- n 1)))))
```

The *display, printf*, and *newline* procedures do not produce output values. Instead, they are applied to produce *side effects.* A side effect is something that changes the state of a computation. In this case, the side effect is printing in the Interactions window. Side effects make reasoning about what programs do much more complicated since the order in which events happen now matters. We will mostly avoid using procedures with side effects until Chapter 9, but printing procedures are so useful that we introduce them here.

side effects

4.5.2 Tracing

DrRacket provides a more automated way to observe applications of procedures. We can use tracing to observe the start of a procedure evaluation (including the procedure inputs) and the completion of the evaluation (including the output). To use tracing, it is necessary to first load the tracing library by evaluating this expression:

```
(require racket/trace)
```

This defines the *trace* procedure that takes one input, a constructed procedure (trace does not work for primitive procedures). After evaluating (*trace proc*), the interpreter will print out the procedure name and its inputs at the beginning of every application of *proc* and the value of the output at the end of the application evaluation. If there are other applications before the first application finishes evaluating, these will be printed indented so it is possible to match up the beginning and end of each application evaluation. For example (the trace outputs are shown in `typewriter` font),

```
> (trace factorial)
> (factorial 2)
(factorial 2)
|(factorial 1)
| (factorial 0)
| 1
|1
2
2
```

The trace shows that (*factorial* 2) is evaluated first; within its evaluation, (*factorial* 1) and then (*factorial* 0) are evaluated. The outputs of each of these applications is lined up vertically below the application entry trace.

Exploration 4.2: Recipes for π

The value π is the defined as the ratio between the circumference of a circle and its diameter. One way to calculate the approximate value of π is the Gregory-Leibniz series (which was actually discovered by the Indian mathematician Mādhava in the 14th century):

$$\pi = \frac{4}{1} - \frac{4}{3} + \frac{4}{5} - \frac{4}{7} + \frac{4}{9} - \cdots$$

This summation converges to π. The more terms that are included, the closer the computed value will be to the actual value of π.

a. [★] Define a procedure *compute-pi* that takes as input n, the number of terms to include and outputs an approximation of π computed using the first n terms of the Gregory-Leibniz series. (*compute-pi* 1) should evaluate to 4 and (*compute-pi* 2) should evaluate to 2 2/3. For higher terms, use the built-in procedure *exact->inexact* to see the decimal value. For example,

(*exact->inexact* (*compute-pi* 10000))

evaluates (after a long wait!) to 3.1414926535900434.

The Gregory-Leibniz series is fairly simple, but it takes an awful long time to converge to a good approximation for π — only one digit is correct after 10 terms, and after summing 10000 terms only the first four digits are correct.

Mādhava discovered another series for computing the value of π that converges much more quickly:

$$\pi = \sqrt{12} * (1 - \frac{1}{3 * 3} + \frac{1}{5 * 3^2} - \frac{1}{7 * 3^3} + \frac{1}{9 * 3^4} - \ldots)$$

Mādhava computed the first 21 terms of this series, finding an approximation of π that is correct for the first 12 digits: 3.14159265359.

b. [★★] Define a procedure *cherry-pi* that takes as input n, the number of terms to include and outputs an approximation of π computed using the first n terms of the Mādhava series. (Continue reading for hints.)

To define *faster-pi*, first define two helper functions: *faster-pi-helper*, that takes one input, n, and computes the sum of the first n terms in the series without the $\sqrt{12}$ factor, and *faster-pi-term* that takes one input n and computes the value of the nth term in the series (without alternating the adding and subtracting). (*faster-pi-term* 1) should evaluate to 1 and (*faster-pi-term* 2) should evaluate to 1/9. Then, define *faster-pi* as:

```
(define (faster-pi terms) (* (sqrt 12) (faster-pi-helper terms)))
```

This uses the built-in *sqrt* procedure that takes one input and produces as output an approximation of its square root. The accuracy of the *sqrt* procedure[7] limits the number of digits of π that can be correctly computed using this method (see Exploration 4.1 for ways to compute a more accurate approximation for the square root of 12). You should be able to get a few more correct digits than Mādhava was able to get without a computer 600 years ago, but to get more digits would need a more accurate *sqrt* procedure or another method for computing π.

The built-in *expt* procedure takes two inputs, a and b, and produces a^b as its output. You could also define your own procedure to compute a^b for any integer inputs a and b.

c. [★★★] Find a procedure for computing enough digits of π to find the *Feynman point* where there are six consecutive 9 digits. This point is named for Richard Feynman, who quipped that he wanted to memorize π to that point so he could recite it as "... nine, nine, nine, nine, nine, nine, and so on".

[7] To test its accuracy, try evaluating (*square* (*sqrt* 12)).

Exploration 4.3: Recursive Definitions and Games

Many games can be analyzed by thinking recursively. For this exploration, we consider how to develop a winning strategy for some two-player games. In all the games, we assume player 1 moves first, and the two players take turns until the game ends. The game ends when the player who's turn it is cannot move; the other player wins. A strategy is a *winning strategy* if it provides a way to always select a move that wins the game, regardless of what the other player does.

One approach for developing a winning strategy is to work backwards from the winning position. This position corresponds to the base case in a recursive definition. If the game reaches a winning position for player 1, then player 1 wins. Moving back one move, if the game reaches a position where it is player 2's move, but all possible moves lead to a winning position for player 1, then player 1 is guaranteed to win. Continuing backwards, if the game reaches a position where it is player 1's move, and there is a move that leads to a position where all possible moves for player 2 lead to a winning position for player 1, then player 1 is guaranteed to win.

The first game we will consider is called *Nim*. Variants on Nim have been played widely over many centuries, but no one is quite sure where the name comes from. We'll start with a simple variation on the game that was called *Thai 21* when it was used as an Immunity Challenge on *Survivor*.

In this version of Nim, the game starts with a pile of 21 stones. One each turn, a player removes one, two, or three stones. The player who removes the last stone wins, since the other player cannot make a valid move on the following turn.

a. What should the player who moves first do to ensure she can always win the game? (Hint: start with the base case, and work backwards. Think about a game starting with 5 stones first, before trying 21.)

b. Suppose instead of being able to take 1 to 3 stones with each turn, you can take 1 to n stones where n is some number greater than or equal to 1. For what values of n should the first player always win (when the game starts with 21 stones)?

A standard Nim game starts with three heaps. At each turn, a player removes any number of stones from any one heap (but may not remove stones from more than one heap). We can describe the state of a 3-heap game of Nim using three numbers, representing the number of stones in each heap. For example, the *Thai 21* game starts with the state (21 0 0) (one heap with 21 stones, and two empty heaps).[8]

c. What should the first player do to win if the starting state is (2 1 0)?

d. Which player should win if the starting state is (2 2 2)?

e. [*] Which player should win if the starting state is (5 6 7)?

f. [**] Describe a strategy for always winning a winnable game of Nim starting from any position.[9]

---

[8]With the standard Nim rules, this would not be an interesting game since the first player can simply win by removing all 21 stones from the first heap.

[9]If you get stuck, you'll find many resources about Nim on the Internet; but, you'll get a lot more out of this if you solve it yourself.

The final game we consider is the "Corner the Queen" game invented by Rufus Isaacs.[10] The game is played using a single Queen on a arbitrarily large chessboard as shown in Figure 4.5.

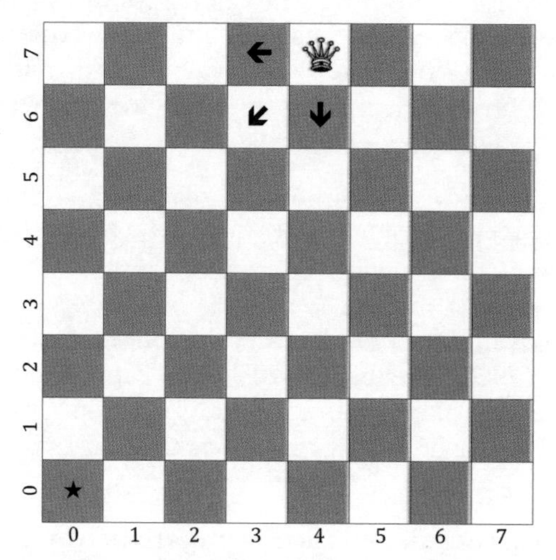

Figure 4.5. Cornering the Queen.

On each turn, a player moves the Queen one or more squares in either the left, down, or diagonally down-left direction (unlike a standard chess Queen, in this game the queen may not move right, up or up-right). As with the other games, the last player to make a legal move wins. For this game, once the Queen reaches the bottom left square marked with the ⋆, there are no moves possible. Hence, the player who moves the Queen onto the ⋆ wins the game. We name the squares using the numbers on the sides of the chessboard with the column number first. So, the Queen in the picture is on square (4 7).

g. Identify all the starting squares for which the first played to move can win right away. (Your answer should generalize to any size square chessboard.)

h. Suppose the Queen is on square (2 1) and it is your move. Explain why there is no way you can avoid losing the game.

i. Given the shown starting position (with the Queen at (4 7), would you rather be the first or second player?

j. [⋆] Describe a strategy for winning the game (when possible). Explain from which starting positions it is not possible to win (assuming the other player always makes the right move).

k. [⋆] Define a variant of Nim that is essentially the same as the "Corner the Queen" game. (This game is known as "Wythoff's Nim".)

Developing winning strategies for these types of games is similar to defining a recursive procedure that solves a problem. We need to identify a base case from which it is obvious how to win, and a way to make progress fro m a large input towards that base case.

[10]Described in Martin Gardner, *Penrose Tiles to Trapdoor Ciphers. . .And the Return of Dr Matrix*, The Mathematical Association of America, 1997.

4.6 Summary

By breaking problems down into simpler problems we can develop solutions to complex problems. Many problems can be solved by combining instances of the same problem on simpler inputs. When we define a procedure to solve a problem this way, it needs to have a predicate expression to determine when the base case has been reached, a consequent expression that provides the value for the base case, and an alternate expression that defines the solution to the given input as an expression using a solution to a smaller input.

Our general recursive problem solving strategy is:

I'd rather be an optimist and a fool than a pessimist and right.
Albert Einstein

1. **Be optimistic!** Assume you can solve it.
2. Think of the simplest version of the problem, something you can already solve. This is the base case.
3. Consider how you would solve a big version of the problem by using the result for a slightly smaller version of the problem. This is the recursive case.
4. Combine the base case and the recursive case to solve the problem.

For problems involving numbers, the base case is often when the input value is zero. The problem size is usually reduced is by subtracting 1 from one of the inputs.

In the next chapter, we introduce more complex data structures. For problems involving complex data, the same strategy will work but with different base cases and ways to shrink the problem size.

5 Data

From a bit to a few hundred megabytes, from a microsecond to half an hour of computing confronts us with the completely baffling ratio of 10^9! .... By evoking the need for deep conceptual hierarchies, the automatic computer confronts us with a radically new intellectual challenge that has no precedent in our history.
Edsger Dijkstra

For all the programs so far, we have been limited to simple data such as numbers and Booleans. We call this *scalar* data since it has no structure. As we saw in Chapter 1, we can represent all discrete data using just (enormously large) whole numbers. For example, we could represent the text of a book using only one (very large!) number, and manipulate the characters in the book by changing the value of that number. But, it would be very difficult to design and understand computations that use numbers to represent complex data.

scalar

We need more complex data structures to better model structured data. We want to represent data in ways that allow us to think about the problem we are trying to solve, rather than the details of how data is represented and manipulated.

This chapter covers techniques for building data structures and for defining procedures that manipulate structured data, and introduces data abstraction as a tool for managing program complexity.

5.1 Types

All data in a program has an associated type. Internally, all data is stored just as a sequence of bits, so the type of the data is important to understand what it means. We have seen several different types of data already: Numbers, Booleans, and Procedures (we use initial capital letters to signify a datatype).

A *datatype* defines a set (often infinite) of possible values. The Boolean datatype contains the two Boolean values, *true* and *false*. The Number type includes the infinite set of all whole numbers (it also includes negative numbers and rational numbers). We think of the set of possible Numbers as infinite, even though on any particular computer there is some limit to the amount of memory available, and hence, some largest number that can be represented. On any real computer, the number of possible values of any data type is always finite. But, we can imagine a computer large enough to represent any given number.

datatype

The type of a value determines what can be done with it. For example, a Number can be used as one of the inputs to the primitive procedures $+$, $*$, and $=$. A Boolean can be used as the first subexpression of an if expression and as the input to the *not* procedure (—not— can also take a Number as its input, but for all Number value inputs the output is false), but cannot be used as the input to $+$, $*$, or $=$.[1]

A Procedure can be the first subexpression in an application expression. There are infinitely many different types of Procedures, since the type of a Procedure depends on its input and output types. For example, recall *bigger* procedure from Chapter 3:

```
(define (bigger a b) (if (> a b) a b))
```

It takes two Numbers as input and produces a Number as output. We denote this type as:

$$\text{Number} \times \text{Number} \rightarrow \text{Number}$$

The inputs to the procedure are shown on the left side of the arrow. The type of each input is shown in order, separated by the $\times$ symbol.[2] The output type is given on the right side of the arrow.

From its definition, it is clear that the *bigger* procedure takes two inputs from its parameter list. How do we know the inputs must be Numbers and the output is a Number?

The body of the *bigger* procedure is an if expression with the predicate expression ($>$ *a b*). This applies the $>$ primitive procedure to the two inputs. The type of the $>$ procedure is Number $\times$ Number $\rightarrow$ Boolean. So, for the predicate expression to be valid, its inputs must both be Numbers. This means the input values to *bigger* must both be Numbers. We know the output of the *bigger* procedure will be a Number by analyzing the consequent and alternate subexpressions: each evaluates to one of the input values, which must be a Number.

Starting with the primitive Boolean, Number, and Procedure types, we can build arbitrarily complex datatypes. This chapter introduces mechanisms for building complex datatypes by combining the primitive datatypes.

Exercise 5.1. Describe the type of each of these expressions.

a. 17

b. (**lambda** (*a*) (> *a* 0))

c. ((**lambda** (*a*) (> *a* 0)) 3)

d. (**lambda** (*a*) (**lambda** (*b*) (> *a b*)))

e. (**lambda** (*a*) *a*)

[1] The primitive procedure *equal?* is a more general comparison procedure that can take as inputs any two values, so could be used to compare Boolean values. For example, (*equal? false false*) evaluates to true and (*equal? true* 3) is a valid expression that evaluates to *false*.

[2] The notation using $\times$ to separate input types makes sense if you think about the number of different inputs to a procedure. For example, consider a procedure that takes two Boolean values as inputs, so its type is Boolean $\times$ Boolean $\rightarrow$ Value. Each Boolean input can be one of two possible values. If we combined both inputs into one input, there would be 2×2 different values needed to represent all possible inputs.

Exercise 5.2. Define or identify a procedure that has the given type.

a. Number × Number → Boolean

b. Number → Number

c. (Number → Number) × (Number → Number)
→ (Number → Number)

d. Number → (Number → (Number → Number))

5.2 Pairs

The simplest structured data construct is a *Pair*. We draw a Pair as two boxes, each containing a value. We call each box of a Pair a *cell*. Here is a Pair where the first cell has the value 37 and the second cell has the value 42:

Pair

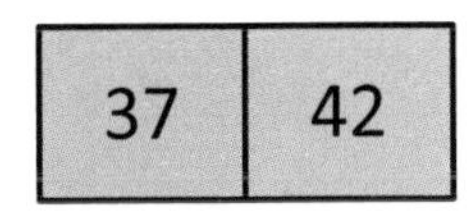

Scheme provides built-in procedures for constructing a Pair, and for extracting each cell from a Pair:

cons: Value × Value → Pair
: Evaluates to a Pair whose first cell is the first input and second cell is the second input. The inputs can be of any type.

car: Pair → Value
: Evaluates to the first cell of the input, which must be a Pair.

cdr: Pair → Value
: Evaluates to the second cell of input, which must be a Pair.

These rather unfortunate names come from the original LISP implementation on the IBM 704. The name *cons* is short for "construct". The name *car* is short for "Contents of the *A*ddress part of the *R*egister" and the name *cdr* (pronounced "could-er") is short for "Contents of the *D*ecrement part of the *R*egister". The designers of the original LISP implementation picked the names because of how pairs could be implemented on the IBM 704 using a single register to store both parts of a pair, but it is a mistake to name things after details of their implementation (see Section 5.6). Unfortunately, the names stuck.

We can construct the Pair shown above by evaluating (*cons* 37 42). DrRacket displays a Pair by printing the value of each cell separated by a dot: (37 . 42). The interactions below show example uses of *cons*, *car*, and *cdr*.

```
> (define mypair (cons 37 42))
> (car mypair)
37
> (cdr mypair)
42
```

The values in the cells of a Pair can be any type, including other Pairs. For example, this definition defines a Pair where each cell of the Pair is itself a Pair:

```
(define doublepair (cons (cons 1 2) (cons 3 4)))
```

We can use the *car* and *cdr* procedures to access components of the *doublepair* structure: (*car doublepair*) evaluates to the Pair (1 . 2), and (*cdr doublepair*) evaluates to the Pair (3 . 4).

We can compose multiple *car* and *cdr* applications to extract components from nested pairs:

```
> (cdr (car doublepair))
2
> (car (cdr doublepair))
3
> ((fcompose cdr cdr) doublepair)
4
> (car (car (car doublepair)))
car: expects argument of type <pair>; given 1
```

fcompose from Section 4.2.1

The last expression produces an error when it is evaluated since *car* is applied to the scalar value 1. The *car* and *cdr* procedures can only be applied to an input that is a Pair. Hence, an error results when we attempt to apply *car* to a scalar value. This is an important property of data: the type of data (e.g., a Pair) defines how it can be used (e.g., passed as the input to *car* and *cdr*). Every procedure expects a certain type of inputs, and typically produces an error when it is applied to values of the wrong type.

We can draw the value of *doublepair* by nesting Pairs within cells:

Drawing Pairs within Pairs within Pairs can get quite difficult, however. For instance, try drawing (*cons* 1 (*cons* 2 (*cons* 3 (*cons* 4 5)))) this way.

Instead, we us arrows to point to the contents of cells that are not simple values. This is the structure of *doublepair* shown using arrows:

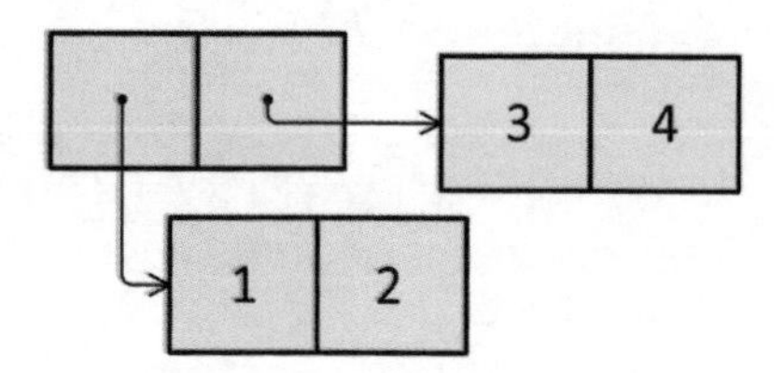

Using arrows to point to cell contents allows us to draw arbitrarily complicated data structures such as (*cons* 1 (*cons* 2 (*cons* 3 (*cons* 4 5)))), keeping the cells reasonable sizes:

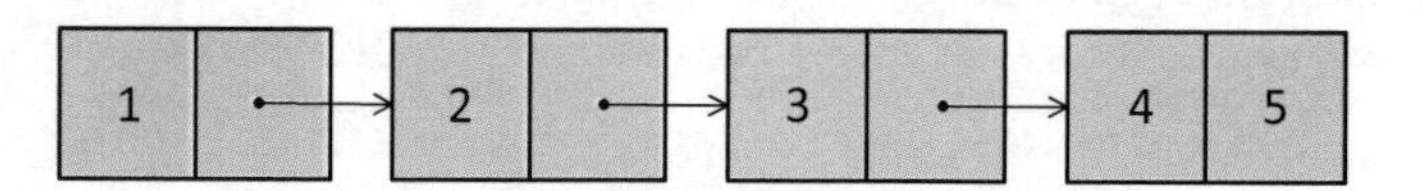

Exercise 5.3. Suppose the following definition has been executed:

```
(define tpair
  (cons (cons (cons 1 2) (cons 3 4))
        5))
```

Draw the structure defined by *tpair*, and give the value of each of the following expressions.

a. (*cdr tpair*)

b. (*car* (*car* (*car tpair*)))

c. (*cdr* (*cdr* (*car tpair*)))

d. (*car* (*cdr* (*cdr tpair*)))

Exercise 5.4. Write expressions that extract each of the four elements from *fstruct* defined by (**define** *fstruct* (*cons* 1 (*cons* 2 (*cons* 3 4)))).

Exercise 5.5. Give an expression that produces the structure shown below.

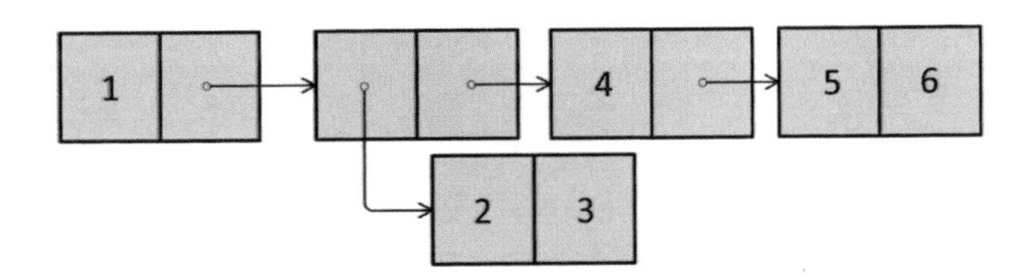

5.2.1 Making Pairs

Although Scheme provides the built-in procedures *cons*, *car*, and *cdr* for creating Pairs and accessing their cells, there is nothing magical about these procedures. We can define procedures with the same behavior ourselves using the subset of Scheme introduced in Chapter 3.

Here is one way to define the pair procedures (we prepend an *s* to the names to avoid confusion with the built-in procedures):

```
(define (scons a b) (lambda (w) (if w a b)))
(define (scar pair) (pair true))
(define (scdr pair) (pair false))
```

The *scons* procedure takes the two parts of the Pair as inputs, and produces as output a procedure. The output procedure takes one input, a selector that determines which of the two cells of the Pair to output. If the selector is true, the value of the if expression is the value of the first cell; if the selector is false, it is the value of the second cell. The *scar* and *scdr* procedures apply a procedure constructed by *scons* to either *true* (to select the first cell in *scar*) or *false* (to select the second cell in *scdr*).

Exercise 5.6. Convince yourself the definitions of *scons*, *scar*, and *scdr* above work as expected by following the evaluation rules to evaluate

```
(scar (scons 1 2))
```

Exercise 5.7. Show the corresponding definitions of *tcar* and *tcdr* that provide the pair selection behavior for a pair created using *tcons* defined as:

```
(define (tcons a b) (lambda (w) (if w b a)))
```

5.2.2 Triples to Octuples

Pairs are useful for representing data that is composed of two parts such as a calendar date (composed of a number and month), or a playing card (composed of a rank and suit). But, what if we want to represent data composed of more than two parts such as a date (composed of a number, month, and year) or a poker hand consisting of five playing cards? For more complex data structures, we need data structures that have more than two components.

A *triple* has three components. Here is one way to define a triple datatype:

```
(define (make-triple a b c)
  (lambda (w) (if (= w 0) a (if (= w 1) b c))))
(define (triple-first t) (t 0))
(define (triple-second t) (t 1))
(define (triple-third t) (t 2))
```

Since a triple has three components we need three different selector values.

Another way to make a triple would be to combine two Pairs. We do this by making a Pair whose second cell is itself a Pair:

```
(define (make-triple a b c) (cons a (cons b c)))
(define (triple-first t) (car t))
(define (triple-second t) (car (cdr t)))
(define (triple-third t) (cdr (cdr t)))
```

Similarly, we can define a *quadruple* as a Pair whose second cell is a triple:

```
(define (make-quad a b c d) (cons a (make-triple b c d)))
(define (quad-first q) (car q))
(define (quad-second q) (triple-first (cdr q))
(define (quad-third q) (triple-second (cdr q))
(define (quad-fourth q) (triple-third (cdr q))
```

We could continue in this manner defining increasingly large tuples.

> A *triple* is a Pair whose second cell is a Pair.
> A *quadruple* is a Pair whose second cell is a *triple*.
> A *quintuple* is a Pair whose second cell is a *quadruple*.
> ...
> An $n + 1$-*uple* is a Pair whose second cell is an n-*uple*.

Building from the simple Pair, we can construct tuples containing any number of components.

Exercise 5.8. Define a procedure that constructs a quintuple and procedures for selecting the five elements of a quintuple.

Exercise 5.9. Another way of thinking of a triple is as a Pair where the first cell is a Pair and the second cell is a scalar. Provide definitions of *make-triple, triple-first, triple-second,* and *triple-third* for this construct.

5.3 Lists

In the previous section, we saw how to construct arbitrarily large tuples from Pairs. This way of managing data is not very satisfying since it requires defining different procedures for constructing and accessing elements of every length tuple. For many applications, we want to be able to manage data of any length such as all the items in a web store, or all the bids on a given item. Since the number of components in these objects can change, it would be very painful to need to define a new tuple type every time an item is added. We need a data type that can hold *any* number of items.

This definition almost provides what we need:

> An *any-uple* is a Pair whose second cell is an *any-uple*.

This seems to allow an *any-uple* to contain any number of elements. The problem is we have no stopping point. With only the definition above, there is no way to construct an *any-uple* without already having one.

The situation is similar to defining *MoreDigits* as zero or more digits in Chapter 2, defining *MoreExpressions* in the Scheme grammar in Chapter 3 as zero or more *Expressions*, and recursive composition in Chapter 4.

Recall the grammar rules for *MoreExpressions*:

MoreExpressions ::⇒ *Expression MoreExpressions*
MoreExpressions ::⇒ ϵ

The rule for constructing an *any-uple* is analogous to the first *MoreExpression* replacement rule. To allow an *any-uple* to be constructed, we also need a construction rule similar to the second rule, where *MoreExpression* can be replaced with nothing. Since it is hard to type and read nothing in a program, Scheme has a name for this value: *null*.

null

DrRacket will print out the value of *null* as (). It is also known as the *empty list*, since it represents the List containing no elements. The built-in procedure *null?* takes one input parameter and evaluates to true if and only if the value of that parameter is null.

Using null, we can now define a *List*:

List

> A *List* is either (1) null or (2) a Pair whose second cell is a *List*.

Symbolically, we define a List as:

List ::⇒ null
List ::⇒ (*cons Value List*)

These two rules define a List as a data structure that can contain any number of elements. Starting from null, we can create Lists of any length:

- *null* evaluates to a List containing no elements.
- (*cons* 1 *null*) evaluates to a List containing one element.
- (*cons* 1 (*cons* 2 *null*)) evaluates to a List containing two elements.
- (*cons* 1 (*cons* 2 (*cons* 3 *null*))) evaluates to a 3-element List.

Scheme provides a convenient procedure, *list*, for constructing a List. The *list* procedure takes zero or more inputs, and evaluates to a List containing those inputs in order. The following expressions are equivalent to the corresponding expressions above: (*list*), (*list* 1), (*list* 1 2), and (*list* 1 2 3).

Lists are just a collection of Pairs, so we can draw a List using the same box and arrow notation we used to draw structures created with Pairs. Here is the structure resulting from (*list* 1 2 3):

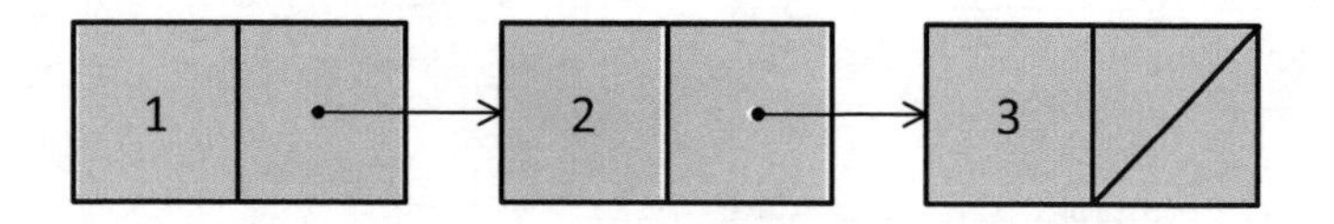

There are three Pairs in the List, the second cell of each Pair is a List. For the third Pair, the second cell is the List *null*, which we draw as a slash through the final cell in the diagram.

Table 5.1 summarizes some of the built-in procedures for manipulating Pairs and Lists.

Exercise 5.10. For each of the following expressions, explain whether or not the expression evaluates to a List. Check your answers with a Scheme interpreter by using the *list?* procedure.

a. *null*

b. (*cons* 1 2)

c. (*cons null null*)

d. (*cons* (*cons* (*cons* 1 2) 3) *null*)

e. (*cdr* (*cons* 1 (*cons* 2 (*cons null null*))))

f. (*cons* (*list* 1 2 3) 4)

	Type	**Output**
cons	Value × Value → Pair	a Pair consisting of the two inputs
car	Pair → Value	the first cell of the input Pair
cdr	Pair → Value	the second cell of the input Pair
list	zero or more Values → List	a List containing the inputs
null?	Value → Boolean	true if the input is null, otherwise false
pair?	Value → Boolean	true if the input is a Pair, otherwise false
list?	Value → Boolean	true if the input is a List, otherwise false

Table 5.1. Selected Built-In Scheme Procedures for Lists and Pairs.

5.4 List Procedures

Since the List data structure is defined recursively, it is natural to define recursive procedures to examine and manipulate lists. Whereas most recursive procedures on inputs that are Numbers usually used 0 as the base case, for lists the most common base case is *null*. With numbers, we make progress by subtracting 1; with lists, we make progress by using *cdr* to reduce the length of the input List by one element for each recursive application. This means we often break problems involving Lists into figuring out what to do with the first element of the List and the result of applying the recursive procedure to the rest of the List.

We can specialize our general problem solving strategy from Chapter 3 for procedures involving lists:

1. **Be *very* optimistic!** Since lists themselves are recursive data structures, most problems involving lists can be solved with recursive procedures.
2. Think of the simplest version of the problem, something you can already solve. This is the base case. For lists, this is usually the empty list.
3. Consider how you would solve a big version of the problem by using the result for a slightly smaller version of the problem. This is the recursive case. For lists, the smaller version of the problem is usually the rest (*cdr*) of the List.
4. Combine the base case and the recursive case to solve the problem.

Next we consider procedures that examine lists by walking through their elements and producing a scalar value. Section 5.4.2 generalizes these procedures. In Section 5.4.3, we explore procedures that output lists.

5.4.1 Procedures that Examine Lists

All of the example procedures in this section take a single List as input and produce a scalar value that depends on the elements of the List as output. These procedures have base cases where the List is empty, and recursive cases that apply the recursive procedure to the *cdr* of the input List.

Example 5.1: Length

How many elements are in a given List?[3] Our standard recursive problem solving technique is to "Think of the simplest version of the problem, something you can already solve." For this procedure, the simplest version of the problem is when the input is the empty list, *null*. We know the length of the empty list is 0. So, the base case test is (*null? p*) and the output for the base case is 0.

For the recursive case, we need to consider the structure of all lists other than *null*. Recall from our definition that a List is either *null* or (*cons Value List*). The base case handles the *null* list; the recursive case must handle a List that is a Pair of an element and a List. The length of this List is one more than the length of the List that is the *cdr* of the Pair.

[3]Scheme provides a built-in procedure *length* that takes a List as its input and outputs the number of elements in the List. Here, we will define our own *list-length* procedure that does this (without using the built-in *length* procedure). As with many other examples and exercises in this chapter, it is instructive to define our own versions of some of the built-in list procedures.

```
(define (list-length p)
   (if (null? p)
      0
      (+ 1 (list-length (cdr p)))))
```

Here are a few example applications of our *list-length* procedure:

```
> (list-length null)
0
> (list-length (cons 0 null))
1
> (list-length (list 1 2 3 4))
4
```

Example 5.2: List Sums and Products

First, we define a procedure that takes a List of numbers as input and produces as output the sum of the numbers in the input List. As usual, the base case is when the input is *null*: the sum of an empty list is 0. For the recursive case, we need to add the value of the first number in the List, to the sum of the rest of the numbers in the List.

```
(define (list-sum p)
   (if (null? p) 0 (+ (car p) (list-sum (cdr p)))))
```

We can define *list-product* similarly, using * in place of +. The base case result cannot be 0, though, since then the final result would always be 0 since any number multiplied by 0 is 0. We follow the mathematical convention that the product of the empty list is 1.

```
(define (list-product p)
   (if (null? p) 1 (* (car p) (list-product (cdr p)))))
```

Exercise 5.11. Define a procedure *is-list?* that takes one input and outputs true if the input is a List, and false otherwise. Your procedure should behave identically to the built-in *list?* procedure, but you should not use *list?* in your definition.

Exercise 5.12. Define a procedure *list-max* that takes a List of non-negative numbers as its input and produces as its result the value of the greatest element in the List (or 0 if there are no elements in the input List). For example, (*list-max* (*list* 1 1 2 0)) should evaluate to 2.

5.4.2 Generic Accumulators

The *list-length*, *list-sum*, and *list-product* procedures all have very similar structures. The base case is when the input is the empty list, and the recursive case involves doing something with the first element of the List and recursively calling the procedure with the rest of the List:

```
(define (Recursive-Procedure p)
   (if (null? p)
      Base-Case-Result
      (Accumulator-Function (car p) (Recursive-Procedure (cdr p)))))
```

We can define a generic accumulator procedure for lists by making the base case result and accumulator function inputs:

```
(define (list-accumulate f base p)
  (if (null? p)
      base
      (f (car p) (list-accumulate f base (cdr p)))))
```

We can use *list-accumulate* to define *list-sum* and *list-product*:

```
(define (list-sum p) (list-accumulate + 0 p))
(define (list-product p) (list-accumulate * 1 p))
```

Defining the *list-length* procedure is a bit less natural. The recursive case in the original *list-length* procedure is (+ 1 (*list-length* (*cdr p*))); it does not use the value of the first element of the List. But, *list-accumulate* is defined to take a procedure that takes two inputs—the first input is the first element of the List; the second input is the result of applying *list-accumulate* to the rest of the List. We should follow our usual strategy: be optimistic! Being optimistic as in recursive definitions, the value of the second input should be the length of the rest of the List. Hence, we need to pass in a procedure that takes two inputs, ignores the first input, and outputs one more than the value of the second input:

```
(define (list-length p)
  (list-accumulate (lambda (el length-rest) (+ 1 length-rest)) 0 p))
```

Exercise 5.13. Use *list-accumulate* to define *list-max* (from Exercise 5.12).

Exercise 5.14. [★] Use *list-accumulate* to define *is-list?* (from Exercise 5.11).

Example 5.3: Accessing List Elements

The built-in *car* procedure provides a way to get the first element of a list, but what if we want to get the third element? We can do this by taking the *cdr* twice to eliminate the first two elements, and then using *car* to get the third:

```
(car (cdr (cdr p)))
```

We want a more general procedure that can access any selected list element. It takes two inputs: a List, and an index Number that identifies the element. If we start counting from 1 (it is often more natural to start from 0), then the base case is when the index is 1 and the output should be the first element of the List:

```
(if (= n 1) (car p) ...)
```

For the recursive case, we make progress by eliminating the first element of the list. We also need to adjust the index: since we have removed the first element of the list, the index should be reduced by one. For example, instead of wanting the third element of the original list, we now want the second element of the *cdr* of the original list.

```
(define (list-get-element p n)
  (if (= n 1)
      (car p)
      (list-get-element (cdr p) (- n 1))))
```

What happens if we apply *list-get-element* to an index that is larger than the size of the input List (for example, (*list-get-element* (*list* 1 2) 3))?

The first recursive call is (*list-get-element* (*list* 2) 2). The second recursive call is (*list-get-element* (*list*) 1). At this point, *n* is 1, so the base case is reached and (*car p*) is evaluated. But, *p* is the empty list (which is not a Pair), so an error results.

A better version of *list-get-element* would provide a meaningful error message when the requested element is out of range. We do this by adding an if expression that tests if the input List is *null*:

```
(define (list-get-element p n)
  (if (null? p)
     (error "Index out of range")
     (if (= n 1) (car p) (list-get-element (cdr p) (- n 1)))))
```

The built-in procedure *error* takes a String as input. The String datatype is a sequence of characters; we can create a String by surrounding characters with double quotes, as in the example. The *error* procedure terminates program execution with a message that displays the input value.

defensive programming

Checking explicitly for invalid inputs is known as *defensive programming*. Programming defensively helps avoid tricky to debug errors and makes it easier to understand what went wrong if there is an error.

Exercise 5.15. Define a procedure *list-last-element* that takes as input a List and outputs the last element of the input List. If the input List is empty, *list-last-element* should produce an error.

Exercise 5.16. Define a procedure *list-ordered?* that takes two inputs, a test procedure and a List. It outputs true if all the elements of the List are ordered according to the test procedure. For example, (*list-ordered?* $<$ (*list* 1 2 3)) evaluates to true, and (*list-ordered?* $<$ (*list* 1 2 3 2)) evaluates to false. Hint: think about what the output should be for the empty list.

5.4.3 Procedures that Construct Lists

The procedures in this section take values (including Lists) as input, and produce a new List as output. As before, the empty list is typically the base case. Since we are producing a List as output, the result for the base case is also usually null. The recursive case will use *cons* to construct a List combining the first element with the result of the recursive application on the rest of the List.

Example 5.4: Mapping

One common task for manipulating a List is to produce a new List that is the result of applying some procedure to every element in the input List.

For the base case, applying any procedure to every element of the empty list produces the empty list. For the recursive case, we use *cons* to construct a List. The first element is the result of applying the mapping procedure to the first element of the input List. The rest of the output List is the result of recursively mapping the rest of the input List.

Here is a procedure that constructs a List that contains the square of every element of the input List:

```
(define (list-square p)
  (if (null? p) null
     (cons (square (car p))
           (list-square (cdr p)))))
```

We generalize this by making the procedure which is applied to each element an input. The procedure *list-map* takes a procedure as its first input and a List as its second input. It outputs a List whose elements are the results of applying the input procedure to each element of the input List.[4]

```
(define (list-map f p)
  (if (null? p) null
     (cons (f (car p))
           (list-map f (cdr p)))))
```

We can use *list-map* to define *square-all*:

```
(define (square-all p) (list-map square p))
```

Exercise 5.17. Define a procedure *list-increment* that takes as input a List of numbers, and produces as output a List containing each element in the input List incremented by one. For example, (*list-increment* 1 2 3) evaluates to (2 3 4).

Exercise 5.18. Use *list-map* and *list-sum* to define *list-length*:

```
(define (list-length p) (list-sum (list-map ____ p)))
```

Example 5.5: Filtering

Consider defining a procedure that takes as input a List of numbers, and evaluates to a List of all the non-negative numbers in the input. For example, (*list-filter-negative* (*list* 1 −3 −4 5 −2 0)) evaluates to (1 5 0).

First, consider the base case when the input is the empty list. If we filter the negative numbers from the empty list, the result is an empty list. So, for the base case, the result should be null.

In the recursive case, we need to determine whether or not the first element should be included in the output. If it should be included, we construct a new List consisting of the first element followed by the result of filtering the remaining elements in the List. If it should not be included, we skip the first element and the result is the result of filtering the remaining elements in the List.

```
(define (list-filter-negative p)
  (if (null? p) null
     (if (>= (car p) 0)
        (cons (car p) (list-filter-negative (cdr p)))
        (list-filter-negative (cdr p)))))
```

Similarly to *list-map*, we can generalize our filter by making the test procedure as an input, so we can use any predicate to determine which elements to include

[4]Scheme provides a built-in *map* procedure. It behaves like this one when passed a procedure and a single List as inputs, but can also work on more than one List input at a time.

in the output List.[5]

```
(define (list-filter test p)
  (if (null? p) null
     (if (test (car p))
        (cons (car p) (list-filter test (cdr p)))
        (list-filter test (cdr p)))))
```

Using the *list-filter* procedure, we can define *list-filter-negative* as:

```
(define (list-filter-negative p) (list-filter (lambda (x) (>= x 0)) p))
```

We could also define the *list-filter* procedure using the *list-accumulate* procedure from Section 5.4.1:

```
(define (list-filter test p)
  (list-accumulate
    (lambda (el rest) (if (test el) (cons el rest) rest))
    null
    p))
```

Exercise 5.19. Define a procedure *list-filter-even* that takes as input a List of numbers and produces as output a List consisting of all the even elements of the input List.

Exercise 5.20. Define a procedure *list-remove* that takes two inputs: a test procedure and a List. As output, it produces a List that is a copy of the input List with all of the elements for which the test procedure evaluates to true removed. For example, (*list-remove* (**lambda** (*x*) (= *x* 0)) (*list* 0 1 2 3)) should evaluates to the List (1 2 3).

Exercise 5.21. [★★] Define a procedure *list-unique-elements* that takes as input a List and produces as output a List containing the unique elements of the input List. The output List should contain the elements in the same order as the input List, but should only contain the first appearance of each value in the input List.

Example 5.6: Append

The *list-append* procedure takes as input two lists and produces as output a List consisting of the elements of the first List followed by the elements of the second List.[6] For the base case, when the first List is empty, the result of appending the lists should just be the second List. When the first List is non-empty, we can produce the result by *cons*-ing the first element of the first List with the result of appending the rest of the first List and the second List.

```
(define (list-append p q)
  (if (null? p) q
     (cons (car p) (list-append (cdr p) q))))
```

[5]Scheme provides a built-in function *filter* that behaves like our *list-filter* procedure.

[6]There is a built-in procedure *append* that does this. The built-in *append* takes any number of Lists as inputs, and appends them all into one List.

Example 5.7: Reverse

The *list-reverse* procedure takes a List as input and produces as output a List containing the elements of the input List in reverse order.[7] For example, (*list-reverse* (*list* 1 2 3)) evaluates to the List (3 2 1). As usual, we consider the base case where the input List is null first. The reverse of the empty list is the empty list. To reverse a non-empty List, we should put the first element of the List at the end of the result of reversing the rest of the List.

The tricky part is putting the first element at the end, since *cons* only puts elements at the beginning of a List. We can use the *list-append* procedure defined in the previous example to put a List at the end of another List. To make this work, we need to turn the element at the front of the List into a List containing just that element. We do this using (*list* (*car p*)).

```
(define (list-reverse p)
  (if (null? p) null
     (list-append (list-reverse (cdr p)) (list (car p)))))
```

Exercise 5.22. Define the *list-reverse* procedure using *list-accumulate*.

Example 5.8: Intsto

For our final example, we define the *intsto* procedure that constructs a List containing the whole numbers between 1 and the input parameter value. For example, (*intsto* 5) evaluates to the List (1 2 3 4 5).

This example combines ideas from the previous chapter on creating recursive definitions for problems involving numbers, and from this chapter on lists. Since the input parameter is not a List, the base case is not the usual list base case when the input is *null*. Instead, we use the input value 0 as the base case. The result for input 0 is the empty list. For higher values, the output is the result of putting the input value at the end of the List of numbers up to the input value minus one.

A first attempt that doesn't quite work is:

```
(define (revintsto n)
  (if (= n 0) null
     (cons n (revintsto (− n 1)))))
```

The problem with this solution is that it is *cons*-ing the higher number to the front of the result, instead of at the end. Hence, it produces the List of numbers in descending order: (*revintsto* 5) evaluates to (5 4 3 2 1).

One solution is to reverse the result by composing *list-reverse* with *revintsto*:

```
(define (intsto n) (list-reverse (revintsto n)))
```

Equivalently, we can use the *fcompose* procedure from Section 4.2:

```
(define intsto (fcompose list-reverse revintsto))
```

Alternatively, we could use *list-append* to put the high number directly at the end of the List. Since the second operand to *list-append* must be a List, we use (*list n*) to make a singleton List containing the value as we did for *list-reverse*.

[7] The built-in procedure *reverse* does this.

```
(define (intsto n)
  (if (= n 0) null
    (list-append (intsto (- n 1)) (list n))))
```

Although all of these procedures are functionally equivalent (for all valid inputs, each function produces exactly the same output), the amount of computing work (and hence the time they take to execute) varies across the implementations. We consider the problem of estimating the running-times of different procedures in Part II.

Exercise 5.23. Define *factorial* using *intsto.*

5.5 Lists of Lists

The elements of a List can be any datatype, including, of course, other Lists. In defining procedures that operate on Lists of Lists, we often use more than one recursive call when we need to go inside the inner Lists.

Example 5.9: Summing Nested Lists

Consider the problem of summing all the numbers in a List of Lists. For example, (*nested-list-sum* (*list* (*list* 1 2 3) (*list* 4 5 6))) should evaluate to 21. We can define *nested-list-sum* using *list-sum* on each List.

```
(define (nested-list-sum p)
  (if (null? p) 0
    (+ (list-sum (car p))
       (nested-list-sum (cdr p)))))
```

This works when we know the input is a List of Lists. But, what if the input can contain arbitrarily deeply nested Lists?

To handle this, we need to recursively sum the inner Lists. Each element in our deep List is either a List or a Number. If it is a List, we should add the value of the sum of all elements in the List to the result for the rest of the List. If it is a Number, we should just add the value of the Number to the result for the rest of the List. So, our procedure involves two recursive calls: one for the first element in the List when it is a List, and the other for the rest of the List.

```
(define (deep-list-sum p)
  (if (null? p) 0
    (+ (if (list? (car p))
           (deep-list-sum (car p))
           (car p))
       (deep-list-sum (cdr p)))))
```

Example 5.10: Flattening Lists

Another way to compute the deep list sum would be to first flatten the List, and then use the *list-sum* procedure.

Flattening a nested list takes a List of Lists and evaluates to a List containing the elements of the inner Lists. We can define *list-flatten* by using *list-append* to append all the inner Lists together.

```
(define (list-flatten p)
  (if (null? p) null
     (list-append (car p) (list-flatten (cdr p)))))
```

This flattens a List of Lists into a single List. To completely flatten a deeply nested List, we use multiple recursive calls as we did with *deep-list-sum*:

```
(define (deep-list-flatten p)
  (if (null? p) null
     (list-append (if (list? (car p))
                       (deep-list-flatten (car p))
                       (list (car p)))
                   (deep-list-flatten (cdr p)))))
```

Now we can define *deep-list-sum* as:

```
(define deep-list-sum (fcompose deep-list-flatten list-sum))
```

Exercise 5.24. [⋆] Define a procedure *deep-list-map* that behaves similarly to *list-map* but on deeply nested lists. It should take two parameters, a mapping procedure, and a List (that may contain deeply nested Lists as elements), and output a List with the same structure as the input List with each value mapped using the mapping procedure.

Exercise 5.25. [⋆] Define a procedure *deep-list-filter* that behaves similarly to *list-filter* but on deeply nested lists.

Exploration 5.1: Pascal's Triangle

Pascal's Triangle (named for Blaise Pascal, although known to many others before him) is shown below:

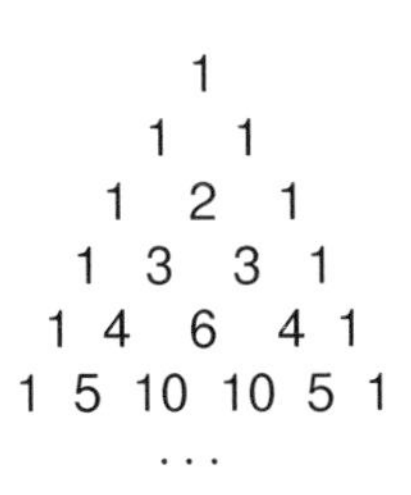

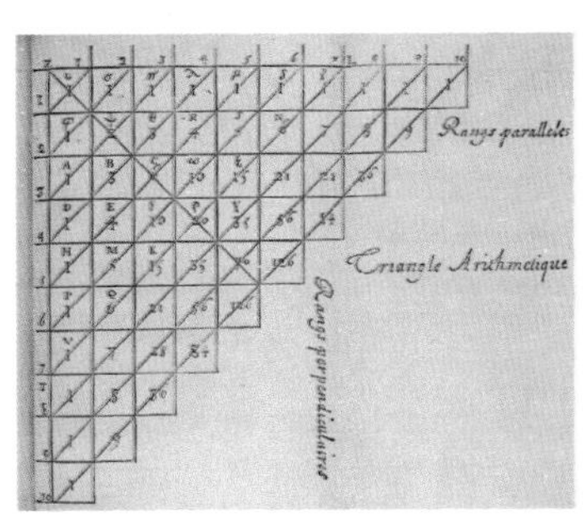

Each number in the triangle is the sum of the two numbers immediately above and to the left and right of it. The numbers in Pascal's Triangle are the coefficients in a binomial expansion. The numbers of the nth row (where the rows are numbered starting from 0) are the coefficients of the binomial expansion of $(x+y)^n$. For example, $(x+y)^2 = x^2 + 2xy + y^2$, so the coefficients are 1 2 1, matching the third row in the triangle; from the fifth row, $(x+y)^4 = x^4 + 4x^3y + 6x^2y^2 + 4xy^3 + y^4$. The values in the triangle also match the number of ways to choose k elements from a set of size n (see Exercise 4.5) — the kth number on the nth row of the triangle gives the number of ways to choose k elements from a set of size n. For example, the third number on the fifth ($n = 4$) row is 6, so there are

6 ways to choose 3 items from a set of size 4.

The goal of this exploration is to define a procedure, *pascals-triangle* to produce Pascal's Triangle. The input to your procedure should be the number of rows; the output should be a list, where each element of the list is a list of the numbers on that row of Pascal's Triangle. For example, (*pascals-triangle* 0) should produce ((1)) (a list containing one element which is a list containing the number 1), and (*pascals-triangle* 4) should produce ((1) (1 1) (1 2 1) (1 3 3 1) (1 4 6 4 1)).

Ambitious readers should attempt to define *pascals-triangle* themselves; the sub-parts below provide some hints for one way to define it.

a. First, define a procedure *expand-row* that expands one row in the triangle. It takes a List of numbers as input, and as output produces a List with one more element than the input list. The first number in the output List should be the first number in the input List; the last number in the output List should be the last number in the input List. Every other number in the output List is the sum of two numbers in the input List. The nth number in the output List is the sum of the $n-1^{th}$ and n^{th} numbers in the input List. For example, (*expand-row* (*list* 1)) evaluates to (1 1); (*expand-row* (*list* 1 1)) evaluates to (1 2 1); and (*expand-row* (*list* 1 4 6 4 1)) evaluates to (1 5 10 10 5 1). This is trickier than the recursive list procedures we have seen so far since the base case is not the empty list. It also needs to deal with the first element specially. To define *expand-row*, it will be helpful to divide it into two procedures, one that deals with the first element of the list, and one that produces the rest of the list:

```
(define (expand-row p) (cons (car p) (expand-row-rest p)))
```

b. Define a procedure *pascals-triangle-row* that takes one input, n, and outputs the nth row of Pascal's Triangle. For example, (*pascals-triangle-row* 0) evaluates to (1) and (*pascals-triangle-row* 3) produces (1 3 3 1).

c. Finally, define *pascals-triangle* with the behavior described above.

5.6 Data Abstraction

The mechanisms we have for constructing and manipulating complex data structures are valuable because they enable us to think about programs closer to the level of the problem we are solving than the low level of how data is stored and manipulated in the computer. Our goal is to hide unnecessary details about how data is represented so we can focus on the important aspects of what the data means and what we need to do with it to solve our problem. The technique of hiding how data is represented from how it is used is known as *data abstraction*.

data abstraction

The datatypes we have seen so far are not very abstract. We have datatypes for representing Pairs, triples, and Lists, but we want datatypes for representing objects closer to the level of the problem we want to solve. A good data abstraction is abstract enough to be used without worrying about details like which cell of the Pair contains which datum and how to access the different elements of a List. Instead, we want to define procedures with meaningful names that manipulate the relevant parts of our data.

The rest of this section is an extended example that illustrates how to solve problems by first identifying the objects we need to model the problem, and then implementing data abstractions that represent those objects. Once the appropriate data abstractions are designed and implemented, the solution to the problem often follows readily. This example also uses many of the list procedures defined earlier in this chapter.

Exploration 5.2: Pegboard Puzzle

For this exploration, we develop a program to solve the infamous pegboard puzzle, often found tormenting unsuspecting diners at pancake restaurants. The standard puzzle is a one-player game played on a triangular board with fifteen holes with pegs in all of the holes except one.

The goal is to remove all but one of the pegs by jumping pegs over one another. A peg may jump over an adjacent peg only when there is a free hole on the other side of the peg. The jumped peg is removed. The game ends when there are no possible moves. If there is only one peg remaining, the player wins (according to the Cracker Barrel version of the game, "Leave only one—you're genius"). If more than one peg remains, the player loses ("Leave four or more'n you're just plain 'eg-no-ra-moose'.").

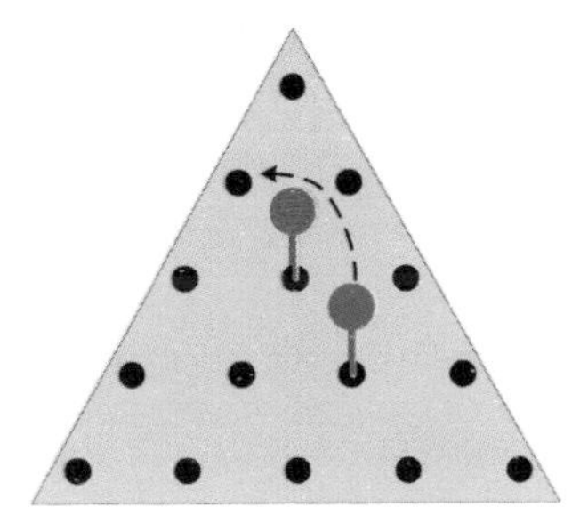

Figure 5.1. Pegboard Puzzle.

The blue peg can jump the red peg as shown, removing the red peg. The resulting position is a winning position.

Our goal is to develop a program that finds a winning solution to the pegboard game from any winnable starting position. We use a *brute force* approach: try all possible moves until we find one that works. Brute force solutions only work on small-size problems. Because they have to try all possibilities they are often too slow for solving large problems, even on the most powerful computers imaginable.[8]

brute force

The first thing to think about to solve a complex problem is what datatypes we need. We want datatypes that represent the things we need to model in our problem solution. For the pegboard game, we need to model the board with its pegs. We also need to model actions in the game like a move (jumping over a peg). The important thing about a datatype is what you can do with it. To design our board datatype we need to think about what we want to do with a board. In the physical pegboard game, the board holds the pegs. The important property we need to observe about the board is which holes on the board contain pegs. For this, we need a way of identifying board positions. We define a datatype

[8]The generalized pegboard puzzle is an example of a class of problems known as *NP-Complete*. This means it is not known whether or not any solution exists that is substantially better than the brute force solution, but it would be extraordinarily surprising (and of momentous significance!) to find one.

for representing positions first, then a datatype for representing moves, and a datatype for representing the board. Finally, we use these datatypes to define a procedure that finds a winning solution.

Position. We identify the board positions using row and column numbers:

```
        (1 1)
      (2 1) (2 2)
    (3 1) (3 2) (3 3)
  (4 1) (4 2) (4 3) (4 4)
(5 1) (5 2) (5 3) (5 4) (5 5)
```

A position has a row and a column, so we could just use a Pair to represent a position. This would work, but we prefer to have a more abstract datatype so we can think about a position's row and column, rather than thinking that a position is a Pair and using the *car* and *cdr* procedures to extract the row and column from the position.

Our Position datatype should provide at least these operations:

make-position: Number × Number → Position
Creates a Position representing the row and column given by the input numbers.
position-get-row: Position → Number
Outputs the row number of the input Position.
position-get-column: Position → Number
Outputs the column number of the input Position.

Since the Position needs to keep track of two numbers, a natural way to implement the Position datatype is to use a Pair. A more defensive implementation of the Position datatype uses a *tagged list*. With a tagged list, the first element of the list is a tag denoting the datatype it represents. All operations check the tag is correct before proceeding. We can use any type to encode the list tag, but it is most convenient to use the built-in Symbol type. Symbols are a quote (') followed by a sequence of characters. The important operation we can do with a Symbol, is test whether it is an exact match for another symbol using the *eq?* procedure.

tagged list

We define the tagged list datatype, *tlist*, using the *list-get-element* procedure from Example 5.3:

```
(define (make-tlist tag p) (cons tag p))
(define (tlist-get-tag p) (car p))

(define (tlist-get-element tag p n)
  (if (eq? (tlist-get-tag p) tag)
    (list-get-element (cdr p) n)
    (error (format "Bad tag: ~a (expected ~a)"
                   (tlist-get-tag p) tag))))
```

The *format* procedure is a built-in procedure similar to the *printf* procedure described in Section 4.5.1. Instead of printing as a side effect, *format* produces a String. For example, (*format* "list: ~a number: ~a." (*list* 1 2 3) 123) evaluates to the String "list: (1 2 3) number: 123.".

This is an example of defensive programming. Using our tagged lists, if we accidentally attempt to use a value that is not a Position as a position, we will get a clear error message instead of a hard-to-debug error (or worse, an unnoticed incorrect result).

Using the tagged list, we define the Position datatype as:

```
(define (make-position row col) (make-tlist 'Position (list row col)))
(define (position-get-row posn) (tlist-get-element 'Position posn 1))
(define (position-get-column posn) (tlist-get-element 'Position posn 2))
```

Here are some example interactions with our Position datatype:

```
> (define pos (make-position 2 1))
> pos
(Position 2 1)
> (get-position-row pos)
2
> (get-position-row (list 1 2))
Bad tag: 1 (expected Position)                Error since input is not a Position.
```

Move. A move involves three positions: where the jumping peg starts, the position of the peg that is jumped and removed, and the landing position. One possibility would be to represent a move as a list of the three positions. A better option is to observe that once any two of the positions are known, the third position is determined. For example, if we know the starting position and the landing position, we know the jumped peg is at the position between them. Hence, we could represent a jump using just the starting and landing positions.

Another possibility is to represent a jump by storing the starting Position and the direction. This is also enough to determine the jumped and landing positions. This approach avoids the difficulty of calculating jumped positions. To do it, we first design a Direction datatype for representing the possible move directions. Directions have two components: the change in the column (we use 1 for right and −1 for left), and the change in the row (1 for down and −1 for up).

We implement the Direction datatype using a tagged list similarly to how we defined Position:

```
(define (make-direction right down)
   (make-tlist 'Direction (list right down)))
(define (direction-get-horizontal dir) (tlist-get-element 'Direction dir 1))
(define (direction-get-vertical dir) (tlist-get-element 'Direction dir 2))
```

The Move datatype is defined using the starting position and the jump direction:

```
(define (make-move start direction)
   (make-tlist 'Move (list start direction)))
(define (move-get-start move) (tlist-get-element 'Move move 1))
(define (move-get-direction move) (tlist-get-element 'Move move 2))
```

We also define procedures for getting the jumped and landing positions of a move. The jumped position is the result of moving one step in the move direction from the starting position. So, it will be useful to define a procedure that takes a Position and a Direction as input, and outputs a Position that is one step in the input Direction from the input Position.

```
(define (direction-step pos dir)
  (make-position
    (+ (position-get-row pos) (direction-get-vertical dir))
    (+ (position-get-column pos) (direction-get-horizontal dir))))
```

Using *direction-step* we can implement procedure to get the middle and landing positions.

```
(define (move-get-jumped move)
  (direction-step (move-get-start move) (move-get-direction move)))
(define (move-get-landing move)
  (direction-step (move-get-jumped move) (move-get-direction move)))
```

Board. The board datatype represents the current state of the board. It keeps track of which holes in the board contain pegs, and provides operations that model adding and removing pegs from the board:

make-board: Number → Board
Outputs a board full of pegs with the input number of rows. (The standard physical board has 5 rows, but our datatype supports any number of rows.)

board-rows: Board → Number
Outputs the number of rows in the input board.

board-valid-position?: Board × Position → Boolean
Outputs *true* if input Position corresponds to a position on the Board; otherwise, *false*.

board-is-winning?: Board → Boolean
Outputs *true* if the Board represents a winning position (exactly one peg); otherwise, *false*.

board-contains-peg?: Position → Boolean
Outputs *true* if the hole at the input Position contains a peg; otherwise, *false*.

board-add-peg: Board × Position → Board
Output a Board containing all the pegs of the input Board and one additional peg at the input Position. If the input Board already has a peg at the input Position, produces an error.

board-remove-peg: Board × Position → Board
Outputs a Board containing all the pegs of the input Board except for the peg at the input Position. If the input Board does not have a peg at the input Position, produces an error.

The procedures for adding and removing pegs change the state of the board to reflect moves in the game, but nothing we have seen so far, however, provides a means for changing the state of an existing object.[9] So, instead of defining these operations to change the state of the board, they actually create a new board that is different from the input board by the one new peg. These procedures take a Board and Position as inputs, and produce as output a Board.

There are lots of different ways we could represent the Board. One possibility is to keep a List of the Positions of the pegs on the board. Another possibility is to

[9]We will introduce mechanisms for changing state in Chapter 9. Allowing state to change breaks the substitution model of evaluation.

keep a List of the Positions of the empty holes on the board. Yet another possibility is to keep a List of Lists, where each List corresponds to one row on the board. The elements in each of the Lists are Booleans representing whether or not there is a peg at that position. The good thing about data abstraction is we could pick any of these representations and change it to a different representation later (for example, if we needed a more efficient board implementation). As long as the procedures for implementing the Board are updated the work with the new representation, all the code that uses the board abstraction should continue to work correctly without any changes.

We choose the third option and represent a Board using a List of Lists where each element of the inner lists is a Boolean indicating whether or not the corresponding position contains a peg. So, *make-board* evaluates to a List of Lists, where each element of the List contains the row number of elements and all the inner elements are true (the initial board is completely full of pegs). First, we define a procedure *make-list-of-constants* that takes two inputs, a Number, *n*, and a Value, *val*. The output is a List of length *n* where each element has the value *val*.

```
(define (make-list-of-constants n val)
  (if (= n 0) null (cons val (make-list-of-constants (− n 1) val))))
```

To make the initial board, we use *make-list-of-constants* to make each row of the board. As usual, a recursive problem solving strategy works well: the simplest board is a board with zero rows (represented as the empty list); for each larger board, we add a row with the right number of elements.

The tricky part is putting the rows in order. This is similar to the problem we faced with *intsto*, and a similar solution using *append-list* works here:

```
(define (make-board rows)
  (if (= rows 0) null
    (list-append (make-board (− rows 1))
                 (list (make-list-of-constants rows true)))))
```

Evaluating (*make-board* 3) produces ((*true*) (*true true*) (*true true true*)).

The *board-rows* procedure takes a Board as input and outputs the number of rows on the board.

```
(define (board-rows board) (length board))
```

The *board-valid-position?* indicates if a Position is on the board. A position is valid if its row number is between 1 and the number of rows on the board, and its column numbers is between 1 and the row number.

```
(define (board-valid-position? board pos)
  (and (>= (position-get-row pos) 1) (>= (position-get-column pos) 1)
       (<= (position-get-row pos) (board-rows board))
       (<= (position-get-column pos) (position-get-row pos))))
```

We need a way to check if a Board represents a winning solution (that is, contains only one peg). We implement a more general procedure to count the number of pegs on a board first. Our board representation used *true* to represent a peg. To count the pegs, we first map the Boolean values used to represent pegs to 1 if there is a peg and 0 if there is no peg. Then, we use *sum-list* to count the number of pegs. Since the Board is a List of Lists, we first use *list-flatten* to put all the pegs in a single List.

```
(define (board-number-of-pegs board)
  (list-sum
   (list-map (lambda (peg) (if peg 1 0)) (list-flatten board))))
```

A board is a winning board if it contains exactly one peg:

```
(define (board-is-winning? board)
    (= (board-number-of-pegs board) 1))
```

The *board-contains-peg?* procedure takes a Board and a Position as input, and outputs a Boolean indicating whether or not that Position contains a peg. To implement *board-contains-peg?* we need to find the appropriate row in our board representation, and then find the element in its list corresponding to the position's column. The *list-get-element* procedure (from Example 5.3) does exactly what we need. Since our board is represented as a List of Lists, we need to use it twice: first to get the row, and then to select the column within that row:

```
(define (board-contains-peg? board pos)
  (list-get-element (list-get-element board (position-get-row pos))
                    (position-get-column pos)))
```

Defining procedures for adding and removing pegs from the board is more complicated. Both of these procedures need to make a board with every row identical to the input board, except the row where the peg is added or removed. For that row, we need to replace the corresponding value. Hence, instead of defining separate procedures for adding and removing we first implement a more general *board-replace-peg* procedure that takes an extra parameter indicating whether a peg should be added or removed at the selected position.

First we consider the subproblem of replacing a peg in a row. The procedure *row-replace-peg* takes as input a List representing a row on the board and a Number indicating the column where the peg should be replaced. We can define *row-replace-peg* recursively: the base case is when the modified peg is at the beginning of the row (the column number is 1); in the recursive case, we copy the first element in the List, and replace the peg in the rest of the list. The third parameter indicates if we are adding or removing a peg. Since *true* values represent holes with pegs, a *true* value indicates that we are adding a peg and *false* means we are removing a peg.

```
(define (row-replace-peg pegs col val)
  (if (= col 1)
     (cons val (cdr pegs))
     (cons (car pegs) (row-replace-peg (cdr pegs) (- col 1) val))))
```

To replace the peg on the board, we use *row-replace-peg* to replace the peg on the appropriate row, and keep all the other rows the same.

```
(define (board-replace-peg board row col val)
  (if (= row 1)
     (cons (row-replace-peg (car board) col val) (cdr board))
     (cons (car board) (board-replace-peg (cdr board) (- row 1) col val))))
```

Both *board-add-peg* and *board-remove-peg* can be defined simply using *board-*

remove-peg. They first check if the operation is valid (adding is valid only if the selected position does not contain a peg, removing is valid only if the selected position contains a peg), and then use *board-replace-peg* to produce the modified board:

```
(define (board-add-peg board pos)
  (if (board-contains-peg? board pos)
     (error (format "Board already contains peg at position: ~a" pos))
     (board-replace-peg board (position-get-row pos)
                                          (position-get-column pos) true)))

(define (board-remove-peg board pos)
  (if (not (board-contains-peg? board pos))
     (error (format "Board does not contain peg at position: ~a" pos))
     (board-replace-peg board (position-get-row pos)
                                          (position-get-column pos) false)))
```

We can now define a procedure that models making a move on a board. Making a move involves removing the jumped peg and moving the peg from the starting position to the landing position. Moving the peg is equivalent to removing the peg from the starting position and adding a peg to the landing position, so the procedures we defined for adding and removing pegs can be composed to model making a move. We add a peg landing position to the board that results from removing the pegs in the starting and jumped positions:

```
(define (board-execute-move board move)
  (board-add-peg
   (board-remove-peg
    (board-remove-peg board (move-get-start move))
    (move-get-jumped move))
   (move-get-landing move)))
```

Finding Valid Moves. Now that we can model the board and simulate making jumps, we are ready to develop the solution. At each step, we try all valid moves on the board to see if any move leads to a winning position (that is, a position with only one peg remaining). So, we need a procedure that takes a Board as its input and outputs a List of all valid moves on the board. We break this down into the problem of producing a list of all conceivable moves (all moves in all directions from all starting positions on the board), filtering that list for moves that stay on the board, and then filtering the resulting list for moves that are legal (start at a position containing a peg, jump over a position containing a peg, and land in a position that is an empty hole).

First, we generate all conceivable moves by creating moves starting from each position on the board and moving in all possible move directions. We break this down further: the first problem is to produce a List of all positions on the board.

We can generate a list of all row numbers using the *intsto* procedure (from Example 5.8). To get a list of all the positions, we need to produce a list of the positions for each row. We do this by mapping each row to the corresponding list:

```
(define (all-positions-helper board)
  (list-map
    (lambda (row) (list-map (lambda (col) (make-position row col))
                            (intsto row)))
    (intsto (board-rows board))))
```

This almost does what we need, except instead of producing one List containing all the positions, it produces a List of Lists for the positions in each row. The *list-flatten* procedure (from Example 5.10) produces a flat list containing all the positions.

```
(define (all-positions board)
  (list-flatten (all-positions-helper board)))
```

For each Position, we find all possible moves starting from that position. We can move in six possible directions on the board: left, right, up-left, up-right, down-left, and down-right.

```
(define all-directions
  (list
   (make-direction −1 0) (make-direction 1 0) ; left, right
   (make-direction −1 −1) (make-direction 0 −1) ; up-left, up-right
   (make-direction 0 1) (make-direction 1 1))) ; down-left, down-right
```

For each position on the board, we create a list of possible moves starting at that position and moving in each possible move directions. This produces a List of Lists, so we use *list-flatten* to flatten the output of the *list-map* application into a single List of Moves.

```
(define (all-conceivable-moves board)
  (list-flatten
    (list-map
      (lambda (pos) (list-map (lambda (dir) (make-move pos dir))
                              all-directions))
      (all-positions board))))
```

The output produced by *all-conceivable-moves* includes moves that fly off the board. We use the *list-filter* procedure to remove those moves, to get the list of moves that stay on the board:

```
(define (all-board-moves board)
  (list-filter
   (lambda (move) (board-valid-position? board (move-get-landing move)))
   (all-conceivable-moves board)))
```

Finally, we need to filter out the moves that are not legal moves. A legal move must start at a position that contains a peg, jump over a position that contains a peg, and land in an empty hole. We use *list-filter* similarly to how we kept only the moves that stay on the board:

```
(define (all-legal-moves board)
  (list-filter
    (lambda (move)
      (and
       (board-contains-peg? board (move-get-start move))
       (board-contains-peg? board (move-get-jumped move))
       (not (board-contains-peg? board (move-get-landing move)))))
   (all-board-moves board)))
```

Winning the Game. Our goal is to find a sequence of moves that leads to a winning position, starting from the current board. If there is a winning sequence of moves, we can find it by trying all possible moves on the current board. Each of these moves leads to a new board. If the original board has a winning sequence of moves, at least one of the new boards has a winning sequence of moves. Hence, we can solve the puzzle by recursively trying all moves until finding a winning position.

```
(define (solve-pegboard board)
  (if (board-is-winning? board)
     null ; no moves needed to reach winning position
     (try-moves board (all-legal-moves board))))
```

If there is a sequence of moves that wins the game starting from the input Board, *solve-pegboard* outputs a List of Moves representing a winning sequence. This could be null, in the case where the input board is already a winning board. If there is no sequence of moves to win from the input board, *solve-pegboard* outputs false.

It remains to define the *try-moves* procedure. It takes a Board and a List of Moves as inputs. If there is a sequence of moves that starts with one of the input moves and leads to a winning position it outputs a List of Moves that wins; otherwise, it outputs false.

The base case is when there are no moves to try. When the input list is *null* it means there are no moves to try. We output *false* to mean this attempt did not lead to a winning board. Otherwise, we try the first move. If it leads to a winning position, *try-moves* should output the List of Moves that starts with the first move and is followed by the rest of the moves needed to solve the board resulting from taking the first move (that is, the result of *solve-pegboard* applied to the Board resulting from taking the first move). If the first move doesn't lead to a winning board, it tries the rest of the moves by calling *try-moves* recursively.

```
(define (try-moves board moves)
  (if (null? moves)
     false ; didn't find a winner
     (if (solve-pegboard (board-execute-move board (car moves)))
        (cons (car moves)
              (solve-pegboard (board-execute-move board (car moves))))
        (try-moves board (cdr moves)))))
```

Evaluating (*solve-pegboard* (*make-board* 5)) produces false since there is no way to win starting from a completely full board. Evaluating (*solve-pegboard* (*board-remove-peg* (*make-board* 5) (*make-position* 1 1))) takes about three minutes to produce this sequence of moves for winning the game starting from a 5-row board with the top peg removed:

((*Move* (*Position* 3 1) (*Direction* 0 −1))
(*Move* (*Position* 3 3) (*Direction* −1 0))
(*Move* (*Position* 1 1) (*Direction* 1 1))
(*Move* (*Position* 4 1) (*Direction* 0 −1))
... ; 8 moves elided
(*Move* (*Position* 5 1) (*Direction* 1 1)))

a. [*] Change the implementation to use a different Board representation, such as keeping a list of the Positions of each hole on the board. Only the procedures with names starting with *board-* should need to change when the Board representation is changed. Compare your implementation to this one.

b. [*] The standard pegboard puzzle uses a triangular board, but there is no reason the board has to be a triangle. Define a more general pegboard puzzle solver that works for a board of any shape.

c. [**] The described implementation is very inefficient. It does lots of redundant computation. For example, *all-possible-moves* evaluates to the same value every time it is applied to a board with the same number of rows. It is wasteful to recompute this over and over again to solve a given board. See how much faster you can make the pegboard solver. Can you make it fast enough to solve the 5-row board in less than half the original time? Can you make it fast enough to solve a 7-row board?

5.7 Summary of Part I

To conclude Part I, we revisit the three main themes introduced in Section 1.4.

Recursive definitions. We have seen many types of recursive definitions and used them to solve problems, including the pegboard puzzle. Recursive grammars provide a compact way to define a language; recursive procedure definitions enable us to solve problems by optimistically assuming a smaller problem instance can be solved and using that solution to solve the problem; recursive data structures such as the list type allow us to define and manipulate complex data built from simple components. All recursive definitions involve a base case. For grammars, the base case provides a way to stop the recursive replacements by produce a terminal (or empty output) directly; for procedures, the base case provides a direct solution to a small problem instance; for data structures, the base case provides a small instance of the data type (e.g., *null*). We will see many more examples of recursive definitions in the rest of this book.

universal programming language

Universality. All of the programs we have can be created from the simple subset of Scheme introduced in Chapter 3. This subset is a *universal programming language*: it is powerful enough to describe all possible computations. We can generate all the programs using the simple Scheme grammar, and interpret their meaning by systematically following the evaluation rules. We have also seen the universality of code and data. Procedures can take procedures as inputs, and produce procedures as outputs.

Abstraction. Abstraction hides details by giving things names. Procedural abstraction defines a procedure; by using inputs, a short procedure definition can abstract infinitely many different information processes. Data abstraction hides the details of how data is represented by providing procedures that abstractly create and manipulate that data. As we develop programs to solve more complex problems, it is increasingly important to use abstraction well to manage complexity. We need to break problems down into smaller parts that can be solved separately. Solutions to complex problems can be developed by thinking about what objects need to be modeled, and designing data abstractions the implement those models. Most of the work in solving the problem is defining the right datatypes; once we have the datatypes we need to model the problem well, we are usually well along the path to a solution.

With the tools from Part I, you can define a procedure to do any possible computation. In Part II, we examine the costs of executing procedures.

6 Machines

It is unworthy of excellent people to lose hours like slaves in the labor of calculation which could safely be relegated to anyone else if machines were used.
Gottfried Wilhelm von Leibniz, 1685

The first five chapters focused on ways to use language to describe procedures. Although finding ways to describe procedures succinctly and precisely would be worthwhile even if we did not have machines to carry out those procedures, the tremendous practical value we gain from being able to describe procedures comes from the ability of computers to carry out those procedures astoundingly quickly, reliably, and inexpensively. As a very rough approximation, a typical laptop gives an individual computing power comparable to having every living human on the planet working for you without ever making a mistake or needing a break.

This chapter introduces computing machines. Computers are different from other machines in two key ways:

1. Whereas other machines amplify or extend our *physical* abilities, computers amplify and extend our *mental* abilities.
2. Whereas other machines are designed for a few specific tasks, computers can be *programmed* to perform many tasks. The simple computer model introduced in this chapter can perform *all* possible computations.

The next section gives a brief history of computing machines, from prehistoric calculating aids to the design of the first universal computers. Section 6.2 explains how machines can implement logic. Section 6.3 introduces a simple abstract model of a computing machine that is powerful enough to carry out any algorithm.

We provide only a very shallow introduction to how machines can implement computations. Our primary goal is not to convey the details of how to design and build an efficient computing machine (although that is certainly a worthy goal that is often pursued in later computing courses), but to gain sufficient understanding of the properties nearly all conceivable computing machines share to be able to predict properties about the costs involved in carrying out a particular procedure. The following chapters use this to reason about the costs of various procedures. In Chapter 12, we use it to reason about the range of problems that can and cannot be solved by any mechanical computing machine.

6.1 History of Computing Machines

The goal of early machines was to carry out some physical process with less effort than would be required by a human. These machines took physical things as inputs, performed physical actions on those things, and produced some physical output. For instance, a cotton gin takes as input raw cotton, mechanically separates the cotton seed and lint, and produces the separated products as output.

The first big leap toward computing machines was the development of machines whose purpose is abstract rather than physical. Instead of producing physical things, these machines used physical things to *represent* information. The output of the machine is valuable because it can be interpreted as information, not for its direct physical effect.

Our first example is not a machine, but using fingers to count. The base ten number system used by most human cultures reflects using our ten fingers for counting.[1] Successful shepherds needed to find ways to count higher than ten. Shepherds used stones to represent numbers, making the cognitive leap of using a physical stone to represent some quantity of sheep. A shepherd would count sheep by holding stones in his hand that represent the number of sheep.

Suan Pan

More complex societies required more counting and more advanced calculating. The Inca civilization in Peru used knots in collections of strings known as *khipu* to keep track of thousands of items for a hierarchical system of taxation. Many cultures developed forms of abaci, including the ancient Mesopotamians and Romans. An *abacus* performs calculations by moving beads on rods. The Chinese *suan pan* ("calculating plate") is an abacus with a beam subdividing the rods, typically with two beads above the bar (each representing 5), and five beads below the beam (each representing 1). An operator can perform addition, subtraction, multiplication, and division by following mechanical processes using an abacus.

Pascaline
David Monniaux

All of these machines require humans to move parts to perform calculations. As machine technology improved, automatic calculating machines were built where the operator only needed to set up the inputs and then turn a crank or use some external power source to perform the calculation. The first automatic calculating machine to be widely demonstrated was the *Pascaline*, built by then nineteen-year old French mathematician Blaise Pascal (also responsible for Pascal's triangle from Exploration 5.1) to replace the tedious calculations he had to do to manage his father's accounts. The Pascaline had five wheels, each representing one digit of a number, linked by gears to perform addition with carries. Gottfried Wilhelm von Leibniz built the first machine capable of performing all four basic arithmetic operations (addition, subtraction, multiplication, and division) fully mechanically in 1694.

Over the following centuries, more sophisticated mechanical calculating machines were developed but these machines could still only perform one operation at a time. Performing a series of calculations was a tedious and error-prone process in which a human operator had to set up the machine for each arith-

[1] Not all human cultures use base ten number systems. For example, many cultures including the Maya and Basque adopted base twenty systems counting both fingers and toes. This was natural in warm areas, where typical footwear left the toes uncovered.

metic operation, record the result, and reset the machine for the next calculation.

The big breakthrough was the conceptual leap of programmability. A machine is *programmable* if its inputs not only control the values it operates on, but the operations it performs.

The first programmable computing machine was envisioned (but never successfully built) in the 1830s by Charles Babbage. Babbage was born in London in 1791 and studied mathematics at Cambridge. In the 1800s, calculations were done by looking up values in large books of mathematical and astronomical tables. These tables were computed by hand, and often contained errors. The calculations were especially important for astronomical navigation, and when the values were incorrect a ship would miscalculate its position at sea (sometimes with tragic consequences).

We got nothing for our £17,000 but Mr. Babbage's grumblings. We should at least have had a clever toy for our money.
Richard Sheepshanks, *Letter to the Board of Visitors of the Greenwich Royal Observatory*, 1854

Babbage sought to develop a machine to mechanize the calculations to compute these tables. Starting in 1822, he designed a steam-powered machine known as the Difference Engine to compute polynomials needed for astronomical calculations using Newton's method of successive differences (a generalization of Heron's method from Exploration 4.1). The Difference Engine was never fully completed. but led Babbage to envision a more general calculating machine.

This new machine, the Analytical Engine, designed between 1833 and 1844, was the first general-purpose computer envisioned. It was designed so that it could be programmed to perform any calculation. One breakthrough in Babbage's design was to feed the machine's outputs back into its inputs. This meant the engine could perform calculations with an arbitrary number of steps by cycling outputs back through the machine.

Analytical Engine
Science Museum, London

The Analytical Engine was programmed using punch cards, based on the cards that were used by Jacquard looms. Each card could describe an instruction such as loading a number into a variable in the store, moving values, performing arithmetic operations on the values in the store, and, most interestingly, jumping forward and backwards in the instruction cards. The Analytical Engine supported conditional jumps where the jump would be taken depending on the state of a lever in the machine (this is essentially a simple form of the if expression).

In 1842, Charles Babbage visited Italy and described the Analytical Engine to Luigi Menabrea, an Italian engineer, military officer, and mathematician who would later become Prime Minister of Italy. Menabrea published a description of Babbage's lectures in French. Ada Augusta Byron King (also known as Ada, Countess of Lovelace) translated the article into English.

Ada

In addition to the translation, Ada added a series of notes to the article. The notes included a program to compute Bernoulli numbers, the first detailed program for the Analytical Engine. Ada was the first to realize the importance and interest in creating the programs themselves, and envisioned how programs could be used to do much more than just calculate mathematical functions. This was the first computer program ever described, and Ada is recognized as the first computer programmer.

Despite Babbage's design, and Ada's vision, the Analytical Engine was never completed. It is unclear whether the main reason for the failure to build a working Analytical Engine was due to limitations of the mechanical components available at the time, or due to Babbage's inability to work with his engineer collaborator or to secure continued funding.

On two occasions I have been asked by members of Parliament, "Pray, Mr. Babbage, if you put into the machine wrong figures, will the right answers come out?" I am not able rightly to apprehend the kind of confusion of ideas that could provoke such a question.
Charles Babbage

The first working programmable computers would not appear for nearly a hundred years. Advances in electronics enabled more reliable and faster components than the mechanical components used by Babbage, and the desperation brought on by World War II spurred the funding and efforts that led to working general-purpose computing machines.

The remaining conceptual leap is to treat the program itself as data. In Babbage's Analytical Engine, the program is a stack of cards and the data are numbers stored in the machine. The machine cannot alter its own program.

The idea of treating the program as just another kind of data the machine can process was developed in theory by Alan Turing in the 1930s (Section 6.3 of this chapter describes his model of computing), and first implemented by the Manchester Small-Scale Experimental Machine (built by a team at Victoria University in Manchester) in 1948.

This computer (and all general-purpose computers in use today) stores the program itself in the machine's memory. Thus, the computer can create new programs by writing into its own memory. This power to change its own program is what makes stored-program computers so versatile.

Exercise 6.1. Babbage's design for the Analytical Engine called for a store holding 1000 variables, each of which is a 50-digit (decimal) number. How many bits could the store of Babbage's Analytical Engine hold?

6.2 Mechanizing Logic

Boolean logic

This section explains how machines can compute, starting with simple logical operations. We use *Boolean logic*, in which there are two possible values: *true* (often denoted as 1), and *false* (often denoted as 0). The Boolean datatype in Scheme is based on Boolean logic. Boolean logic is named for George Boole, a self-taught British mathematician who published *An investigation into the Laws of Thought, on Which are founded the Mathematical Theories of Logic and Probabilities* in 1854. Before Boole's work, logic focused on natural language discourse. Boole made logic a formal language to which the tools of mathematics could be applied.

George Boole

We illustrate how logical functions can be implemented mechanically by describing some logical machines. Modern computers use electrons to compute because they are small (more than a billion billion billion (10^{31}) electrons fit within the volume of a grain of sand), fast (approaching the speed of light), and cheap (more than a billion billion (10^{22}) electrons come out of a power outlet for less than a cent). They are also invisible and behave in somewhat mysterious ways, however, so we will instead consider how to compute with wine (or your favorite colored liquid). The basic notions of mechanical computation don't depend on the medium we use to compute, only on our ability to use it to represent values and to perform simple logical operations.

6.2.1 Implementing Logic

To implement logic using a machine, we need physical ways of representing the two possible values. We use a full bottle of wine to represent *true* and an empty bottle of wine to represent *false*. If the value of an input is *true*, we pour a bottle of wine in the input nozzle; for *false* inputs we do nothing. Similarly, electronic computers typically use presence of voltage to represent *true*, and absence of voltage to represent *false*.

And. A logical *and* function takes two inputs and produces one output. The output is *true* if both of the inputs are *true*; otherwise the output is *false*. We define a *logical-and* procedure using an if expression:[2]

```
(define (logical-and a b) (if a b false))
```

To design a mechanical implementation of the logical *and* function, we want a simpler definition that does not involve implementing something as complex as an if expression.

A different way to define a function is by using a table to show the corresponding output value for each possible pair of input values. This approach is limited to functions with a small number of possible inputs; we could not define addition on integers this way, since there are infinitely many possible different numbers that could be used as inputs. For functions in Boolean logic, there are only two possible values for each input (*true* and *false*) so it is feasible to list the outputs for all possible inputs.

We call a table defining a Boolean function a *truth table*. If there is one input, the table needs two entries, showing the output value for each possible input. When there are two inputs, the table needs four entries, showing the output value for all possible combinations of the input values. The truth table for the logical *and* function is:

truth table

A	*B*	*(and A B)*
false	*false*	*false*
true	*false*	*false*
false	*true*	*false*
true	*true*	*true*

We design a machine that implements the function described by the truth table: if both inputs are *true* (represented by full bottles of wine in our machine), the output should be *true*; if either input is *false*, the output should be *false* (an empty bottle). One way to do this is shown in Figure 6.1. Both inputs pour into a basin. The output nozzle is placed at a height corresponding to one bottle of wine in the collection basin, so the output bottle will fill (representing *true*), only if both inputs are true.

The design in Figure 6.1 would probably not work very well in practice. Some of the wine is likely to spill, so even when both inputs are *true* the output might not be a full bottle of wine. What should a $\frac{3}{4}$ full bottle of wine represent? What about a bottle that is half full?

[2]Scheme provides a special form *and* that performs the same function as the logical *and* function. It is a special form, though, since the second input expression is not evaluated unless the first input expression evaluates to *true*.

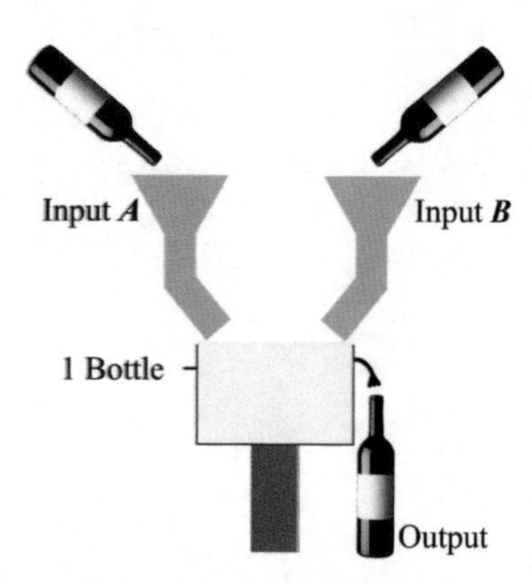

Figure 6.1. Computing *and* with wine.

digital abstraction The solution is the *digital abstraction*. Although there are many different quantities of wine that could be in a bottle, regardless of the actual quantity the value is interpreted as only one of two possible values: *true* or *false*. If the bottle has more than a given threshold, say half full, it represents *true*; otherwise, it represents *false*. This means an infinitely large set of possible values are abstracted as meaning *true*, so it doesn't matter which of the values above half full it is.

The digital abstraction provides a transition between the continuous world of physical things and the logical world of discrete values. It is much easier to design computing systems around discrete values than around continuous values; by mapping a range of possible continuous values to just two discrete values, we give up a lot of information but gain in simplicity and reliability. Nearly all computing machines today operate on discrete values using the digital abstraction.

Or. The logical *or* function takes two inputs, and outputs true if any of the inputs are true:[3]

A	*B*	(*or A B*)
false	*false*	*false*
true	*false*	*true*
false	*true*	*true*
true	*true*	*true*

Try to invent your own design for a machine that computes the *or* function before looking at one solution in Figure 6.2(a).

Implementing not. The output of the *not* function is the opposite of the value of its input:

A	(*not A*)
false	*true*
true	*false*

[3]Scheme provides a special form *or* that implements the logical *or* function, similarly to the *and* special form. If the first input evaluates to true, the second input is not evaluated and the value of the *or* expression is true.

It is not possible to produce a logical *not* without some other source of wine; it needs to create wine (to represent *true*) when there is none input (representing *false*). To implement the *not* function, we need the notion of a *source current* and a *clock*. The source current injects a bottle of wine on each clock tick. The clock ticks periodically, on each operation. The inputs need to be set up before the clock tick. When the clock ticks, a bottle of wine is sent through the source current, and the output is produced. Figure 6.2(b) shows one way to implement the *not* function.

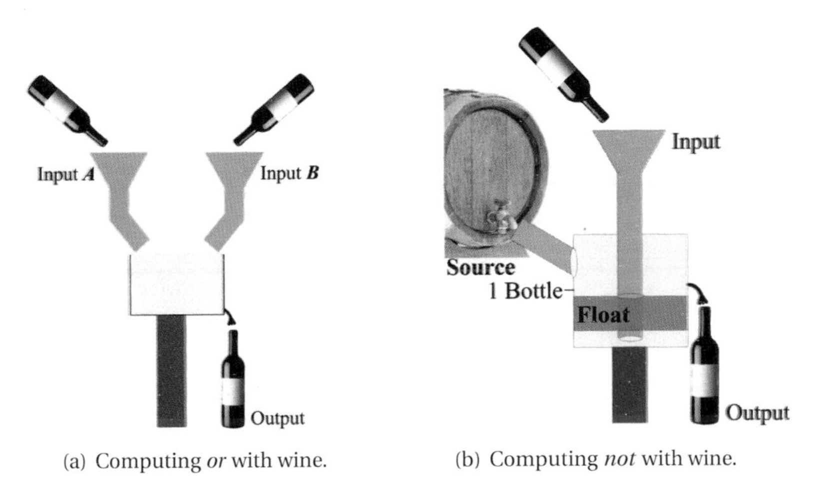

(a) Computing *or* with wine.

(b) Computing *not* with wine.

Figure 6.2. Computing logical *or* and *not* with wine

(a) The *or* machine is similar to the *and* machine in design, except we move the output nozzle to the bottom of the basin, so if either input is *true*, the output is *true*; when both inputs are *true*, some wine is spilled but the logical result is still *true*.

(b) The *not* machine uses a clock. Before the clock tick, the input is set. If the input is *true*, the float is lifted, blocking the source opening; if the input i *false*, the float rests on the bottom of the basin. When the clock ticks, the source wine is injected. If the float is up (because of the *true* input), the opening is blocked, and the output is empty (*false*). If the float is down (because of the *false* input), the opening is open, the source wine will pour across the float, filling the output (representing *true*). (This design assumes wine coming from the source does not leak under the float, which might be hard to build in a real system.)

6.2.2 Composing Operations

We can implement *and*, *or* and *not* using wine, but is that enough to perform interesting computations? In this subsection, we consider how simple logical functions can be combined to implement any logical function; in the following subsection, we see how basic arithmetic operations can be built from logical functions.

We start by making a three-input conjunction function. The *and3* of three inputs is *true* if and only if all three inputs are *true*. One way to make the three-input *and3* is to follow the same idea as the two-input *and* where all three inputs pour into the same basin, but make the basin with the output nozzle above the two bottle level.

Another way to implement a three-input *and3* is to compose two of the two-input *and* functions, similarly to how we composed procedures in Section 4.2.

Building *and3* by composing two two-input *and* functions allows us to construct a three-input *and3* without needing to design any new structures, as shown in Figure 6.3. The output of the first *and* function is fed into the second *and* function as its first input; the third input is fed directly into the second *and* function as its second input. We could write this as (*and* (*and A B*) *C*).

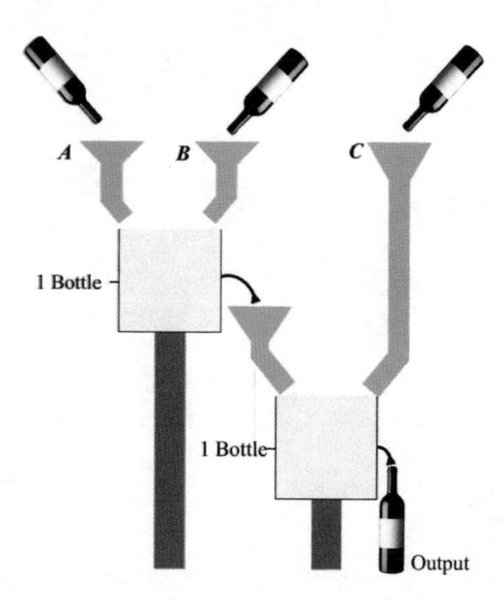

Figure 6.3. Computing *and3* by composing two *and* functions.

Composing logical functions also allows us to build new logical functions. Consider the *xor* (exclusive or) function that takes two inputs, and has output *true* when exactly one of the inputs is *true*:

A	*B*	(*xor A B*)
false	*false*	*false*
true	*false*	*true*
false	*true*	*true*
true	*true*	*false*

Can we build *xor* by composing the functions we already have?

The *xor* is similar to *or*, except for the result when both inputs are *true*. So, we could compute (*xor A B*) as (*and* (*or A B*) (*not* (*and A B*))). Thus, we can build an *xor* machine by composing the designs we already have for *and*, *or*, and *not*.

We can compose any pair of functions where the outputs for the first function are consistent with the input for the second function. One particularly important function known as *nand* results from *not* and *and*:

A	*B*	(*nand A B*)
false	*false*	*true*
true	*false*	*true*
false	*true*	*true*
true	*true*	*false*

All Boolean logic functions can be implemented using just the *nand* function. One way to prove this is to show how to build all logic functions using just *nand*. For example, we can implement *not* using *nand* where the one input to the *not* function is used for both inputs to the *nand* function:

$$(not\ A) \equiv (nand\ A\ A)$$

Now that we have shown how to implement *not* using *nand*, it is easy to see how to implement *and* using *nand*:

$$(and\ A\ B) \equiv (not\ (nand\ A\ B))$$

Implementing *or* is a bit trickier. Recall that *A or B* is *true* if any one of the inputs is *true*. But, *A nand B* is *true* if both inputs are *false*, and *false* if both inputs are *true*. To compute *or* using only *nand* functions, we need to invert both inputs:

$$(or\ A\ B) \equiv (nand\ (not\ A)\ (not\ B))$$

To complete the proof, we would need to show how to implement all the other Boolean logic functions. We omit the details here, but leave some of the other functions as exercises. The universality of the *nand* function makes it very useful for implementing computing devices. Trillions of *nand* gates are produced in silicon every day.

Exercise 6.2. Define a Scheme procedure, *logical-or*, that takes two inputs and outputs the logical or of those inputs.

Exercise 6.3. What is the meaning of composing *not* with itself? For example, (*not* (*not A*)).

Exercise 6.4. Define the *xor* function using only *nand* functions.

Exercise 6.5. [★] Our definition of (*not A*) as (*nand A A*) assumes there is a way to produce two copies of a given input. Design a component for our wine machine that can do this. It should take one input, and produce two outputs, both with the same value as the input. (Hint: when the input is *true*, we need to produce two full bottles as outputs, so there must be a source similarly to the *not* component.)

Exercise 6.6. [★] The digital abstraction works fine as long as actual values stay close to the value they represent. But, if we continue to compute with the outputs of functions, the actual values will get increasingly fuzzy. For example, if the inputs to the *and3* function in Figure 6.3 are initially all $\frac{3}{4}$ full bottles (which should be interpreted as *true*), the basin for the first *and* function will fill to $1\frac{1}{2}$, so only $\frac{1}{2}$ bottle will be output from the first *and*. When combined with the third input, the second basin will contain $1\frac{1}{4}$ bottles, so only $\frac{1}{4}$ will spill into the output bottle. Thus, the output will represent *false*, even though all three inputs represent *true*. The solution to this problem is to use an *amplifier* to restore values to their full representations. Design a wine machine amplifier that takes one input and produces a strong representation of that input as its output. If that input represents *true* (any value that is half full or more), the amplifier should output *true*, but with a strong, full bottle representation. If that input represents *false* (any value that is less than half full), the amplifier should output a strong *false* value (completely empty).

6.2.3 Arithmetic

Not only is the *nand* function complete for Boolean logical functions, it is also enough to implement all discrete arithmetic functions. First, consider the problem of adding two one-bit numbers.

There are four possible pairs of inputs:

A		B		r_1	r_0
0	+	0	=	0	0
0	+	1	=	0	1
1	+	0	=	0	1
1	+	1	=	1	0

We can compute each of the two output bits as a logical function of the two input bits. The right output bit, r_0, is 1 if exactly one of the input bits is 1:

$$r_0 = (or\ (and\ (not\ A)\ B)\ (and\ A\ (not\ B)))$$

This is what the *xor* function computes, so:

$$r_0 = (xor\ A\ B)$$

The left output bit, r_1, is 0 for all inputs except when both inputs are 1:

$$r_1 = (and\ A\ B)$$

Since we have already seen how to implement *and*, *or*, *xor*, and *not* using only *nand* functions, this means we can implement a one-bit adder using only *nand* functions.

Adding larger numbers requires more logical functions. Consider adding two n-bit numbers:

$$\begin{array}{cccccccc} & & a_{n-1} & a_{n-2} & \cdots & a_1 & a_0 \\ + & & b_{n-1} & b_{n-2} & \cdots & b_1 & b_0 \\ \hline = & r_n & r_{n-1} & r_{n-2} & \cdots & r_1 & r_0 \end{array}$$

The elementary school algorithm for adding decimal numbers is to sum up the digits from right to left. If the result in one place is more than one digit, the additional tens are carried to the next digit. We use c_k to represent the carry digit in the kth column.

$$
\begin{array}{cccccccc}
 & c_n & c_{n-1} & c_{n-2} & \cdots & c_1 & \\
 & & a_{n-1} & a_{n-2} & \cdots & a_1 & a_0 \\
+ & & b_{n-1} & b_{n-2} & \cdots & b_1 & b_0 \\
\hline
= & r_n & r_{n-1} & r_{n-2} & \cdots & r_1 & r_0
\end{array}
$$

The algorithm for addition is:

- Initially, $c_0 = 0$.
- Repeat for each digit k from 0 to n:
    1. $v_1 v_0 = a_k + b_k + c_k$ (if there is no digit a_k or b_k use 0).
    2. $r_k = v_0$.
    3. $c_{k+1} = v_1$.

This is perhaps the first interesting algorithm most people learn: if followed correctly, it is guaranteed to produce the correct result, and to always finish, for any two input numbers.

Step 1 seems to require already knowing how to perform addition, since it uses $+$. But, the numbers added are one-digit numbers (and c_k is 0 or 1). Hence, there are a finite number of possible inputs for the addition in step 1: 10 decimal digits for $a_k \times 10$ decimal digits for $b_k \times 2$ possible values of c_k. We can memorize the 100 possibilities for adding two digits (or write them down in a table), and easily add one as necessary for the carry. Hence, computing this addition does not require a general addition algorithm, just a specialized method for adding one-digit numbers.

We can use the same algorithm to sum binary numbers, except it is simpler since there are only two binary digits. Without the carry bit, the result bit, r_k, is 1 if (*xor* a_k b_k). If the carry bit is 1, the result bit should flip. So,

$$r_k = (\mathit{xor}\ (\mathit{xor}\ a_k\ b_k)\ c_k)$$

This is the same as adding $a_k + b_k + c_k$ base two and keeping only the right digit.

The carry bit is 1 if the sum of the input bits and previous carry bit is greater than 1. This happens when any two of the bits are 1:

$$c_{k+1} = (\mathit{or}\ (\mathit{and}\ a_k\ b_k)\ (\mathit{and}\ a_k\ c_k)\ (\mathit{and}\ b_k\ c_k))$$

As with elementary school decimal addition, we start with $c_0 = 0$, and proceed through all the bits from right to left.

We can propagate the equations through the steps to find a logical equation for each result bit in terms of just the input bits. First, we simplify the functions for the first result and carry bits based on knowing $c_0 = 0$:

$$r_0 = (\mathit{xor}\ (\mathit{xor}\ a_0\ b_0)\ c_0) = (\mathit{xor}\ a_0\ b_0)$$
$$c_1 = (\mathit{or}\ (\mathit{and}\ a_0\ b_0)\ (\mathit{and}\ a_0\ c_0)\ (\mathit{and}\ b_0\ c_0)) = (\mathit{and}\ a_0\ b_0)$$

Then, we can derive the functions for r_1 and c_2:

$$r_1 = (\mathit{xor}\ (\mathit{xor}\ a_1\ b_1)\ c_1) = (\mathit{xor}\ (\mathit{xor}\ a_1\ b_1)\ (\mathit{and}\ a_0\ b_0))$$
$$c_2 = (\mathit{or}\ (\mathit{and}\ a_1\ b_1)\ (\mathit{and}\ a_1\ c_1)\ (\mathit{and}\ b_1\ c_1))$$
$$= (\mathit{or}\ (\mathit{and}\ a_1\ b_1)\ (\mathit{and}\ a_1\ (\mathit{and}\ a_0\ b_0))\ (\mathit{and}\ b_1\ (\mathit{and}\ a_0\ b_0)))$$

As we move left through the digits, the terms get increasingly complex. But, for any number of digits, we can always find functions for computing the result bits using only logical functions on the input bits. Hence, we can implement addition for any length binary numbers using only *nand* functions.

We can also implement multiplication, subtraction, and division using only *nand* functions. We omit the details here, but the essential approach of breaking down our elementary school arithmetic algorithms into functions for computing each output bit works for all of the arithmetic operations.

Exercise 6.7. Adding logically.

a. What is the logical formula for r_3?

b. Without simplification, how many functions will be composed to compute the addition result bit r_4?

c. [★] Is it possible to compute r_4 with fewer logical functions?

Exercise 6.8. Show how to compute the result bits for binary multiplication of two 2-bit inputs using only logical functions.

Exercise 6.9. [★] Show how to compute the result bits for binary multiplication of two inputs of any length using only logical functions.

6.3 Modeling Computing

By composing the logic functions, we could build a wine computer to perform any Boolean function. And, we can perform any discrete arithmetic function using only Boolean functions. For a useful computer, though, we need programmability. We would like to be able to make the inputs to the machine describe the logical functions that it should perform, rather than having to build a new machine for each desired function. We could, in theory, construct such a machine using wine, but it would be awfully complicated. Instead, we consider programmable computing machines abstractly.

Recall in Chapter 1, we defined a computer as a machine that can:

1. Accept input.
2. Execute a mechanical procedure.
3. Produce output.

So, our model of a computer needs to model these three things.

Modeling input. In real computers, input comes in many forms: typing on a keyboard, moving a mouse, packets coming in from the network, an accelerometer in the device, etc.

For our model, we want to keep things as simple as possible, though. From a computational standpoint, it doesn't really matter how the input is collected. We can represent any discrete input with a sequence of bits. Input devices like keyboards are clearly discrete: there are a finite number of keys, and each key could be assigned a unique number. Input from a pointing device like a mouse could be continuous, but we can always identify some minimum detected movement distance, and record the mouse movements as discrete numbers of move units and directions. Richer input devices like a camera or microphone can also produce discrete output by discretizing the input using a process similar to the image storage in Chapter 1. So, the information produced by any input device can be represented by a sequence of bits.

The virtual shopping spree was a first for the President who has a reputation for being "technologically challenged." But White House sources insist that the First Shopper used his own laptop and even "knew how to use the mouse."
BusinessWeek, 22 December 1999

For real input devices, the time an event occurs is often crucial. When playing a video game, it does not just matter that the mouse button was clicked, it matters a great deal *when* the click occurs. How can we model inputs where time matters using just our simple sequence of bits?

One way would be to divide time into discrete quanta and encode the input as zero or one events in each quanta. A more efficient way would be to add a timestamp to each input. The timestamps are just numbers (e.g., the number of milliseconds since the start time), so can be written down just as sequences of bits.

Thus, we can model a wide range of complex input devices with just a finite sequence of bits. The input must be finite, since our model computer needs all the input before it starts processing. This means our model is not a good model for computations where the input is infinite, such as a web server intended to keep running and processing new inputs (e.g., requests for a web page) forever. In practice, though, this isn't usually a big problem since we can make the input finite by limiting the time the server is running in the model.

A finite sequence of bits can be modeled using a long, narrow, tape that is divided into squares, where each square contains one bit of the input.

Modeling output. Output from computers effects the physical world in lots of very complex ways: displaying images on a screen, printing text on a printer, sending an encoded web page over a network, sending an electrical signal to an anti-lock brake to increase the braking pressure, etc.

We don't attempt to model the physical impact of computer outputs; that would be far too complicated, but it is also one step beyond modeling the computation itself. Instead, we consider just the information content of the output. The information in a picture is the same whether it is presented as a sequence of bits or an image projected on a screen, its just less pleasant to look at as a sequence of bits. So, we can model the output just like we modeled the input: a sequence of bits written on a tape divided into squares.

Modeling processing. Our processing model should be able to model every possible mechanical procedure since we want to model a universal computer, but should be as simple as possible.

One thing our model computer needs is a way to keep track of what it is doing. We can think of this like scratch paper: a human would not be able to do a long computation without keeping track of intermediate values on scratch paper, and a computer has the same need. In Babbage's Analytical Engine, this was called the *store*, and divided into a thousand variables, each of which could store a fifty decimal digit number. In the Apollo Guidance Computer, the working memory was divided into banks, each bank holding 1024 words. Each word was 15 bits (plus one bit for error correction). In current 32-bit processors, such as the x86, memory is divided into pages, each containing 1024 32-bit words.

For our model machine, we don't want to have arbitrary limits on the amount of working storage. So, we model the working storage with an infinitely long tape. Like the input and output tapes, it is divided into squares, and each square can contain one symbol. For our model computer, it is useful to think about having an infinitely long tape, but of course, no real computer has infinite amounts of working storage. We can, however, imagine continuing to add more memory to a real computer as needed until we have enough to solve a given problem, and adding more if we need to solve a larger problem.

Our model now involves separate tapes for input, output, and a working tape. We can simplify the model by using a single tape for all three. At the beginning of the execution, the tape contains the input (which must be finite). As processing is done, the input is read and the tape is used as the working tape. Whatever is on the tape and the end of the execution is the output.

We also need a way for our model machine to interface with the tape. We imagine a tape head that contacts a single square on the tape. On each processing step, the tape head can read the symbol in the current square, write a symbol in the current square, and move one square either left or right.

The final thing we need is a way to model actually doing the processing. In our model, this means controlling what the tape head does: at each step, it needs to decide what to write on the tape, and whether to move left or right, or to finish the execution.

In early computing machines, processing meant performing one of the basic arithmetic operations (addition, subtraction, multiplication, or division). We don't want to have to model anything as complex as multiplication in our model machine, however. The previous section showed how addition and other arithmetic operations can be built from simpler logical operations. To carry out a complex operation as a composition of simple operations, we need a way to keep track of enough state to know what to do next. The machine state is just a number that keeps track of what the machine is doing. Unlike the tape, it is limited to a finite number. There are two reasons why the machine state number must be finite: first, we need to be able to write down the program for the machine by explaining what it should do in each state, which would be difficult if there were infinitely many states.

We also need rules to control what the tape head does. We can think of each rule as a mapping from the current observed state of the machine to what to do next. The input for a rule is the symbol in the current tape square and the current state of the machine; the output of each rule is three things: the symbol to write on the current tape square, the direction for the tape head to move (left, right, or halt), and the new machine state. We can describe the program for the machine by listing the rules. For each machine state, we need a rule for each possible symbol on the tape.

6.3.1 Turing Machines

This abstract model of a computer was invented by Alan Turing in the 1930s and is known as a *Turing Machine*. Turing's model is depicted in Figure 6.4. An infinite tape divided into squares is used as the input, working storage, and output. The tape head can read the current square on the tape, write a symbol into the current tape square, and move left or right one position. The tape head

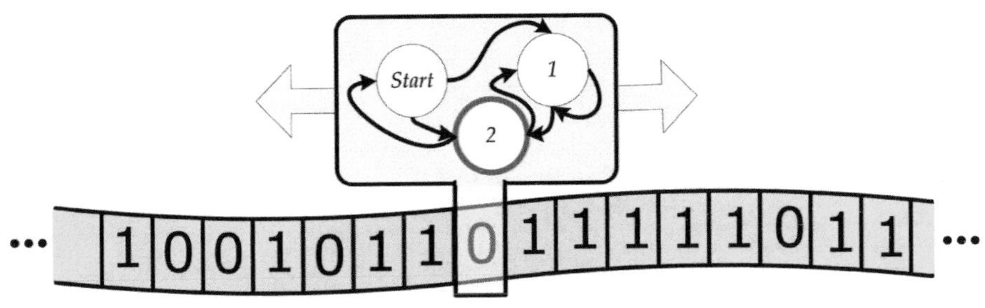

Figure 6.4. Turing Machine model.

keeps track of its internal state, and follows rules matching the current state and current tape square to determine what to do next.

Turing's model is by far the most widely used model for computers today. Turing developed this model in 1936, before anything resembling a modern computer existed. Turing did not develop his model as a model of an automatic computer, but instead as a model for what could be done by a human following mechanical rules. He devised the infinite tape to model the two-dimensional graph paper students use to perform arithmetic. He argued that the number of machine states must be limited by arguing that a human could only keep a limited amount of information in mind at one time.

Turing's model is equivalent to the model we described earlier, but instead of using only bits as the symbols on the tape, Turing's model uses members of any finite set of symbols, known as the *alphabet* of the tape. Allowing the tape alphabet to contain any set of symbols instead of just the two binary digits makes it easier to describe a Turing Machine that computes a particular function, but does not change the power of the model. That means, every computation that could be done with a Turing Machine using any alphabet set, could also be done by some Turing Machine using only the binary digits.

We could show this by describing an algorithm that takes in a description of a Turing Machine using an arbitrarily large alphabet, and produces a Turing Machine that uses only two symbols to simulate the input Turing Machine. As we saw in Chapter 1, we can map each of the alphabet symbols to a finite sequence of binary digits.

Mapping the rules is more complex: since each original input symbol is now spread over several squares, we need extra states and rules to read the equivalent of one original input. For example, suppose our original machine uses 16 alphabet symbols, and we map each symbol to a 4-bit sequence. If the original machine used a symbol `X`, which we map to the sequence of bits `1011`, we would need four states for every state in the original machine that has a rule using `X` as input. These four states would read the `1`, `0`, `1`, `1` from the tape. The last state now corresponds to the state in the original machine when an `X` is read from the tape. To follow the rule, we also need to use four states to write the bit sequence corresponding to the original write symbol on the tape. Then, simulating moving one square left or right on the original Turing Machine, now requires moving four squares, so requires four more states. Hence, we may need 12 states for each transition rule of the original machine, but can simulate everything it does using only two symbols.

universal computing machine

The Turing Machine model is a *universal computing machine*. This means every algorithm can be implemented by some Turing Machine. Chapter 12 explores more deeply what it means to simulate every possible Turing Machine and explores the set of problems that can be solved by a Turing Machine.

Any physical machine has a limited amount of memory. If the machine does not have enough space to store a trillion bits, there is no way it can do a computation whose output would exceed a trillion bits. Nevertheless, the simplicity and robustness of the Turing Machine model make it a useful way to think about computing even if we cannot build a truly universal computing machine.

Turing's model has proven to be remarkably robust. Despite being invented before anything resembling a modern computer existed, nearly every computing machine ever imagined or built can be modeled well using Turing's simple model. The important thing about the model is that we can simulate any computer using a Turing Machine. Any step on any computer that operates using standard physics and be simulated with a finite number of steps on a Turing Machine. This means if we know how many steps it takes to solve some problem on a Turing Machine, the number of steps it takes on any other machine is at most some multiple of that number. Hence, if we can reason about the number of steps required for a Turing Machine to solve a given problem, then we can make strong and general claims about the number of steps it would take *any* standard computer to solve the problem. We will show this more convincingly in Chapter 12, but for now we assert it, and use it to reason about the cost of executing various procedures in the following chapter.

Example 6.1: Balancing Parentheses

We define a Turing Machine that solves the problem of checking parentheses are well-balanced. For example, in a Scheme expression, every opening left parenthesis must have a corresponding closing right parenthesis. For example, `(()(()))()` is well-balanced, but `(()))(()` is not. Our goal is to design a Turing Machine that takes as input a string of parentheses (with a `#` at the beginning and end to mark the endpoints) and produces as output a `1` on the tape if the input string is well-balanced, and a `0` otherwise. For this problem, the output is what is written in the square under the tape head; it doesn't matter what is left on the rest of the tape.

Our strategy is to find matching pairs of parentheses and cross them out by writing an `X` on the tape in place of the parenthesis. If all the parentheses are crossed out at the end, the input was well-balanced, so the machine writes a `1` as its output and halts. If not, the input was not well-balanced, and the machine writes a 0 as its output and halts. The trick to the matching is that a closing parenthesis always matches the first open parenthesis found moving to the left from the closing parenthesis. The plan for the machine is to move the tape head to the right (without changing the input) until a closing parenthesis is found. Cross out that closing parenthesis by replacing it with an `X`, and move to the left until an open parenthesis is found. This matches the closing parenthesis, so it is replaced with an `X`. Then, continue to the right searching for the next closing parenthesis. If the end of the tape (marked with a `#`) is found, check the tape has no remaining open parenthesis.

We need three internal states: *LookForClosing*, in which the machine continues to the right until it finds a closing parenthesis (this is the start state); *LookForOpen*, in which the machine continues to the left until it finds the balancing open parenthesis; and *CheckTape*, in which the machine checks there are no unbalanced open parentheses on the tape starting from the right end of the tape and moving towards the left end. The full rules are shown in Figure 6.5.

State	Read	Next State	Write	Move	
LookForClosing	)	*LookForOpen*	X	←	*Found closing.*
LookForClosing	(	*LookForClosing*	(	→	*Keep looking.*
LookForClosing	X	*LookForClosing*	X	→	*Keep looking.*
LookForClosing	#	*CheckTape*	#	←	*End of tape.*
LookForOpen	)	-	X	Error	*Shouldn't happen.*
LookForOpen	(	*LookForClosing*	X	→	*Found open.*
LookForOpen	X	*LookForOpen*	X	←	*Keep looking.*
LookForOpen	#	-	0	Halt	*Reached beginning.*
CheckTape	)	-	0	Error	*Shouldn't happen.*
CheckTape	(	-	0	Halt	*Unbalanced open.*
CheckTape	X	*CheckTape*	X	←	*Keep checking.*
CheckTape	#	-	1	Halt	*Finished checking.*

Figure 6.5. Rules for checking balanced parentheses Turing Machine.

Another way to depict a Turing Machine is to show the states and rules graphically. Each state is a node in the graph. For each rule, we draw an edge on the graph between the starting state and the next state, and label the edge with the read and write tape symbols (separated by a /), and move direction.

Figure 6.6 shows the same Turing Machine as a state graph. When reading a symbol in a given state produces an error (such as when a) is encountered in the *LookForOpen* state), it is not necessary to draw an edge on the graph. If there is no outgoing edge for the current read symbol for the current state in the state graph, execution terminates with an error.

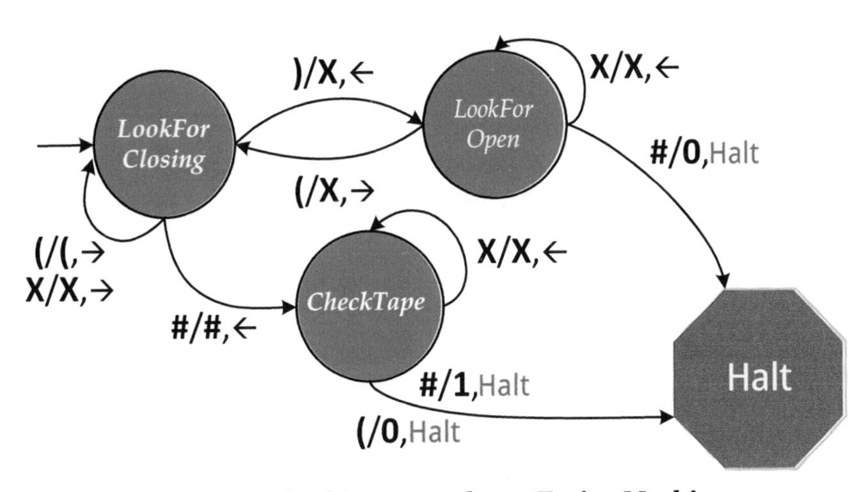

Figure 6.6. Checking parentheses Turing Machine.

Exercise 6.10. Follow the rules to simulate the checking parentheses Turing Machine on each input (assume the beginning and end of the input are marked with a #):

a.)

b. ()

c. *empty input*

d. (()(()))()

e. (()))(()

Exercise 6.11. [★] Design a Turing Machine for adding two arbitrary-length binary numbers. The input is of the form $a_{n-1} \ldots a_1 a_0 + b_{m-1} \ldots b_1 b_0$ (with # markers at both ends) where each a_k and b_k is either 0 or 1. The output tape should contain bits that represent the sum of the two inputs.

Profile: Alan Turing

Alan Turing
Image from Bletchley Park Ltd.

Alan Turing was born in London in 1912, and developed his computing model while at Cambridge in the 1930s. He developed the model to solve a famous problem posed by David Hilbert in 1928. The problem, known as the *Entscheidungsproblem* (German for "decision problem") asked for an algorithm that could determine the truth or falsehood of a mathematical statement. To solve the problem, Turing first needed a formal model of an algorithm. For this, he invented the Turing Machine model described above, and defined an algorithm as any Turing Machine that is guaranteed to eventually halt on any input. With the model, Turing was able to show that there are some problems that cannot be solved by *any* algorithm. We return to this in Chapter 12 and explain Turing's proof and examples of problems that cannot be solved.

Bombe
Rebuilt at Bletchley Park

After publishing his solution to the *Entscheidungsproblem* in 1936, Turing went to Princeton and studied with Alonzo Church (inventor of the Lambda calculus, on which Scheme is based). With the start of World War II, Turing joined the highly secret British effort to break Nazi codes at Bletchley Park. Turing was instrumental in breaking the Enigma code which was used by the Nazi's to communicate with field units and submarines. Turing designed an electro-mechanical machine known as a *bombe* for searching possible keys to decrypt Enigma-encrypted messages. The machines used logical operations to search the possible rotor settings on the Enigma to find the settings that were most likely to have generated an intercepted encrypted message. Bletchley Park was able to break thousands of Enigma messages during the war. The Allies used the knowledge gained from them to avoid Nazi submarines and gain a tremendous tactical advantage.

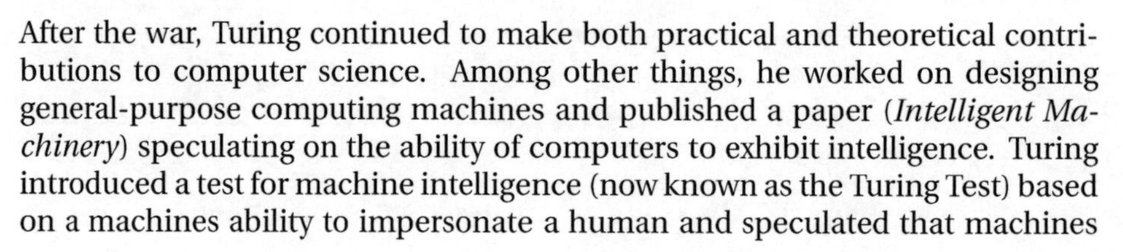

After the war, Turing continued to make both practical and theoretical contributions to computer science. Among other things, he worked on designing general-purpose computing machines and published a paper (*Intelligent Machinery*) speculating on the ability of computers to exhibit intelligence. Turing introduced a test for machine intelligence (now known as the Turing Test) based on a machines ability to impersonate a human and speculated that machines would be able to pass the test within 50 years (that is, by the year 2000). Turing also studied morphogenesis (how biological systems grow) including why Fibonacci numbers appear so often in plants.

In 1952, Turing's house was broken into, and Turing reported the crime to the police. The investigation revealed that Turing was a homosexual, which at the time was considered a crime in Britain. Turing did not attempt to hide his homosexuality, and was convicted and given a choice between serving time in prison and taking hormone treatments. He accepted the treatments, and has his security clearance revoked. In 1954, at the age of 41, Turing was found dead in an apparent suicide, with a cynide-laced partially-eaten apple next to him. The codebreaking effort at Bletchley Park was kept secret for many years after the war (Turing's report on Enigma was not declassified until 1996), so Turing never received public recognition for his contributions to the war effort. In September 2009, instigated by an on-line petition, British Prime Minister Gordon Brown issued an apology for how the British government treated Alan Turing.

6.4 Summary

The power of computers comes from their programmability. Universal computers can be programmed to execute any algorithm. The Turing Machine model provides a simple, abstract, model of a computing machine. Every algorithm can be implemented as a Turing Machine, and a Turing Machine can simulate any other reasonable computer.

As the first computer programmer, Ada deserves the last word:

> *By the word operation, we mean any process which alters the mutual relation of two or more things, be this relation of what kind it may. This is the most general definition, and would include all subjects in the universe. In abstract mathematics, of course operations alter those particular relations which are involved in the considerations of number and space, and the results of operations are those peculiar results which correspond to the nature of the subjects of operation. But the science of operations, as derived from mathematics more especially, is a science of itself, and has its own abstract truth and value; just as logic has its own peculiar truth and value, independently of the subjects to which we may apply its reasonings and processes....*
>
> *The operating mechanism can even be thrown into action independently of any object to operate upon (although of course no result could then be developed). Again, it might act upon other things besides number, were objects found whose mutual fundamental relations could be expressed by those of the abstract science of operations, and which should be also susceptible of adaptations to the action of the operating notation and mechanism of the engine. Supposing, for instance, that the fundamental relations of pitched sounds in the science of harmony and of musical composition were susceptible of such expression and adaptations, the engine might compose elaborate and scientific pieces of music of any degree of complexity or extent.*
>
> Ada, Countess of Lovelace, *Sketch of The Analytical Engine*, 1843

7 Cost

A LISP programmer knows the value of everything, but the cost of nothing.
Alan Perlis

I told my dad that someday I'd have a computer that I could write programs on. He said that would cost as much as a house. I said, "Well, then I'm going to live in an apartment."
Steve Wozniak

This chapter develops tools for reasoning about the cost of evaluating a given expression. Predicting the cost of executing a procedure has practical value (for example, we can estimate how much computing power is needed to solve a particular problem or decide between two possible implementations), but also provides deep insights into the nature of procedures and problems.

The most commonly used cost metric is time. Other measures of cost include the amount of memory needed and the amount of energy consumed. Indirectly, these costs can often be translated into money: the rate of transactions a service can support, or the price of the computer needed to solve a problem.

7.1 Empirical Measurements

We can measure the cost of evaluating a given expression empirically. If we are primarily concerned with time, we could just use a stopwatch to measure the evaluation time. For more accurate results, we use the built-in (*time Expression*) special form.[1] Evaluating (*time Expression*) produces the value of the input expression, but also prints out the time required to evaluate the expression (shown in our examples using *slanted* font). It prints out three time values:

cpu time
: The time in milliseconds the processor ran to evaluate the expression. CPU is an abbreviation for "central processing unit", the computer's main processor.

real time
: The actual time in milliseconds it took to evaluate the expression. Since other processes may be running on the computer while this expression is evaluated, the real time may be longer than the CPU time, which only counts the time the processor was working on evaluating this expression.

[1] The *time* construct must be a special form, since the expression is not evaluated before entering *time* as it would be with the normal application rule. If it were evaluated normally, there would be no way to time how long it takes to evaluate, since it would have already been evaluated before *time* is applied.

gc time
The time in milliseconds the interpreter spent on garbage collection to evaluate the expression. Garbage collection is used to reclaim memory that is storing data that will never be used again.

For example, using the definitions from Chapter 5,

```
(time (solve-pegboard (board-remove-peg (make-board 5)
                                        (make-position 1 1))))
```

prints: *cpu time: 141797 real time: 152063 gc time: 765*. The real time is 152 seconds, meaning this evaluation took just over two and a half minutes. Of this time, the evaluation was using the CPU for 142 seconds, and the garbage collector ran for less than one second.

Here are two more examples:

```
> (time (car (list-append (intsto 1000) (intsto 100))))
cpu time: 531 real time: 531 gc time: 62
1
> (time (car (list-append (intsto 1000) (intsto 100))))
cpu time: 609 real time: 609 gc time: 0
1
```

The two expressions evaluated are identical, but the reported time varies. Even on the same computer, the time needed to evaluate the same expression varies. Many properties unrelated to our expression (such as where things happen to be stored in memory) impact the actual time needed for any particular evaluation. Hence, it is dangerous to draw conclusions about which procedure is faster based on a few timings.

Another limitation of this way of measuring cost is it only works if we wait for the evaluation to complete. If we try an evaluation and it has not finished after an hour, say, we have no idea if the actual time to finish the evaluation is sixty-one minutes or a quintillion years. We could wait another minute, but if it still hasn't finished we don't know if the execution time is sixty-two minutes or a quintillion years. The techniques we develop allow us to predict the time an evaluation needs without waiting for it to execute.

There's no sense in being precise when you don't even know what you're talking about.
John von Neumann

Finally, measuring the time of a particular application of a procedure does not provide much insight into how long it will take to apply the procedure to different inputs. We would like to understand how the evaluation time scales with the size of the inputs so we can understand which inputs the procedure can sensibly be applied to, and can choose the best procedure to use for different situations. The next section introduces mathematical tools that are helpful for capturing how cost scales with input size.

Exercise 7.1. Suppose you are defining a procedure that needs to append two lists, one short list, *short* and one very long list, *long*, but the order of elements in the resulting list does not matter. Is it better to use (*list-append short long*) or (*list-append long short*)? (A good answer will involve both experimental results and an analytical explanation.)

Exploration 7.1: Multiplying Like Rabbits

Filius Bonacci was an Italian monk and mathematician in the 12th century. He published a book, *Liber Abbaci*, on how to calculate with decimal numbers that introduced Hindu-Arabic numbers to Europe (replacing Roman numbers) along with many of the algorithms for doing arithmetic we learn in elementary school. It also included the problem for which *Fibonacci* numbers are named:[2]

> *A pair of newly-born male and female rabbits are put in a field. Rabbits mate at the age of one month and after that procreate every month, so the female rabbit produces a new pair of rabbits at the end of its second month. Assume rabbits never die and that each female rabbit produces one new pair (one male, one female) every month from her second month on. How many pairs will there be in one year?*

Filius Bonacci

We can define a function that gives the number of pairs of rabbits at the beginning of the nth month as:

$$Fibonacci(n) = \begin{cases} 1 & : \; n = 1 \\ 1 & : \; n = 2 \\ Fibonacci(n-1) + Fibonacci(n-2) & : \; n > 1 \end{cases}$$

The third case follows from Bonacci's assumptions: all the rabbits alive at the beginning of the previous month are still alive (the $Fibonacci(n-1)$ term), and all the rabbits that are at least two months old reproduce (the $Fibonacci(n-2)$ term).

The sequence produced is known as the Fibonacci sequence:

$$1, 1, 2, 3, 5, 8, 13, 21, 34, 55, 89, 144, 233, 377, \ldots$$

After the first two 1s, each number in the sequence is the sum of the previous two numbers. Fibonacci numbers occur frequently in nature, such as the arrangement of florets in the sunflower (34 spirals in one direction and 55 in the other) or the number of petals in common plants (typically 1, 2, 3, 5, 8, 13, 21, or 34), hence the rarity of the four-leaf clover.

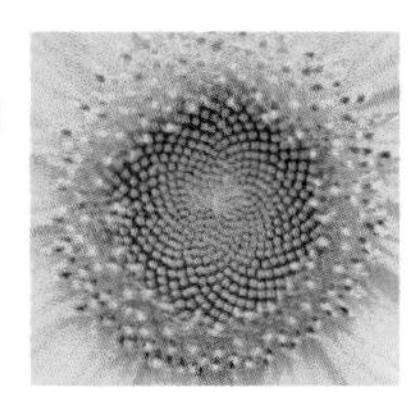

Translating the definition of the *Fibonacci* function into a Scheme procedure is straightforward; we combine the two base cases using the *or* special form:

```
(define (fibo n)
  (if (or (= n 1) (= n 2)) 1
     (+ (fibo (- n 1)) (fibo (- n 2)))))
```

Applying *fibo* to small inputs works fine:

```
> (time (fibo 10))
cpu time: 0 real time: 0 gc time: 0
55
> (time (fibo 30))
cpu time: 2156 real time: 2187 gc time: 0
832040
```

[2] Although the sequence is named for Bonacci, it was probably not invented by him. The sequence was already known to Indian mathematicians with whom Bonacci studied.

But when we try to determine the number of rabbits in five years by computing (*fibo* 60), our interpreter just hangs without producing a value.

The *fibo* procedure is defined in a way that guarantees it eventually completes when applied to a non-negative whole number: each recursive call reduces the input by 1 or 2, so both recursive calls get closer to the base case. Hence, we always make progress and must eventually reach the base case, unwind the recursive applications, and produce a value. To understand why the evaluation of (*fibo* 60) did not finish in our interpreter, we need to consider how much work is required to evaluate the expression.

To evaluate (*fibo* 60), the interpreter follows the if expressions to the recursive case, where it needs to evaluate (+ (*fibo* 59) (*fibo* 58)). To evaluate (*fibo* 59), it needs to evaluate (*fibo* 58) again and also evaluate (*fibo* 57). To evaluate (*fibo* 58) (which needs to be done twice), it needs to evaluate (*fibo* 57) and (*fibo* 56). So, there is one evaluation of (*fibo* 60), one evaluation of (*fibo* 59), two evaluations of (*fibo* 58), and three evaluations of (*fibo* 57).

The total number of evaluations of the *fibo* procedure for each input is itself the Fibonacci sequence! To understand why, consider the evaluation tree for (*fibo* 4) shown in Figure 7.1. The only direct number values are the 1 values that result from evaluations of either (*fibo* 1) or (*fibo* 2). Hence, the number of 1 values must be the value of the final result, which just sums all these numbers. For (*fibo* 4), there are 5 leaf applications, and 3 more inner applications, for 8 (= $Fibonacci(5)$) total recursive applications. The number of evaluations of applications of *fibo* needed to evaluate (*fibo* 60) is the 61st Fibonacci number — 2,504,730,781,961 — over two and a half trillion applications of *fibo*!

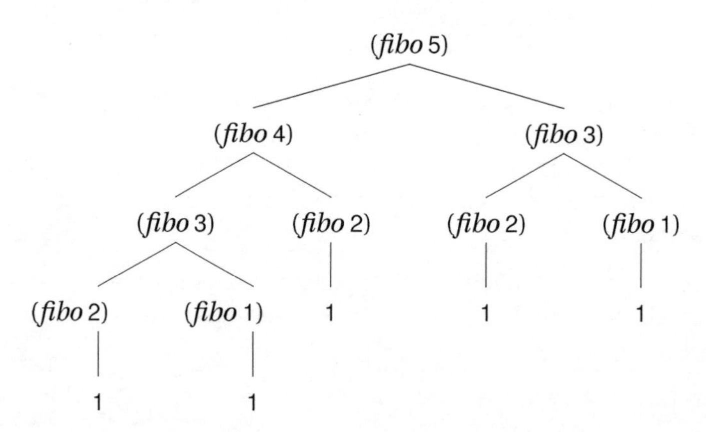

Figure 7.1. Evaluation of *fibo* procedure.

Although our *fibo* definition is *correct*, it is ridiculously inefficient and only finishes for input numbers below about 40. It involves a tremendous amount of duplicated work: for the (*fibo* 60) example, there are two evaluations of (*fibo* 58) and over a trillion evaluations of (*fibo* 1) and (*fibo* 2).

We can avoid this duplicated effort by building up to the answer starting from the base cases. This is more like the way a human would determine the numbers in the Fibonacci sequence: we find the next number by adding the previous two numbers, and stop once we have reached the number we want.

The *fast-fibo* procedure computes the nth Fibonacci number, but avoids the duplicate effort by computing the results building up from the first two Fibonacci numbers, instead of working backwards.

```
(define (fast-fibo n)
  (define (fibo-iter a b left)
    (if (<= left 0) b
        (fibo-iter b (+ a b) (- left 1))))
  (fibo-iter 1 1 (- n 2)))
```

This is a form of what is known as *dynamic programming*. The definition is still recursive, but unlike the original definition the problem is broken down differently. Instead of breaking the problem down into a slightly smaller instance of the original problem, with dynamic programming we build up from the base case to the desired solution. In the case of Fibonacci, the *fast-fibo* procedure builds up from the two base cases until reaching the desired answer. The additional complexity is we need to keep track of when to stop; we do this using the *left* parameter.

dynamic programming

The helper procedure, *fibo-iter* (short for iteration), takes three parameters: *a* is the value of the previous-previous Fibonacci number, *b* is the value of the previous Fibonacci number, and *left* is the number of iterations needed before reaching the target. The initial call to *fibo-iter* passes in 1 as *a* (the value of *Fibonacci*(1)), and 1 as *b* (the value of *Fibonacci*(2)), and (− *n* 2) as *left* (we have $n-2$ more iterations to do to reach the target, since the first two Fibonacci numbers were passed in as *a* and *b* we are now working on *Fibonacci*(2)). Each recursive call to *fibo-iter* reduces the value passed in as *left* by one, and advances the values of *a* and *b* to the next numbers in the Fibonacci sequence.

The *fast-fibo* procedure produces the same output values as the original *fibo* procedure, but requires far less work to do so. The number of applications of *fibo-iter* needed to evaluate (*fast-fibo* 60) is now only 59. The value passed in as *left* for the first application of *fibo-iter* is 58, and each recursive call reduces the value of *left* by one until the zero case is reached. This allows us to compute the expected number of rabbits in 5 years is 1548008755920 (over 1.5 Trillion)[3].

7.2 Orders of Growth

As illustrated by the Fibonacci exploration, the same problem can be solved by procedures that require vastly different resources. The important question in understanding the resources required to evaluate a procedure application is *how the required resources scale with the size of the input.* For small inputs, both Fibonacci procedures work using with minimal resources. For large inputs, the first Fibonacci procedure never finishes, but the fast Fibonacci procedure finishes effectively instantly.

In this section, we introduce three functions computer scientists use to capture

[3]Perhaps Bonacci's assumptions are not a good model for actual rabbit procreation. This result suggests that in about 10 years the mass of all the rabbits produced from the initial pair will exceed the mass of the Earth, which, although scary, seems unlikely!

the important properties of how resources required grow with input size. Each function takes as input a function, and produces as output a set of functions:

$O(f)$ ("big oh")
: The set of functions that grow *no faster* than f grows.

$\Theta(f)$ (theta)
: The set of functions that grow *as fast* as f grows.

$\Omega(f)$ (omega)
: The set of functions that grow *no slower* than f grows.

These functions capture the asymptotic behavior of functions, that is, how they behave as the inputs get arbitrarily large. To understand how the time required to evaluate a procedure increases as the inputs to that procedure increase, we need to know the asymptotic behavior of a function that takes the size of input to the target procedure as its input and outputs the number of steps to evaluate the target procedure on that input.

Remember that accumulated knowledge, like accumulated capital, increases at compound interest: but it differs from the accumulation of capital in this; that the increase of knowledge produces a more rapid rate of progress, whilst the accumulation of capital leads to a lower rate of interest. Capital thus checks its own accumulation: knowledge thus accelerates its own advance. Each generation, therefore, to deserve comparison with its predecessor, is bound to add much more largely to the common stock than that which it immediately succeeds.
Charles Babbage, 1851

Figure 7.2 depicts the sets O, Θ, Ω for some function f. Next, we define each function and provide some examples. Section 7.3 illustrates how to analyze the time required to evaluate applications of procedures using these notations.

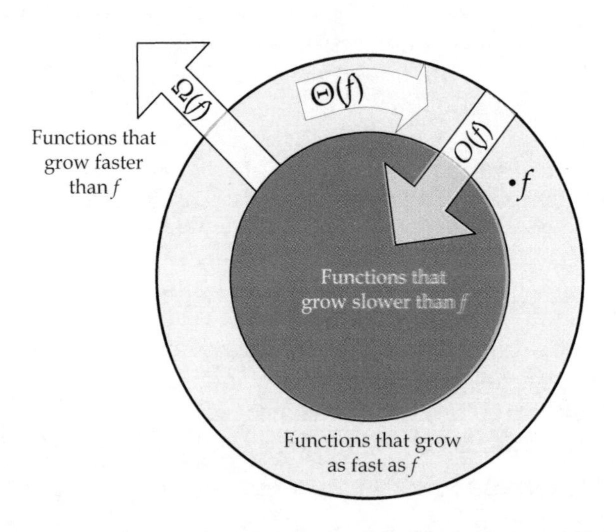

Figure 7.2. Visualization of the sets $O(f)$, $\Omega(f)$, and $\Theta(f)$.

7.2.1 Big *O*

The first notation we introduce is O, pronounced "big oh". The O function takes as input a function, and produces as output the set of all functions that grow no faster than the input function. The set $O(f)$ is the set of all functions that grow as fast as, or slower than, f grows. In Figure 7.2, the $O(f)$ set is represented by everything inside the outer circle.

To define the meaning of O precisely, we need to consider what it means for a function to *grow*. We want to capture how the output of the function increases as the input to the function increases. First, we consider a few examples; then we provide a formal definition of O.

$f(n) = n + 12$ and $g(n) = n - 7$
: No matter what n value we use, the value of $f(n)$ is greater than the value of $g(n)$. This doesn't matter for the growth rates, though. What matters is how the difference between $g(n)$ and $f(n)$ changes as the input values increase. No matter what values we choose for n_1 and n_2, we know $g(n_1) - f(n_1) = g(n_2) - f(n_2) = -19$. Thus, the growth rates of f and g are identical and $n - 7$ is in the set $O(n + 12)$, and $n + 12$ is in the set $O(n - 7)$.

$f(n) = 2n$ and $g(n) = 3n$
: The difference between $g(n)$ and $f(n)$ is n. This difference increases as the input value n increases, but it increases by the same amount as n increases. So, the growth rate as n increases is $\frac{n}{n} = 1$. The value of $2n$ is always within a constant multiple of $3n$, so they grow asymptotically at the same rate. Hence, $2n$ is in the set $O(3n)$ and $3n$ is in the set $O(2n)$. x

$f(n) = n$ and $g(n) = n^2$
: The difference between $g(n)$ and $f(n)$ is $n^2 - n = n(n-1)$. The growth rate as n increases is $\frac{n(n-1)}{n} = n - 1$. The value of $n - 1$ increases as n increases, so g grows faster than f. This means n^2 is *not* in $O(n)$ since n^2 grows faster than n. The function n is in $O(n^2)$ since n grows slower than n^2 grows.

$f(n) = Fibonacci(n)$ and $g(n) = n$
: The *Fibonacci* function grows very rapidly. The value of $Fibonacci(n+2)$ is more than *double* the value of $Fibonacci(n)$ since

$$Fibonacci(n+2) = Fibonacci(n+1) + Fibonacci(n)$$

and $Fibonacci(n+1) > Fibonacci(n)$. The rate of increase is multiplicative, and must be at least a factor of $\sqrt{2} \approx 1.414$ (since increasing by one twice more than doubles the value). (In fact, the rate of increase is a factor of $\phi = (1 + \sqrt{5})/2 \approx 1.618$, also known as the "golden ratio". This is a rather remarkable result, but explaining why is beyond the scope of this book.) This is much faster than the growth rate of n, which increases by one when we increase n by one. So, n is in the set $O(Fibonacci(n))$, but $Fibonacci(n)$ is not in the set $O(n)$.

Some of the example functions are plotted in Figure 7.3. The O notation reveals the asymptotic behavior of functions. The functions plotted are the same in both graphs, but the scale of the horizontal axis is different. In the first graph, the

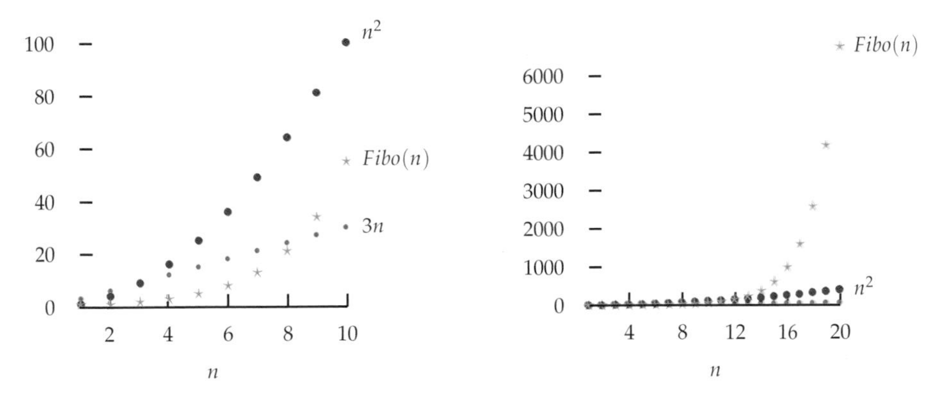

Figure 7.3. Orders of Growth.

rightmost value of n^2 is greatest; for higher input values, the value of *Fibonacci*(n) is greatest. In the second graph, the values of *Fibonacci*(n) for input values up to 20 are so large that the other functions appear as nearly flat lines on the graph.

Definition of O**.** The function g is a member of the set $O(f)$ if and only if there exist positive constants c and n_0 such that, for all values $n \geq n_0$,

$$g(n) \leq cf(n).$$

We can show g is in $O(f)$ using the definition of $O(f)$ by choosing positive constants for the values of c and n_0, and showing that the property $g(n) \leq cf(n)$ holds for all values $n \geq n_0$. To show g is not in $O(f)$, we need to explain how, for any choices of c and n_0, we can find values of n that are greater than n_0 such that $g(n) \leq cf(n)$ does not hold.

Example 7.1: O Examples

We now show the claimed properties are true using the formal definition.

$n-7$ is in $O(n+12)$
: Choose $c = 1$ and $n_0 = 1$. Then, we need to show $n - 7 \leq 1(n+12)$ for all values $n \geq 1$. This is true, since $n - 7 > n + 12$ for all values n.

$n+12$ is in $O(n-7)$
: Choose $c = 2$ and $n_0 = 26$. Then, we need to show $n + 12 \leq 2(n-7)$ for all values $n \geq 26$. The equation simplifies to $n + 12 \leq 2n - 14$, which simplifies to $26 \leq n$. This is trivially true for all values $n \geq 26$.

$2n$ is in $O(3n)$
: Choose $c = 1$ and $n_0 = 1$. Then, $2n \leq 3n$ for all values $n \geq 1$.

$3n$ is in $O(2n)$
: Choose $c = 2$ and $n_0 = 1$. Then, $3n \leq 2(2n)$ simplifies to $n \leq 4/3n$ which is true for all values $n \geq 1$.

n is in $O(n^2)$
: Choose $c = 1$ and $n_0 = 1$. Then $n \leq n^2$ for all values $n \geq 1$.

n^2 is **not** in $O(n)$
: We need to show that no matter what values are chosen for c and n_0, there are values of $n \geq n_0$ such that the inequality $n^2 \leq cn$ does not hold. For any value of c, we can make $n^2 > cn$ by choosing $n > c$.

n is in $O($*Fibonacci*$(n))$
: Choose $c = 1$ and $n_0 = 3$. Then $n \leq$ *Fibonacci*(n) for all values $n \geq n_0$.

Fibonacci(n) is **not** in $O(n-2)$
: No matter what values are chosen for c and n_0, there are values of $n \geq n_0$ such that *Fibonacci*$(n) > c(n)$. We know *Fibonacci*$(12) = 144$, and, from the discussion above, that:

$$\mathit{Fibonacci}(n+2) > 2 * \mathit{Fibonacci}(n)$$

This means, for $n > 12$, we know *Fibonacci*$(n) > n^2$. So, no matter what value is chosen for c, we can choose $n = c$. Then, we need to show

$$\mathit{Fibonacci}(n) > n(n)$$

The right side simplifies to n^2. For $n > 12$, we know *Fibonacci*$(n) > n^2$. Hence, we can always choose an n that contradicts the *Fibonacci*$(n) \leq cn$ inequality by choosing an n that is greater than n_0, 12, and c.

For all of the examples where g is in $O(f)$, there are many acceptable choices for c and n_0. For the given c values, we can always use a higher n_0 value than the selected value. It only matters that there is some finite, positive constant we can choose for n_0, such that the required inequality, $g(n) \leq cf(n)$ holds for all values $n \geq n_0$. Hence, our proofs work equally well with higher values for n_0 than we selected. Similarly, we could always choose higher c values with the same n_0 values. The key is just to pick any appropriate values for c and n_0, and show the inequality holds for all values $n \geq n_0$.

Proving that a function is not in $O(f)$ is usually tougher. The key to these proofs is that the value of n that invalidates the inequality is selected *after* the values of c and n_0 are chosen. One way to think of this is as a game between two adversaries. The first player picks c and n_0, and the second player picks n. To show the property that g is not in $O(f)$, we need to show that no matter what values the first player picks for c and n_0, the second player can always find a value n that is greater than n_0 such that $g(n) > cf(n)$.

Exercise 7.2. For each of the g functions below, answer whether or not g is in the set $O(n)$. Your answer should include a proof. If g is in $O(n)$ you should identify values of c and n_0 that can be selected to make the necessary inequality hold. If g is not in $O(n)$ you should argue convincingly that no matter what values are chosen for c and n_0 there are values of $n \geq n_0$ such the inequality in the definition of O does not hold.

a. $g(n) = n + 5$

b. $g(n) = .01n$

c. $g(n) = 150n + \sqrt{n}$

d. $g(n) = n^{1.5}$

e. $g(n) = n!$

Exercise 7.3. [⋆] Given f is some function in $O(h)$, and g is some function not in $O(h)$, which of the following must always be true:

a. For all positive integers m, $f(m) \leq g(m)$.

b. For some positive integer m, $f(m) < g(m)$.

c. For some positive integer m_0, and all positive integers $m > m_0$,

$$f(m) < g(m).$$

7.2.2 Omega

The set $\Omega(f)$ (omega) is the set of functions that grow no *slower* than f grows. So, a function g is in $\Omega(f)$ if g grows as fast as f or faster. Constrast this with $O(f)$, the set of all functions that grow no *faster* than f grows. In Figure 7.2, $\Omega(f)$ is the set of all functions outside the darker circle.

The formal definition of $\Omega(f)$ is nearly identical to the definition of $O(f)$: the only difference is the $\leq$ comparison is changed to $\geq$.

Definition of $\Omega(f)$. The function g is a member of the set $\Omega(f)$ if and only if there exist positive constants c and n_0 such that, for all values $n \geq n_0$,

$$g(n) \geq cf(n).$$

Example 7.2: Ω Examples

We repeat selected examples from the previous section with Ω instead of O. The strategy is similar: we show g is in $\Omega(f)$ using the definition of $\Omega(f)$ by choosing positive constants for the values of c and n_0, and showing that the property $g(n) \geq cf(n)$ holds for all values $n \geq n_0$. To show g is not in $\Omega(f)$, we need to explain how, for any choices of c and n_0, we can find a choice for $n \geq n_0$ such that $g(n) < cf(n)$.

$n-7$ is in $\Omega(n+12)$
: Choose $c = \frac{1}{2}$ and $n_0 = 26$. Then, we need to show $n - 7 \geq \frac{1}{2}(n+12)$ for all values $n \geq 26$. This is true, since the inequality simplifies $\frac{n}{2} \geq 13$ which holds for all values $n \geq 26$.

$2n$ is in $\Omega(3n)$
: Choose $c = \frac{1}{3}$ and $n_0 = 1$. Then, $2n \geq \frac{1}{3}(3n)$ simplifies to $n \geq 0$ which holds for all values $n \geq 1$.

n is not in $\Omega(n^2)$
: Whatever values are chosen for c and n_0, we can choose $n \geq n_0$ such that $n \geq cn^2$ does not hold. Choose $n > \frac{1}{c}$ (note that c must be less than 1 for the inequality to hold for any positive n, so if c is not less than 1 we can just choose $n \geq 2$). Then, the right side of the inequality cn^2 will be greater than n, and the needed inequality $n \geq cn^2$ does not hold.

n is not in $\Omega(\mathit{Fibonacci}(n))$
: No matter what values are chosen for c and n_0, we can choose $n \geq n_0$ such that $n \geq \mathit{Fibonacci}(n)$ does not hold. The value of $\mathit{Fibonacci}(n)$ more than doubles every time n is increased by 2 (see Section 7.2.1), but the value of $c(n)$ only increases by $2c$. Hence, if we keep increasing n, eventually $\mathit{Fibonacci}(n+1) > c(n-2)$ for any choice of c.

Exercise 7.4. Repeat Exercise 7.2 using Ω instead of O.

Exercise 7.5. For each part, identify a function g that satisfies the property.

a. g is in $O(n^2)$ but not in $\Omega(n^2)$.

b. g is not in $O(n^2)$ but is in $\Omega(n^2)$.

c. g is in both $O(n^2)$ and $\Omega(n^2)$.

7.2.3 Theta

The function $\Theta(f)$ denotes the set of functions that grow at the same rate as f. It is the intersection of the sets $O(f)$ and $\Omega(f)$. Hence, a function g is in $\Theta(f)$ if and only if g is in $O(f)$ and g is in $\Omega(f)$. In Figure 7.2, $\Theta(f)$ is the ring between the outer and inner circles.

An alternate definition combines the inequalities for O and Ω:

Definition of $\Theta(f)$. The function g is a member of the set $\Theta(f)$ if any only if there exist positive constants c_1, c_2, and n_0 such that, for all values $n \geq n_0$,

$$c_1 f(n) \geq g(n) \geq c_2 f(n).$$

If $g(n)$ is in $\Theta(f(n))$, then the sets $\Theta(f(n))$ and $\Theta(g(n))$ are identical. If $g(n) \in \Theta(f(n))$ then g and f grow at the same rate,

Example 7.3: Θ Examples

Determining membership in $\Theta(f)$ is simple once we know membership in $O(f)$ and $\Omega(f)$.

$n - 7$ is in $\Theta(n + 12)$
Since $n-7$ is in $O(n+12)$ and $n-7$ is in $\Omega(n+12)$ we know $n-7$ is in $\Theta(n+12)$. Intuitively, $n - 7$ increases at the same rate as $n + 12$, since adding one to n adds one to both function outputs. We can also show this using the definition of $\Theta(f)$: choose $c_1 = 1$, $c_2 = \frac{1}{2}$, and $n_0 = 38$.

$2n$ is in $\Theta(3n)$
$2n$ is in $O(3n)$ and in $\Omega(3n)$. Choose $c_1 = 1$, $c_2 = \frac{1}{3}$, and $n_0 = 1$.

n is **not** in $\Theta(n^2)$
n is not in $\Omega(n^2)$. Intuitively, n grows slower than n^2 since increasing n by one always increases the value of the first function, n, by one, but increases the value of n^2 by $2n + 1$, a value that increases as n increases.

n^2 is **not** in $\Theta(n)$: n^2 is not in $O(n)$.

$n - 2$ is **not** in $\Theta(\mathit{Fibonacci}(n + 1))$: $n - 2$ is not in $\Omega(n)$.

$\mathit{Fibonacci}(n)$ is **not** in $\Theta(n)$: $\mathit{Fibonacci}(n + 1)$ is not in $O(n - 2)$.

Properties of O, Ω, and Θ. Because O, Ω, and Θ are concerned with the asymptotic properties of functions, that is, how they grow as inputs approach infinity, many functions that are different when the actual output values matter generate identical sets with the O, Ω, and Θ functions. For example, we saw $n - 7$ is in $\Theta(n + 12)$ and $n + 12$ is in $\Theta(n - 7)$. In fact, every function that is in $\Theta(n - 7)$ is also in $\Theta(n + 12)$.

More generally, if we could prove g is in $\Theta(an + k)$ where a is a positive constant and k is any constant, then g is also in $\Theta(n)$. Thus, the set $\Theta(an + k)$ is equivalent to the set $\Theta(n)$.

We prove $\Theta(an + k) \equiv \Theta(n)$ using the definition of Θ. To prove the sets are equivalent, we need to show inclusion in both directions.

$\Theta(n) \subseteq \Theta(an + k)$: For any function g, if g is in $\Theta(n)$ then g is in $\Theta(an + k)$. Since g is in $\Theta(n)$ there exist positive constants c_1, c_2, and n_0 such that $c_1 n \geq g(n) \geq c_2 n$. To show g is also in $\Theta(an + k)$ we find d_1, d_2, and m_0 such that $d_1(an + k) \geq g(n) \geq d_2(an + k)$ for all $n \geq m_0$. Simplifying the inequalities, we need $(ad_1)n + kd_1 \geq g(n) \geq (ad_2)n + kd_2$. Ignoring the constants for now, we can pick $d_1 = \frac{c_1}{a}$ and $d_2 = \frac{c_2}{a}$. Since g is in $\Theta(n)$, we know

$$(a\frac{c_1}{a})n \geq g(n) \geq (a\frac{c_2}{a})n$$

is satisfied. As for the constants, as n increases they become insignificant. Adding one to d_1 and d_2 adds an to the first term and k to the second term. Hence, as n grows, an becomes greater than k.

$\Theta(an + k) \subseteq \Theta(k)$: For any function g, if g is in $\Theta(an + k)$ then g is in $\Theta(n)$. Since g is in $\Theta(an + k)$ there exist positive constants c_1, c_2, and n_0 such that $c_1(an+k) \geq g(n) \geq c_2(an+k)$. Simplifying the inequalities, we have $(ac_1)n + kc_1 \geq g(n) \geq (ac_2)n + kc_2$ or, for some different positive constants $b_1 = ac_1$ and $b_2 = ac_2$ and constants $k_1 = kc_1$ and $k_2 = kc_2$, $b_1 n + k_1 \geq g(n) \geq b_2 n + k_2$. To show g is also in $\Theta(n)$, we find d_1, d_2, and m_0 such that $d_1 n \geq g(n) \geq d_2 n$ for all $n \geq m_0$. If it were not for the constants, we already have this with $d_1 = b_1$ and $d_2 = b_2$. As before, the constants become inconsequential as n increases.

This property also holds for the O and Ω operators since our proof for Θ also proved the property for the O and Ω inequalities.

This result can be generalized to any polynomial. The set $\Theta(a_0 + a_1 n + a_2 n^2 + ... + a_k n^k)$ is equivalent to $\Theta(n^k)$. Because we are concerned with the asymptotic growth, only the highest power term of the polynomial matters once n gets big enough.

Exercise 7.6. Repeat Exercise 7.2 using Θ instead of O.

Exercise 7.7. Show that $\Theta(n^2 - n)$ is equivalent to $\Theta(n^2)$.

Exercise 7.8. [★] Is $\Theta(n^2)$ equivalent to $\Theta(n^{2.1})$? Either prove they are identical, or prove they are different.

Exercise 7.9. [★] Is $\Theta(2^n)$ equivalent to $\Theta(3^n)$? Either prove they are identical, or prove they are different.

7.3 Analyzing Procedures

By considering the asymptotic growth of functions, rather than their actual outputs, the O, Ω, and Θ operators allow us to hide constants and factors that change depending on the speed of our processor, how data is arranged in memory, and the specifics of how our interpreter is implemented. Instead, we can consider the essential properties of how the running time of the procedures increases with the size of the input.

This section explains how to measure input sizes and running times. To understand the growth rate of a procedure's running time, we need a function that maps the size of the inputs to the procedure to the amount of time it takes to evaluate the application. First we consider how to measure the input size; then, we consider how to measure the running time. In Section 7.3.3 we consider *which* input of a given size should be used to reason about the cost of applying a procedure. Section 7.4 provides examples of procedures with different growth rates. The growth rate of a procedure's running time gives us an understanding of how the running time increases as the size of the input increases.

7.3.1 Input Size

Procedure inputs may be many different types: Numbers, Lists of Numbers, Lists of Lists, Procedures, etc. Our goal is to characterize the input size with a single number that does not depend on the types of the input.

We use the Turing machine to model a computer, so the way to measure the size of the input is the number of characters needed to write the input on the tape. The characters can be from any fixed-size alphabet, such as the ten decimal digits, or the letters of the alphabet. The number of different symbols in the tape alphabet does not matter for our analysis since we are concerned with orders of growth not absolute values. Within the O, Ω, and Θ operators, a constant factor does not matter (e.g., $\Theta(n) \equiv \Theta(17n + 523)$). This means is doesn't matter whether we use an alphabet with two symbols or an alphabet with 256 symbols. With two symbols the input may be 8 times as long as it is with a 256-symbol alphabet, but the constant factor does not matter inside the asymptotic operator.

Thus, we measure the size of the input as the number of symbols required to write the number on a Turing Machine input tape. To figure out the input size of a given type, we need to think about how many symbols it would require to write down inputs of that type.

Booleans. There are only two Boolean values: *true* and *false*. Hence, the length of a Boolean input is fixed.

Numbers. Using the decimal number system (that is, 10 tape symbols), we can write a number of magnitude n using $\log_{10} n$ digits. Using the binary number system (that is, 2 tape symbols), we can write it using $\log_2 n$ bits. Within the asymptotic operators, the base of the logarithm does not matter (as long as it is a constant) since it changes the result by a constant factor. We can see this from the argument above — changing the number of symbols in the input alphabet changes the input length by a constant factor which has no impact within the asymptotic operators.

Lists. If the input is a List, the size of the input is related to the number of elements in the list. If each element is a constant size (for example, a list of numbers where each number is between 0 and 100), the size of the input list is some constant multiple of the number of elements in the list. Hence, the size of an input that is a list of n elements is cn for some constant c. Since $\Theta(cn) = \Theta(n)$, the size of a List input is $\Theta(n)$ where n is the number of elements in the List. If List elements can vary in size, then we need to account for that in the input size. For example, suppose the input is a List of Lists, where there are n elements in each inner List, and there are n List elements in the main List. Then, there are n^2 total elements and the input size is in $\Theta(n^2)$.

7.3.2 Running Time

We want a measure of the running time of a procedure that satisfies two properties: (1) it should be robust to ephemeral properties of a particular execution or computer, and (2) it should provide insights into how long it takes evaluate the procedure on a wide range of inputs.

To estimate the running time of an evaluation, we use the number of steps required to perform the evaluation. The actual number of steps depends on the details of how much work can be done on each step. For any particular processor, both the time it takes to perform a step and the amount of work that can be done in one step varies. When we analyze procedures, however, we usually don't want to deal with these details. Instead, what we care about is how the running time changes as the input size increases. This means we can count anything we want as a "step" as long as each step is the approximately same size and the time a step requires does not depend on the size of the input.

The clearest and simplest definition of a step is to use one Turing Machine step. We have a precise definition of exactly what a Turing Machine can do in one step:

it can read the symbol in the current square, write a symbol into that square, transition its internal state number, and move one square to the left or right. Counting Turing Machine steps is very precise, but difficult because we do not usually start with a Turing Machine description of a procedure and creating one is tedious.

Time makes more converts than reason.
Thomas Paine

Instead, we usually reason directly from a Scheme procedure (or any precise description of a procedure) using larger steps. As long as we can claim that whatever we consider a step could be simulated using a constant number of steps on a Turing Machine, our larger steps will produce the same answer within the asymptotic operators. One possibility is to count the number of times an evaluation rule is used in an evaluation of an application of the procedure. The amount of work in each evaluation rule may vary slightly (for example, the evaluation rule for an if expression seems more complex than the rule for a primitive) but does not depend on the input size.

Hence, it is reasonable to assume all the evaluation rules to take constant time. This does not include any additional evaluation rules that are needed to apply one rule. For example, the evaluation rule for application expressions includes evaluating every subexpression. Evaluating an application constitutes one work unit for the application rule itself, plus all the work required to evaluate the subexpressions. In cases where the bigger steps are unclear, we can always return to our precise definition of a step as one step of a Turing Machine.

7.3.3 Worst Case Input

A procedure may have different running times for inputs of the same size.

For example, consider this procedure that takes a List as input and outputs the first positive number in the list:

```
(define (list-first-pos p)
  (if (null? p) (error "No positive element found")
    (if (> (car p) 0) (car p) (list-first-pos (cdr p)))))
```

If the first element in the input list is positive, evaluating the application of *list-first-pos* requires very little work. It is not necessary to consider any other elements in the list if the first element is positive. On the other hand, if none of the elements are positive, the procedure needs to test each element in the list until it reaches the end of the list (where the base case reports an error).

worst case

In our analyses we usually consider the *worst case* input. For a given size, the worst case input is the input for which evaluating the procedure takes the most work. By focusing on the worst case input, we know the maximum running time for the procedure. Without knowing something about the possible inputs to the procedure, it is safest to be pessimistic about the input and not assume any properties that are not known (such as that the first number in the list is positive for the *first-pos* example).

In some cases, we also consider the *average case* input. Since most procedures can take infinitely many inputs, this requires understanding the distribution of possible inputs to determine an “average” input. This is often necessary when we are analyzing the running time of a procedure that uses another helper procedure. If we use the worst-case running time for the helper procedure, we will grossly overestimate the running time of the main procedure. Instead, since we know how the main procedure uses the helper procedure, we can more precisely estimate the actual running time by considering the actual inputs. We see an example of this in the analysis of how the $+$ procedure is used by *list-length* in Section 7.4.2.

7.4 Growth Rates

Since our goal is to understand how the running time of an application of a procedure is related to the size of the input, we want to devise a function that takes as input a number that represents the size of the input and outputs the maximum number of steps required to complete the evaluation on an input of that size. Symbolically, we can think of this function as:

$$\textit{Max-Steps}_{\textit{Proc}}: \textit{Number} \rightarrow \textit{Number}$$

where *Proc* is the name of the procedure we are analyzing. Because the output represents the *maximum* number of steps required, we need to consider the worst-case input of the given size.

Because of all the issues with counting steps exactly, and the uncertainty about how much work can be done in one step on a particular machine, we cannot usually determine the exact function for $\textit{Max-Steps}_{\textit{Proc}}$. Instead, we characterize the running time of a procedure with a set of functions denoted by an asymptotic operator. Inside the O, Ω, and Θ operators, the actual time needed for each step does not matter since the constant factors are hidden by the operator; what matters is how the number of steps required grows as the size of the input grows.

Hence, we will characterize the running time of a procedure using a set of functions produced by one of the asymptotic operators. The Θ operator provides the most information. Since $\Theta(f)$ is the intersection of $O(f)$ (no faster than) and $\Omega(f)$ (no slower than), knowing that the running time of a procedure is in $\Theta(f)$ for some function f provides much more information than just knowing it is in $O(f)$ or just knowing that it is in $\Omega(f)$. Hence, our goal is to characterize the running time of a procedure using the set of functions defined by $\Theta(f)$ of some function f.

The rest of this section provides examples of procedures with different growth rates, from slowest (no growth) through increasingly rapid growth rates. The growth classes described are important classes that are commonly encountered when analyzing procedures, but these are only examples of growth classes. Between each pair of classes described here, there are an unlimited number of different growth classes.

7.4.1 No Growth: Constant Time

If the running time of a procedure does not increase when the size of the input increases, the procedure must be able to produce its output by looking at only a constant number of symbols in the input. Procedures whose running time does not increase with the size of the input are known as *constant time* procedures. Their running time is in $O(1)$ — it does not grow at all. By convention, we use $O(1)$ instead of $\Theta(1)$ to describe constant time. Since there is no way to grow slower than not growing at all, $O(1)$ and $\Theta(1)$ are equivalent.

constant time

We cannot do much in constant time, since we cannot even examine the whole input. A constant time procedure must be able to produce its output by examining only a fixed-size part of the input. Recall that the input size measures the number of squares needed to represent the input. No matter how long the input is, a constant time procedure can look at no more than some fixed number of squares on the tape, so cannot even read the whole input.

An example of a constant time procedure is the built-in procedure *car*. When *car* is applied to a non-empty list, it evaluates to the first element of that list. No matter how long the input list is, all the *car* procedure needs to do is extract the first component of the list. So, the running time of *car* is in $O(1)$.[4] Other built-in procedures that involve lists and pairs that have running times in $O(1)$ include *cons*, *cdr*, *null?*, and *pair?*. None of these procedures need to examine more than the first pair of the list.

7.4.2 Linear Growth

linearly

When the running time of a procedure increases by a constant amount when the size of the input grows by one, the running time of the procedure grows *linearly* with the input size. If the input size is n, the running time is in $\Theta(n)$. If a procedure has running time in $\Theta(n)$, doubling the size of the input will approximately double the execution time.

An example of a procedure that has linear growth is the elementary school addition algorithm from Section 6.2.3. To add two d-digit numbers, we need to perform a constant amount of work for each digit. The number of steps required grows linearly with the size of the numbers (recall from Section 7.3.1 that the *size* of a number is the number of input symbols needed to represent the number).

Many procedures that take a List as input have linear time growth. A procedure that does something that takes constant time with every element in the input List, has running time that grows linearly with the size of the input since adding one element to the list increases the number of steps by a constant amount. Next, we analyze three list procedures, all of which have running times that scale linearly with the size of their input.

Example 7.4: Append

Consider the *list-append* procedure (from Example 5.6):

```
(define (list-append p q)
   (if (null? p) q (cons (car p) (list-append (cdr p) q))))
```

Since *list-append* takes two inputs, we need to be careful about how we refer to the input size. We use n_p to represent the number of elements in the first input, and n_q to represent the number of elements in the second input. So, our goal is to define a function $\textit{Max-Steps}_{\textit{list-append}}(n_p, n_q)$ that captures how the maximum number of steps required to evaluate an application of *list-append* scales with the size of its input.

---

[4] Since we are speculating based on what *car* does, not examining how *car* a particular Scheme interpreter actually implements it, we cannot say definitively that its running time is in $O(1)$. It would be rather shocking, however, for an implementation to implement *car* in a way such that its running time that is not in $O(1)$. The implementation of *scar* in Section 5.2.1 is constant time: regardless of the input size, evaluating an application of it involves evaluating a single application expression, and then evaluating an if expression.

To analyze the running time of *list-append*, we examine its body which is an if expression. The predicate expression applies the *null?* procedure with is constant time since the effort required to determine if a list is *null* does not depend on the length of the list. When the predicate expression evaluates to true, the alternate expression is just q, which can also be evaluated in constant time.

Next, we consider the alternate expression. It includes a recursive application of *list-append*. Hence, the running time of the alternate expression is the time required to evaluate the recursive application plus the time required to evaluate everything else in the expression. The other expressions to evaluate are applications of *cons*, *car*, and *cdr*, all of which is are constant time procedures.

So, we can defined the total running time recursively as:

$$\textit{Max-Steps}_{\textit{list-append}}(n_p, n_q) = C + \textit{Max-Steps}_{\textit{list-append}}(n_p - 1, n_q)$$

where C is some constant that reflects the time for all the operations besides the recursive call. Note that the value of n_q does not matter, so we simplify this to:

$$\textit{Max-Steps}_{\textit{list-append}}(n_p) = C + \textit{Max-Steps}_{\textit{list-append}}(n_p - 1).$$

This does not yet provide a useful characterization of the running time of *list-append* though, since it is a circular definition. To make it a recursive definition, we need a base case. The base case for the running time definition is the same as the base case for the procedure: when the input is *null*. For the base case, the running time is constant:

$$\textit{Max-Steps}_{\textit{list-append}}(0) = C_0$$

where C_0 is some constant.

To better characterize the running time of *list-append*, we want a closed form solution. For a given input n, $\textit{Max-Steps}(n)$ is $C + C + C + C + \ldots + C + C_0$ where there are $n - 1$ of the C terms in the sum. This simplifies to $(n-1)C + C_0 = nC - C + C_0 = nC + C_2$. We do not know what the values of C and C_2 are, but within the asymptotic notations the constant values do not matter. The important property is that the running time scales linearly with the value of its input. Thus, the running time of *list-append* is in $\Theta(n_p)$ where n_p is the number of elements in the first input.

Usually, we do not need to reason at quite this low a level. Instead, to analyze the running time of a recursive procedure it is enough to determine the amount of work involved in each recursive call (excluding the recursive application itself) and multiply this by the number of recursive calls. For this example, there are n_p recursive calls since each call reduces the length of the p input by one until the base case is reached. Each call involves only constant-time procedures (other than the recursive application), so the amount of work involved in each call is constant. Hence, the running time is in $\Theta(n_p)$. Equivalently, the running time for the *list-append* procedure scales linearly with the length of the first input list.

Example 7.5: Length

Consider the *list-length* procedure from Example 5.1:

```
(define (list-length p) (if (null? p) 0 (+ 1 (list-length (cdr p)))))
```

This procedure makes one recursive application of *list-length* for each element in the input *p*. If the input has n elements, there will be $n+1$ total applications of *list-length* to evaluate (one for each element, and one for the *null*). So, the total work is in $\Theta(n \cdot \text{work for each recursive application})$.

To determine the running time, we need to determine how much work is involved in each application. Evaluating an application of *list-length* involves evaluating its body, which is an if expression. To evaluate the if expression, the predicate expression, (*null?* *p*), must be evaluated first. This requires constant time since the *null?* procedure has constant running time (see Section 7.4.1). The consequent expression is the primitive expression, 0, which can be evaluated in constant time. The alternate expression, (+ 1 (*list-length* (*cdr* *p*))), includes the recursive call. There are $n+1$ total applications of *list-length* to evaluate, the total running time is $n+1$ times the work required for each application (other than the recursive application itself).

The remaining work is evaluating (*cdr* *p*) and evaluating the + application. The *cdr* procedure is constant time. Analyzing the running time of the + procedure application is more complicated.

Cost of Addition. Since + is a built-in procedure, we need to think about how it might be implemented. Following the elementary school addition algorithm (from Section 6.2.3), we know we can add any two numbers by walking down the digits. The work required for each digit is constant; we just need to compute the corresponding result and carry bits using a simple formula or lookup table. The number of digits to add is the maximum number of digits in the two input numbers. Thus, if there are b digits to add, the total work is in $\Theta(b)$. In the worst case, we need to look at all the digits in both numbers. In general, we cannot do asymptotically better than this, since adding two arbitrary numbers might require looking at all the digits in both numbers.

But, in the *list-length* procedure the + is used in a very limited way: one of the inputs is always 1. We might be able to add 1 to a number without looking at all the digits in the number. Recall the addition algorithm: we start at the rightmost (least significant) digit, add that digit, and continue with the carry. If one of the input numbers is 1, then once the carry is zero we know now of the more significant digits will need to change. In the worst case, adding one requires changing every digit in the other input. For example, (+ 99999 1) is 100000. In the best case (when the last digit is below 9), adding one requires only examining and changing one digit.

Figuring out the average case is more difficult, but necessary to get a good estimate of the running time of *list-length*. We assume the numbers are represented in binary, so instead of decimal digits we are counting bits (this is both simpler, and closer to how numbers are actually represented in the computer). Approximately half the time, the least significant bit is a 0, so we only need to examine one bit. When the last bit is not a 0, we need to examine the second least significant bit (the second bit from the right): if it is a 0 we are done; if it is a 1, we need to continue.

We always need to examine one bit, the least significant bit. Half the time we also need to examine the second least significant bit. Of those times, half the time we need to continue and examine the next least significant bit. This continues through the whole number. Thus, the expected number of bits we need to examine is,

$$1+\frac{1}{2}\left(1+\frac{1}{2}\left(1+\frac{1}{2}\left(1+\frac{1}{2}(1+\ldots)\right)\right)\right)$$

where the number of terms is the number of bits in the input number, b. Simplifying the equation, we get:

$$1+\frac{1}{2}+\frac{1}{4}+\frac{1}{8}+\frac{1}{16}+\ldots+\frac{1}{2^b}$$

No matter how large b gets, this value is always less than 2. So, on average, the number of bits to examine to add 1 is constant: it does not depend on the length of the input number.

This result generalizes to addition where one of the inputs is any constant value. Adding any constant C to a number n is equivalent to adding one C times. Since adding one is a constant time procedure, adding one C times can also be done in constant time for any constant C.

Excluding the recursive application, the *list-length* application involves applications of two constant time procedures: *cdr* and adding one using $+$. Hence, the total time needed to evaluate one application of *list-length*, excluding the recursive application, is constant.

There are $n+1$ total applications of *list-length* to evaluate total, so the total running time is $c(n+1)$ where c is the amount of time needed for each application. The set $\Theta(c(n+1))$ is identical to the set $\Theta(n)$, so the running time for the length procedure is in $\Theta(n)$ where n is the length of the input list.

Example 7.6: Accessing List Elements

Consider the *list-get-element* procedure from Example 5.3:

```
(define (list-get-element p n)
  (if (= n 1)
      (car p)
      (list-get-element (cdr p) (- n 1))))
```

The procedure takes two inputs, a List and a Number selecting the element of the list to get. Since there are two inputs, we need to think carefully about the input size. We can use variables to represent the size of each input, for example s_p and s_n for the size of p and n respectively. In this case, however, only the size of the first input really matters.

The procedure body is an if expression. The predicate uses the built-in $=$ procedure to compare n to 1. The worst case running time of the $=$ procedure is linear in the size of the input: it potentially needs to look at all bits in the input numbers to determine if they are equal. Similarly to $+$, however, if one of the inputs is a constant, the comparison can be done in constant time. To compare a number of any size to 1, it is enough to look at a few bits. If the least significant bit of the input number is not a 1, we know the result is *false*. If it is a 1, we need to examine a few other bits of the input number to determine if its value is different from 1 (the exact number of bits depends on the details of how numbers are represented). So, the $=$ comparison can be done in constant time.

If the predicate is true, the base case applies the *car* procedure, which has constant running time. The alternate expression involves the recursive calls, as well as evaluating (*cdr p*), which requires constant time, and (− *n* 1). The − procedure is similar to +: for arbitrary inputs, its worst case running time is linear in the input size, but when one of the inputs is a constant the running time is constant. This follows from a similar argument to the one we used for the + procedure (Exercise 7.13 asks for a more detailed analysis of the running time of subtraction). So, the work required for each recursive call is constant.

The number of recursive calls is determined by the value of n and the number of elements in the list p. In the best case, when n is 1, there are no recursive calls and the running time is constant since the procedure only needs to examine the first element. Each recursive call reduces the value passed in as n by 1, so the number of recursive calls scales linearly with n (the actual number is $n - 1$ since the base case is when n equals 1). But, there is a limit on the value of n for which this is true. If the value passed in as n exceeds the number of elements in p, the procedure will produce an error when it attempts to evaluate (*cdr p*) for the empty list. This happens after s_p recursive calls, where s_p is the number of elements in p. Hence, the running time of *list-get-element* does not grow with the length of the input passed as n; after the value of n exceeds the number of elements in p it does not matter how much bigger it gets, the running time does not continue to increase.

Thus, the worst case running time of *list-get-element* grows linearly with the length of the input list. Equivalently, the running time of *list-get-element* is in $\Theta(s_p)$ where s_p is the number of elements in the input list.

Exercise 7.10. Explain why the *list-map* procedure from Section 5.4.1 has running time that is linear in the size of its List input. Assume the procedure input has constant running time.

Exercise 7.11. Consider the *list-sum* procedure (from Example 5.2):

```
(define (list-sum p) (if (null? p) 0 (+ (car p) (list-sum (cdr p)))))
```

What assumptions are needed about the elements in the list for the running time to be linear in the number if elements in the input list?

Exercise 7.12. For the decimal six-digit odometer (shown in the picture on page 142), we measure the amount of work to add one as the total number of wheel digit turns required. For example, going from 000000 to 000001 requires one work unit, but going from 000099 to 000100 requires three work units.

a. What are the worst case inputs?

b. What are the best case inputs?

c. On average, how many work units are required for each mile? Assume over the lifetime of the odometer, the car travels 1,000,000 miles.

d. Lever voting machines were used by the majority of American voters in the 1960s, although they are not widely used today. Most level machines used a three-digit odometer to tally votes. Explain why candidates ended up with 99 votes on a machine far more often than 98 or 100 on these machines.

Exercise 7.13. [★] The *list-get-element* argued by comparison to $+$, that the $-$ procedure has constant running time when one of the inputs is a constant. Develop a more convincing argument why this is true by analyzing the worst case and average case inputs for $-$.

Exercise 7.14. [★] Our analysis of the work required to add one to a number argued that it could be done in constant time. Test experimentally if the DrRacket $+$ procedure actually satisfies this property. Note that one $+$ application is too quick to measure well using the *time* procedure, so you will need to design a procedure that applies $+$ many times without doing much other work.

7.4.3 Quadratic Growth

If the running time of a procedure scales as the square of the size of the input, the procedure's running time grows *quadratically*. Doubling the size of the input approximately quadruples the running time. The running time is in $\Theta(n^2)$ where n is the size of the input.

quadratically

A procedure that takes a list as input has running time that grows quadratically if it goes through all elements in the list once for every element in the list. For example, we can compare every element in a list of length n with every other element using $n(n-1)$ comparisons. This simplifies to $n^2 - n$, but $\Theta(n^2 - n)$ is equivalent to $\Theta(n^2)$ since as n increases only the highest power term matters (see Exercise 7.7).

Example 7.7: Reverse

Consider the *list-reverse* procedure defined in Section 5.4.2:

```
(define (list-reverse p)
  (if (null? p) null (list-append (list-reverse (cdr p)) (list (car p)))))
```

To determine the running time of *list-reverse*, we need to know how many recursive calls there are and how much work is involved in each recursive call. Each recursive application passes in (*cdr p*) as the input, so reduces the length of the input list by one. Hence, applying *list-reverse* to a input list with n elements involves n recursive calls.

The work for each recursive application, excluding the recursive call itself, is applying *list-append*. The first input to *list-append* is the output of the recursive call. As we argued in Example 7.4, the running time of *list-append* is in $\Theta(n_p)$ where n_p is the number of elements in its first input. So, to determine the running time we need to know the length of the first input list to *list-append*. For the first call, (*cdr p*) is the parameter, with length $n-1$; for the second call, there will be $n-2$ elements; and so forth, until the final call where (*cdr p*) has 0 elements. The total number of elements in all of these calls is:

$$(n-1) + (n-2) + \ldots + 1 + 0.$$

The average number of elements in each call is approximately $\frac{n}{2}$. Within the asymptotic operators the constant factor of $\frac{1}{2}$ does not matter, so the average running time for each recursive application is in $\Theta(n)$.

There are n recursive applications, so the total running time of *list-reverse* is n

times the average running time of each recursive application:

$$n \cdot \Theta(n) = \Theta(n^2).$$

Thus, the running time is quadratic in the size of the input list.

Example 7.8: Multiplication

Consider the problem of multiplying two numbers. The elementary school long multiplication algorithm works by multiplying each digit in b by each digit in a, aligning the intermediate results in the right places, and summing the results:

$$\begin{array}{cccccccc}
 & & & & a_{n-1} & \cdots & a_1 & a_0 \\
 & & & \times & b_{n-1} & \cdots & b_1 & b_0 \\
\hline
 & & & & a_{n-1}b_0 & \cdots & a_1b_0 & a_0b_0 \\
 & & & a_{n-1}b_1 & \cdots & a_1b_1 & a_0b_1 & \\
+ & a_{n-1}b_{n-1} & \cdots & a_1b_{n-1} & a_0b_{n-1} & & & \\
\hline
r_{2n-1} & r_{2n-2} & \cdots & \cdots & r_3 & r_2 & r_1 & r_0
\end{array}$$

If both input numbers have n digits, there are n^2 digit multiplications, each of which can be done in constant time. The intermediate results will be n rows, each containing n digits. So, the total number of digits to add is n^2: 1 digit in the ones place, 2 digits in the tens place, ..., n digits in the 10^{n-1}s place, ..., 2 digits in the 10^{2n-3}s place, and 1 digit in the 10^{2n-2}s place. Each digit addition requires constant work, so the total work for all the digit additions is in $\Theta(n^2)$. Adding the work for both the digit multiplications and the digit additions, the total running time for the elementary school multiplication algorithm is quadratic in the number of input digits, $\Theta(n^2)$ where n is the number if digits in the inputs.

This is not the fastest known algorithm for multiplying two numbers, although it was the best algorithm known until 1960. In 1960, Anatolii Karatsuba discovers a multiplication algorithm with running time in $\Theta(n^{\log_2 3})$. Since $\log_2 3 < 1.585$ this is an improvement over the $\Theta(n^2)$ elementary school algorithm. In 2007, Martin Fürer discovered an even faster algorithm for multiplication.[5] It is not yet known if this is the fastest possible multiplication algorithm, or if faster ones exist.

Exercise 7.15. [⋆] Analyze the running time of the elementary school long division algorithm.

Exercise 7.16. [⋆] Define a Scheme procedure that multiplies two multi-digit numbers (without using the built-in $*$ procedure except to multiply single-digit numbers). Strive for your procedure to have running time in $\Theta(n)$ where n is the total number of digits in the input numbers.

Exercise 7.17. [⋆⋆⋆⋆] Devise an asymptotically faster general multiplication algorithm than Fürer's, or prove that no faster algorithm exists.

[5] Martin Fürer, Faster Integer Multiplication, *ACM Symposium on Theory of Computing*, 2007.

7.4.4 Exponential Growth

If the running time of a procedure scales as a power of the size of the input, the procedure's running time grows *exponentially*. When the size of the input increases by one, the running time is multiplied by some constant factor. The growth rate of a function whose output is multiplied by w when the input size, n, increases by one is w^n. Exponential growth is very fast—it is not feasible to evaluate applications of an exponential time procedure on large inputs.

For a surprisingly large number of interesting problems, the best known algorithm has exponential running time. Examples of problems like this include finding the best route between two locations on a map (the problem mentioned at the beginning of Chapter 4), the pegboard puzzle (Exploration 5.2, solving generalized versions of most other games such as Suduko and Minesweeper, and finding the factors of a number. Whether or not it is possible to design faster algorithms that solve these problems is the most important open problem in computer science.

Example 7.9: Factoring

A simple way to find a factor of a given input number is to exhaustively try all possible numbers below the input number to find the first one that divides the number evenly. The *find-factor* procedure takes one number as input and outputs the lowest factor of that number (other than 1):

```
(define (find-factor n)
  (define (find-factor-helper v)
    (if (= (modulo n v) 0) v (find-factor-helper (+ 1 v))))
  (find-factor-helper 2))
```

The *find-factor-helper* procedure takes two inputs, the number to factor and the current guess. Since all numbers are divisible by themselves, the *modulo* test will eventually be *true* for any positive input number, so the maximum number of recursive calls is *n*, the magnitude of the input to *find-factor*. The magnitude of *n* is exponential in its size, so the number of recursive calls is in $\Theta(2^b)$ where b is the number of bits in the input. This means even if the amount of work required for each recursive call were constant, the running time of the *find-factor* procedure is still exponential in the size of its input.

The actual work for each recursive call is not constant, though, since it involves an application of *modulo*. The *modulo* built-in procedure takes two inputs and outputs the remainder when the first input is divided by the second input. Hence, it output is 0 if *n* is divisible by *v*. Computing a remainder, in the worst case, at least involves examining every bit in the input number, so scales at least linearly in the size of its input[6]. This means the running time of *find-factor* is in $\Omega(2^b)$: it grows at least as fast as 2^b.

There are lots of ways we could produce a faster procedure for finding factors: stopping once the square root of the input number is reached since we know there is no need to check the rest of the numbers, skipping even numbers after 2 since if a number is divisible by any even number it is also divisible by 2, or using advanced sieve methods. This techniques can improve the running time by constant factors, but there is no known factoring algorithm that runs in faster than

[6] In fact, it computing the remainder requires performing division, which is quadratic in the size of the input.

exponential time. The security of the widely used RSA encryption algorithm depends on factoring being hard. If someone finds a fast factoring algorithm it would put the codes used to secure Internet commerce at risk.[7]

Example 7.10: Power Set

power set The *power set* of a set S is the set of all subsets of S. For example, the power set of $\{1,2,3\}$ is $\{\{\},\{1\},\{2\},\{3\},\{1,2\},\{1,3\},\{2,3\},\{1,2,3\}\}$.

The number of elements in the power set of S is $2^{|S|}$ (where $|S|$ is the number of elements in the set S).

Here is a procedure that takes a list as input, and produces as output the power set of the elements of the list:

```
(define (list-powerset s)
  (if (null? s) (list null)
     (list-append (list-map (lambda (t) (cons (car s) t))
                                       (list-powerset (cdr s)))
                  (list-powerset (cdr s)))))
```

The *list-powerset* procedure produces a List of Lists. Hence, for the base case, instead of just producing *null*, it produces a list containing a single element, *null*. In the recursive case, we can produce the power set by appending the list of all the subsets that include the first element, with the list of all the subsets that do not include the first element. For example, the powerset of $\{1,2,3\}$ is found by finding the powerset of $\{2,3\}$, which is $\{\{\}, \{2\}, \{3\}, \{2, 3\}\}$, and taking the union of that set with the set of all elements in that set unioned with $\{1\}$.

An application of *list-powerset* involves applying *list-append*, and two recursive applications of (*list-powerset* (*cdr s*)). Increasing the size of the input list by one, *doubles* the total number of applications of *list-powerset* since we need to evaluate (*list-powerset* (*cdr s*)) twice. The number of applications of *list-powerset* is 2^n where n is the length of the input list.[8]

The body of *list-powerset* is an if expression. The predicate applies the constant-time procedure, *null?*. The consequent expression, (*list null*) is also constant time. The alternate expression is an application of *list-append*. From Example 7.4, we know the running time of *list-append* is $\Theta(n_p)$ where n_p is the number of elements in its first input. The first input is the result of applying *list-map* to a procedure and the List produced by (*list-powerset* (*cdr s*)). The length of the list output by *list-map* is the same as the length of its input, so we need to determine the length of (*list-powerset* (*cdr s*)).

We use n_s to represent the number of elements in s. The length of the input list to *map* is the number of elements in the power set of a size $n_s - 1$ set: $2^{n_s - 1}$. But, for each application, the value of n_s is different. Since we are trying to determine the total running time, we can do this by thinking about the total length of all the input lists to *list-map* over all of the *list-powerset*. In the input is a list of length n, the total list length is $2^{n-1} + 2^{n-2} + ... + 2^1 + 2^0$, which is equal to $2^n - 1$. So,

[7]The movie *Sneakers* is a fictional account of what would happen if someone finds a faster than exponential time factoring algorithm.

[8]Observant readers will note that it is not really necessary to perform this evaluation twice since we could do it once and reuse the result. Even with this change, though, the running time would still be in $\Theta(2^n)$.

the running time for all the *list-map* applications is in $\Theta(2^n)$.

The analysis of the *list-append* applications is similar. The length of the first input to *list-append* is the length of the result of the *list-powerset* application, so the total length of all the inputs to append is 2^n.

Other than the applications of *list-map* and *list-append*, the rest of each *list-powerset* application requires constant time. So, the running time required for 2^n applications is in $\Theta(2^n)$. The total running time for *list-powerset* is the sum of the running times for the *list-powerset* applications, in $\Theta(2^n)$; the *list-map* applications, in $\Theta(2^n)$; and the *list-append* applications, in $\Theta(2^n)$. Hence, the total running time is in $\Theta(2^n)$.

In this case, we know there can be no faster than exponential procedure that solves the same problem, since the size of the output is exponential in the size of the input. Since the most work a Turing Machine can do in one step is write one square, the size of the output provides a lower bound on the running time of the Turing Machine. The size of the powerset is 2^n where n is the size of the input set. Hence, the fastest possible procedure for this problem has at least exponential running time.

7.4.5 Faster than Exponential Growth

We have already seen an example of a procedure that grows faster than exponentially in the size of the input: the *fibo* procedure at the beginning of this chapter! Evaluating an application of *fibo* involves $\Theta(\phi^n)$ recursive applications where n is the magnitude of the input parameter. The size of a numeric input is the number of bits needed to express it, so the value n can be as high as $2^b - 1$ where b is the number of bits. Hence, the running time of the *fibo* procedure is in $\Theta(\phi^{2^b})$ where b is the size of the input. This is why we are still waiting for (*fibo* 60) to finish evaluating.

7.4.6 Non-terminating Procedures

All of the procedures so far in the section are algorithms: they may be slow, but they are guaranteed to eventually finish if one can wait long enough. Some procedures never terminate. For example,

```
(define (run-forever) (run-forever))
```

defines a procedure that never finishes. Its body calls itself, never making any progress toward a base case. The running time of this procedure is effectively infinite since it never finishes.

7.5 Summary

Because the speed of computers varies and the exact time required for a particular application depends on many details, the most important property to understand is how the work required scales with the size of the input. The asymptotic operators provide a convenient way of understanding the cost involved in evaluating a procedure applications.

Procedures that can produce an output only touching a fixed amount have constant running times. Procedures whose running times increase by a fixed amount when the input size increases by one have linear (in $\Theta(n)$) running times. Procedures whose running time quadruples when the input size doubles have quadratic (in $\Theta(n^2)$) running times. Procedures whose running time doubles when the input size increases by one have exponential (in $\Theta(2^n)$) running times. Procedures with exponential running time can only be evaluated for small inputs.

Asymptotic analysis, however, must be interpreted cautiously. For large enough inputs, a procedure with running time in $\Theta(n)$ is always faster than a procedure with running time in $\Theta(n^2)$. But, for an input of a particular size, the $\Theta(n^2)$ procedure may be faster. Without knowing the constants that are hidden by the asymptotic operators, there is no way to accurately predict the actual running time on a given input.

Exercise 7.18. Analyze the asymptotic running time of the *list-sum* procedure (from Example 5.2):

```
(define (list-sum p)
  (if (null? p)
     0
     (+ (car p) (list-sum (cdr p)))))
```

You may assume all of the elements in the list have values below some constant (but explain why this assumption is useful in your analysis).

Exercise 7.19. Analyze the asymptotic running time of the *factorial* procedure (from Example 4.1):

```
(define (factorial n) (if (= n 0) 1 (* n (factorial (− n 1)))))
```

Be careful to describe the running time in terms of the *size* (not the magnitude) of the input.

Exercise 7.20. Consider the *intsto* problem (from Example 5.8).

a. [★] Analyze the asymptotic running time of this *intsto* procedure:

```
(define (revintsto n)
  (if (= n 0)
     null
     (cons n (revintsto (− n 1)))))
(define (intsto n) (list-reverse (revintsto n)))
```

b. [★] Analyze the asymptotic running time of this *instto* procedure:

```
(define (intsto n)
   (if (= n 0) null (list-append (intsto (− n 1)) (list n))))
```

c. Which version is better?

d. [★★] Is there an asymptotically faster *intsto* procedure?

Exercise 7.21. Analyze the running time of the *board-replace-peg* procedure (from Exploration 5.2):

```
(define (row-replace-peg pegs col val)
  (if (= col 1) (cons val (cdr pegs))
     (cons (car pegs) (row-replace-peg (cdr pegs) (- col 1) val))))
(define (board-replace-peg board row col val)
  (if (= row 1) (cons (row-replace-peg (car board) col val) (cdr board))
     (cons (car board) (board-replace-peg (cdr board) (- row 1) col val))))
```

Exercise 7.22. Analyze the running time of the *deep-list-flatten* procedure from Section 5.5:

```
(define (deep-list-flatten p)
  (if (null? p) null
     (list-append (if (list? (car p))
                        (deep-list-flatten (car p))
                        (list (car p)))
                     (deep-list-flatten (cdr p)))))
```

Exercise 7.23. [★] Find and correct at least one error in the *Orders of Growth* section of the Wikipedia page on *Analysis of Algorithms* (http://en.wikipedia.org/wiki/Analysis_of_algorithms). This is rated as [★] now (July 2011), since the current entry contains many fairly obvious errors. Hopefully it will soon become a [★★★] challenge, and perhaps, eventually will become impossible!

Sorting and Searching

If you keep proving stuff that others have done, getting confidence, increasing the complexities of your solutions—for the fun of it—then one day you'll turn around and discover that nobody actually did that one! And that's the way to become a computer scientist.
Richard Feynman, *Lectures on Computation*

This chapter presents two extended examples that use the programming techniques from Chapters 2–5 and analysis ideas from Chapters 6–7 to solve some interesting and important problems: sorting and searching. These examples involve some quite challenging problems and incorporate many of the ideas we have seen up to this point in the book. Once you understand them, you are well on your way to thinking like a computer scientist!

8.1 Sorting

The sorting problem takes two inputs: a list of elements and a comparison procedure. It outputs a list containing same elements as the input list ordered according to the comparison procedure. For example, if we sort a list of numbers using $<$ as the comparison procedure, the output is the list of numbers sorted in order from least to greatest.

Sorting is one of the most widely studied problems in computing, and many different sorting algorithms have been proposed. Try to develop a sorting procedure yourself before continuing further. It may be illuminating to try sorting some items by hand an think carefully about how you do it and how much work it is. For example, take a shuffled deck of cards and arrange them in sorted order by ranks. Or, try arranging all the students in your class in order by birthday. Next, we present and analyze three different sorting procedures.

8.1.1 Best-First Sort

A simple sorting strategy is to find the *best* element in the list and put that at the front. The best element is an element for which the comparison procedure evaluates to *true* when applied to that element and every other element. For example, if the comparison function is $<$, the best element is the lowest number in the list. This element belongs at the front of the output list.

The notion of the best element in the list for a given comparison function only makes sense if the comparison function is *transitive*. This means it has the property that for any inputs *a*, *b*, and *c*, if (*cf a b*) and (*cf b c*) are both true, the result of (*cf a c*) must be true. The $<$ function is transitive: $a < b$ and $b < c$ implies

transitive

$a < c$ for all numbers a, b, and c. If the comparison function does not have this property, there may be no way to arrange the elements in a single sorted list. All of our sorting procedures require that the procedure passed as the comparison function is transitive.

Once we can find the best element in a given list, we can sort the whole list by repeatedly finding the best element of the remaining elements until no more elements remain. To define our best-first sorting procedure, we first define a procedure for finding the best element in the list, and then define a procedure for removing an element from a list.

Finding the Best. The best element in the list is either the first element, or the best element from the rest of the list. Hence, we define *list-find-best* recursively. An empty list has no best element, so the base case is for a list that has one element. When the input list has only one element, that element is the best element. If the list has more than one element, the best element is the better of the first element in the list and the best element of the rest of the list.

To pick the better element from two elements, we define the *pick-better* procedure that takes three inputs: a comparison function and two values.

```
(define (pick-better cf p1 p2) (if (cf p1 p2) p1 p2))
```

Assuming the procedure passed as *cf* has constant running time, the running time of *pick-better* is constant. For most of our examples, we use the $<$ procedure as the comparison function. For arbitrary inputs, the running time of $<$ is not constant since in the worst case performing the comparison requires examining every digit in the input numbers. But, if the maximum value of a number in the input list is limited, then we can consider $<$ a constant time procedure since all of the inputs passed to it are below some fixed size.

We use *pick-better* to define *list-find-best*:

```
(define (list-find-best cf p)
  (if (null? (cdr p)) (car p)
     (pick-better cf (car p) (list-find-best cf (cdr p)))))
```

We use n to represent the number of elements in the input list p. An application of *list-find-best* involves $n - 1$ recursive applications since each one passes in *(cdr p)* as the new p operand and the base case stops when the list has one element left. The running time for each application (excluding the recursive application) is constant since it involves only applications of the constant time procedures *null?*, *cdr*, and *pick-better*. So, the total running time for *list-find-best* is in $\Theta(n)$; it scales linearly with the length of the input list.

Deleting an Element. To implement best first sorting, we need to produce a list that contains all the elements of the original list except for the best element, which will be placed at the front of the output list. We define a procedure, *list-delete*, that takes as inputs a List and a Value, and produces a List that contains all the elements of the input list in the original order except for the first element that is equal to the input value.

```
(define (list-delete p el)
  (if (null? p) null
    (if (equal? (car p) el) (cdr p) ; found match, skip this element
      (cons (car p) (list-delete (cdr p) el)))))
```

We use the *equal?* procedure to check if the element matches instead of = so the *list-delete* procedure works on elements that are not just Numbers. The *equal?* procedure behaves identically to = when both inputs are Numbers, but also works sensibly on many other datatypes including Booleans, Characters, Pairs, Lists, and Strings. Since we assume the sizes of the inputs to *equal?* are bounded, we can consider *equal?* to be a constant time procedure (even though it would not be constant time on arbitrary inputs).

The worst case running time for *list-delete* occurs when no element in the list matches the value of *el* (in the best case, the first element matches and the running time does not depend on the length of the input list at all). We use n to represent the number of elements in the input list. There can be up to n recursive applications of *list-delete*. Each application has constant running time since all of the procedures applied (except the recursive call) have constant running times. Hence, the total running time for *list-delete* is in $\Theta(n)$ where n is the length of the input list.

Best-First Sorting. We define *list-sort-best-first* using *list-find-best* and *list-delete*:

```
(define (list-sort-best-first cf p)
  (if (null? p) null
    (cons (list-find-best cf p)
          (list-sort-best-first cf (list-delete p (list-find-best cf p))))))
```

The running time of the *list-sort-best-first* procedure grows quadratically with the length of the input list. We use n to represent the number of elements in the input list. There are n recursive applications since each application of *list-delete* produces an output list that is one element shorter than its input list. In addition to the constant time procedures (*null?* and *cons*), the body of *list-sort-best-first* involves two applications of *list-find-best* on the input list, and one application of *list-delete* on the input list.

Each of these applications has running time in $\Theta(m)$ where m is the length of the input list to *list-find-best* and *list-delete* (we use m here to avoid confusion with n, the length of the first list passed into *list-sort-best-first*). In the first application, this input list will be a list of length n, but in later applications it will be involve lists of decreasing length: $n-1, n-2, \cdots, 1$. Hence, the *average* length of the input lists to *list-find-best* and *list-delete* is approximately $\frac{n}{2}$. Thus, the average running time for each of these applications is in $\Theta(\frac{n}{2})$, which is equivalent to $\Theta(n)$.

There are three applications (two of *list-find-best* and one of *list-delete*) for each application of *list-sort-best-first*, so the total running time for each application is in $\Theta(3n)$, which is equivalent to $\Theta(n)$.

There are n recursive applications, each with average running time in $\Theta(n)$, so the running time for *list-sort-best-first* is in $\Theta(n^2)$. This means doubling the length of the input list quadruples the expected running time, so we predict that sorting a list of 2000 elements to take approximately four times as long as sorting a list of 1000 elements.

Let expression. Each application of the *list-sort-best-first* procedure involves two evaluations of (*list-find-best cf p*), a procedure with running time in $\Theta(n)$ where n is the length of the input list.

The result of both evaluations is the same, so there is no need to evaluate this expression twice. We could just evaluate (*list-find-best cf p*) once and reuse the result. One way to do this is to introduce a new procedure using a lambda expression and pass in the result of (*list-find-best cf p*) as a parameter to this procedure so it can be used twice:

```
(define (list-sort-best-first-nodup cf p)
   (if (null? p) null
      ((lambda (best)
         (cons best (list-sort-best-first-nodup cf (list-delete p best))))
       (list-find-best cf p))))
```

This procedure avoids the duplicate evaluation of (*list-find-best cf p*), but is quite awkward to read and understand.

Scheme provides the let expression special form to avoid this type of duplicate work more elegantly. The grammar for the let expression is:

Expression	::⇒	*LetExpression*
LetExpression	::⇒	(**let** (*Bindings*) *Expression*)
Bindings	::⇒	*Binding Bindings*
Bindings	::⇒	ϵ
Binding	::⇒	(*Name Expression*)

The evaluation rule for the let expression is:

> **Evaluation Rule 6: Let expression.** To evaluate a let expression, evaluate each binding in order. To evaluate each binding, evaluate the binding expression and bind the name to the value of that expression. Then, the value of the let expression is the value of the body expression evaluated with the names in the expression that match binding names substituted with their bound values.

A let expression can be transformed into an equivalent application expression. The let expression

(**let** (($Name_1$ $Expression_1$) ($Name_2$ $Expression_2$)
   $\cdots$ ($Name_k$ $Expression_k$))
 $Expression_{body}$)

is equivalent to the application expression:

((**lambda** ($Name_1$ $Name_2$ $\ldots$ $Name_k$) $Expression_{body}$)
 $Expression_1$ $Expression_2$ $\ldots$ $Expression_k$)

The advantage of the let expression syntax is it puts the expressions next to the names to which they are bound. Using a let expression, we define *list-sort-best-first-let* to avoid the duplicate evaluations:

```
(define (list-sort-best-first-let cf p)
  (if (null? p) null
    (let ((best (list-find-best cf p)))
      (cons best (list-sort-best-first-let cf (list-delete p best))))))
```

This runs faster than *list-sort-best-first* since it avoids the duplicate evaluations, but the asymptotic asymptotic running time is still in $\Theta(n^2)$: there are n recursive applications of *list-sort-best-first-let* and each application involves linear time applications of *list-find-best* and *list-delete*. Using the let expression improves the actual running time by avoiding the duplicate work, but does not impact the asymptotic growth rate since the duplicate work is hidden in the constant factor.

Exercise 8.1. What is the best case input for *list-sort-best-first*? What is its asymptotic running time on the best case input?

Exercise 8.2. Use the *time* special form (Section 7.1) to experimentally measure the evaluation times for the *list-sort-best-first-let* procedure. Do the results match the expected running times based on the $\Theta(n^2)$ asymptotic running time?

You may find it helpful to define a procedure that constructs a list containing n random elements. To generate the random elements use the built-in procedure *random* that takes one number as input and evaluates to a pseudorandom number between 0 and one less than the value of the input number. Be careful in your time measurements that you do not include the time required to generate the input list.

Exercise 8.3. Define the *list-find-best* procedure using the *list-accumulate* procedure from Section 5.4.2 and evaluate its asymptotic running time.

Exercise 8.4. [★] Define and analyze a *list-sort-worst-last* procedure that sorts by finding the worst element first and putting it at the end of the list.

8.1.2 Insertion Sort

The *list-sort-best-first* procedure seems quite inefficient. For every output element, we are searching the whole remaining list to find the best element, but do nothing of value with all the comparisons that were done to find the best element.

An alternate approach is to build up a sorted list as we go through the elements. Insertion sort works by putting the first element in the list in the right place in the list that results from sorting the rest of the elements.

First, we define the *list-insert-one* procedure that takes three inputs: a comparison procedure, an element, and a List. The input List must be sorted according to the comparison function. As output, *list-insert-one* produces a List consisting of the elements of the input List, with the input element inserts in the right place according to the comparison function.

```
(define (list-insert-one cf el p) ; requires: p is sorted by cf
  (if (null? p) (list el)
    (if (cf el (car p)) (cons el p)
      (cons (car p) (list-insert-one cf el (cdr p))))))
```

The running time for *list-insert-one* is in $\Theta(n)$ where n is the number of elements in the input list. In the worst case, the input element belongs at the end of the list and it makes n recursive applications of *list-insert-one*. Each application involves constant work so the overall running time of *list-insert-one* is in $\Theta(n)$.

To sort the whole list, we insert each element into the list that results from sorting the rest of the elements:

```
(define (list-sort-insert cf p)
  (if (null? p) null
    (list-insert-one cf (car p) (list-sort-insert cf (cdr p)))))
```

Evaluating an application of *list-sort-insert* on a list of length n involves n recursive applications. The lengths of the input lists in the recursive applications are $n-1$, $n-2$, ..., 0. Each application involves an application of *list-insert-one* which has linear running time. The average length of the input list over all the applications is approximately $\frac{n}{2}$, so the average running time of the *list-insert-one* applications is in $\Theta(n)$. There are n applications of *list-insert-one*, so the total running time is in $\Theta(n^2)$.

Exercise 8.5. We analyzed the worst case running time of *list-sort-insert* above. Analyze the best case running time. Your analysis should identify the inputs for which *list-sort-insert* runs fastest, and describe the asymptotic running time for the best case input.

Exercise 8.6. Both the *list-sort-best-first-sort* and *list-sort-insert* procedures have asymptotic running times in $\Theta(n^2)$. This tells us how their worst case running times grow with the size of the input, but isn't enough to know which procedure is faster for a particular input. For the questions below, use both analytical and empirical analysis to provide a convincing answer.

a. How do the actual running times of *list-sort-best-first-sort* and *list-sort-insert* on typical inputs compare?

b. Are there any inputs for which *list-sort-best-first* is faster than *list-sort-insert*?

c. For sorting a long list of n random elements, how long does each procedure take? (See Exercise 8.2 for how to create a list of random elements.)

8.1.3 Quicker Sorting

Although insertion sort is typically faster than best-first sort, its running time is still scales quadratically with the length of the list. If it takes 100 milliseconds (one tenth of a second) to sort a list containing 1000 elements using *list-sort-insert*, we expect it will take four ($= 2^2$) times as long to sort a list containing 2000 elements, and a million times ($= 1000^2$) as long (over a day!) to sort a list containing one million ($1000 * 1000$) elements. Yet computers routinely need to sort lists containing many millions of elements (for example, consider processing credit card transactions or analyzing the data collected by a super collider).

The problem with our insertion sort is that it divides the work unevenly into inserting one element and sorting the rest of the list. This is a very unequal division. Any sorting procedure that works by considering one element at a time and putting it in the sorted position as is done by *list-sort-find-best* and *list-sort-insert* has a running time in $\Omega(n^2)$. We cannot do better than this with this strategy since there are n elements, and the time required to figure out where each element goes is in $\Omega(n)$.

To do better, we need to either reduce the number of recursive applications needed (this would mean each recursive call results in more than one element being sorted), or reduce the time required for each application. The approach we take is to use each recursive application to divide the list into two approximately equal-sized parts, but to do the division in such a way that the results of sorting the two parts can be combined directly to form the result. We partition the elements in the list so that all elements in the first part are less than (according to the comparison function) all elements in the second part.

Our first attempt is to modify *insert-one* to partition the list into two parts. This approach does not produce a better-than-quadratic time sorting procedure because of the inefficiency of accessing list elements; however, it leads to insights for producing a quicker sorting procedure.

First, we define a *list-extract* procedure that takes as inputs a list and two numbers indicating the start and end positions, and outputs a list containing the elements of the input list between the start and end positions:

```
(define (list-extract p start end)
  (if (= start 0)
    (if (= end 0) null
      (cons (car p) (list-extract (cdr p) start (- end 1))))
    (list-extract (cdr p) (- start 1) (- end 1))))
```

The running time of the *list-extract* procedure is in $\Theta(n)$ where n is the number of elements in the input list. The worst case input is when the value of *end* is the length of the input list, which means there will be n recursive applications, each involving a constant amount of work.

We use *list-extract* to define procedures for obtaining first and second halves of a list (when the list has an odd number of elements, we put the middle element in the second half of the list):

```
(define (list-first-half p)
  (list-extract p 0 (floor (/ (list-length p) 2))))

(define (list-second-half p)
  (list-extract p (floor (/ (list-length p) 2)) (list-length p)))
```

The *list-first-half* and *list-second-half* procedures use *list-extract* so their running times are linear in the number of elements in the input list.

The *list-insert-one-split* procedure inserts an element in sorted order by first splitting the list in halves and then recursively inserting the new element in the appropriate half of the list:

```
(define (list-insert-one-split cf el p) ; requires: p is sorted by cf
  (if (null? p) (list el)
    (if (null? (cdr p))
      (if (cf el (car p)) (cons el p) (list (car p) el))
      (let ((front (list-first-half p)) (back (list-second-half p)))
        (if (cf el (car back))
          (list-append (list-insert-one-split cf el front) back)
          (list-append front (list-insert-one-split cf el back)))))))
```

In addition to the normal base case when the input list is null, we need a special case when the input list has one element. If the element to be inserted is before this element, the output is produced using *cons*; otherwise, we produce a list of the first (only) element in the list followed by the inserted element.

In the recursive case, we use the *list-first-half* and *list-second-half* procedures to split the input list and bind the results of the first and second halves to the *front* and *back* variables so we do not need to evaluate these expressions more than once.

Since the list passed to *list-insert-one-split* is required to be sorted, the elements in *front* are all less than the first element in *back*. Hence, only one comparison is needed to determine which of the sublists contains the new element: if the element is before the first element in *back* it is in the first half, and we produce the result by appending the result of inserting the element in the front half with the back half unchanged; otherwise, it is in the second half, so we produce the result by appending the front half unchanged with the result of inserting the element in the back half.

To analyze the running time of *list-insert-one-split* we determine the number of recursive calls and the amount of work involved in each application. We use n to denote the number of elements in the input list. Unlike the other recursive list procedures we have analyzed, the number of recursive applications of *list-insert-one-split* does not scale linearly with the length of the input list. The reason for this is that instead of using (*cdr p*) in the recursive call, *list-insert-one-split* passes in either the *front* or *back* value which is the result of (*first-half p*) or (*second-half p*) respectively. The length of the list produced by these procedures is approximately $\frac{1}{2}$ the length of the input list. With each recursive application, the size of the input list is halved. This means, *doubling* the size of the input list only adds one more recursive application. This means the number of recursive calls is logarithmic in the size of the input.

Recall that the *logarithm* ($\log_b$) of a number n is the number x such that $b^x = n$ where b is the *base* of the logarithm. In computing, we most commonly encounter logarithms with base 2. Doubling the input value increases the value of its logarithm base two by one: $\log_2 2n = 1 + \log_2 n$. Changing the base of a logarithm from k to b changes the value by the constant factor (see Section 7.3.1), so inside the asymptotic operators a constant base of a logarithm does not matter. Thus, when the amount of work increases by some constant amount when the input size doubles, we write that the growth rate is in $\Theta(\log n)$ without specifying the base of the logarithm.

Each *list-insert-one-split* application applies *list-append* to a first parameter that is either the front half of the list or the result of inserting the element in the front half of the list. In either case, the length of the list is approximately $\frac{n}{2}$. The running time of *list-append* is in $\Theta(m)$ where m is the length of the first input list. So, the time required for each *list-insert-one-split* application is in $\Theta(n)$ where n is the length of the input list to *list-insert-one-split*.

The lengths of the input lists to *list-insert-one-split* in the recursive calls are approximately $\frac{n}{2}, \frac{n}{4}, \frac{n}{8}, \ldots, 1$, since the length of the list halves with each call. The summation has $\log_2 n$ terms, and the sum of the list is n, so the average length input is $\frac{n}{\log_2 n}$. Hence, the total running time for the *list-append* applications in each application of *list-insert-one-split* is in $\Theta(\log_2 n \times \frac{n}{\log_2 n}) = \Theta(n)$.

The analysis of the applications of *list-first-half* and *list-second-half* is similar: each requires running time in $\Theta(m)$ where m is the length of the input list, which averages $\frac{n}{\log_2 n}$ where n is the length of the input list of *list-insert-one-split*. Hence, the total running time for *list-insert-one-split* is in $\Theta(n)$.

The *list-sort-insert-split* procedure is identical to *list-sort-insert* (except for calling *list-insert-one-split*):

```
(define (list-sort-insert-split cf p)
  (if (null? p) null
    (list-insert-one-split cf (car p) (list-sort-insert-split cf (cdr p)))))
```

Similarly to *list-sort-insert*, *list-sort-insert-split* involves n applications of *list-insert-one-split*, and the average length of the input list is $\frac{n}{2}$. Since *list-sort-insert-split* involves $\Theta(n)$ applications of *list-insert-one-split* with average input list length of $\frac{n}{2}$, the total running time for *list-sort-insert-split* is in $\Theta(n^2)$. Because of the cost of evaluating the *list-append*, *list-first-half*, and *list-second-half* applications, the change to splitting the list in halves has not improved the asymptotic performance; in fact, because of all the extra work in each application, the actual running time is higher than it was for *list-sort-insert*.

The problem with our *list-insert-one-split* procedure is that the *list-first-half* and *list-second-half* procedures have to *cdr* down the whole list to get to the middle of the list, and the *list-append* procedure needs to walk through the entire input list to put the new element in the list. All of these procedures have running times that scale linearly with the length of the input list. To use the splitting strategy effectively, we need is a way to get to the middle of the list quickly. With the standard list representation this is impossible: it requires one *cdr* application to get to the next element in the list, so there is no way to access the middle of the list without using at least $\frac{n}{2}$ applications of *cdr*. To do better, we need to change the way we represent our data. The next subsection introduces such a structure; in Section 8.1.5 shows a way of sorting efficiently using lists directly by changing how we split the list.

8.1.4 Binary Trees

The data structure we will use is known as a *sorted binary tree*. While a list provides constant time procedures for accessing the first element and the rest of the elements, a binary tree provides constant time procedures for accessing the *root* element, the *left* side of the tree, and the *right* side of the tree. The left and right sides of the tree are themselves trees. So, like a list, a binary tree is a recursive data structure.

sorted binary tree

Whereas we defined a List (in Chapter 5) as:

> A *List* is either (1) null or (2) a Pair whose second cell is a *List.*

a Tree is defined as:

> A *Tree* is either (1) null or (2) a triple while first and third parts are both *Trees*.

Symbolically:

Tree ::⇒ *null*
Tree ::⇒ (*make-tree Tree Element Tree*)

The *make-tree* procedure can be defined using *cons* to package the three inputs into a tree:

```
(define (make-tree left element right)
  (cons element (cons left right)))
```

We define selector procedures for extracting the parts of a non-*null* tree:

```
(define (tree-element tree) (car tree))
(define (tree-left tree) (car (cdr tree)))
(define (tree-right tree) (cdr (cdr tree)))
```

The *tree-left* and *tree-right* procedures are constant time procedures that evaluate to the left or right subtrees respectively of a tree.

In a sorted tree, the elements are maintained in a sorted structure. All elements in the left subtree of a tree are less than (according to the comparison function) the value of the root element of the tree; all elements in the right subtree of a tree are greater than or equal to the value of the root element of the tree (the result of comparing them with the root element is false). For example, here is a sorted binary tree containing 6 elements using $<$ as the comparison function:

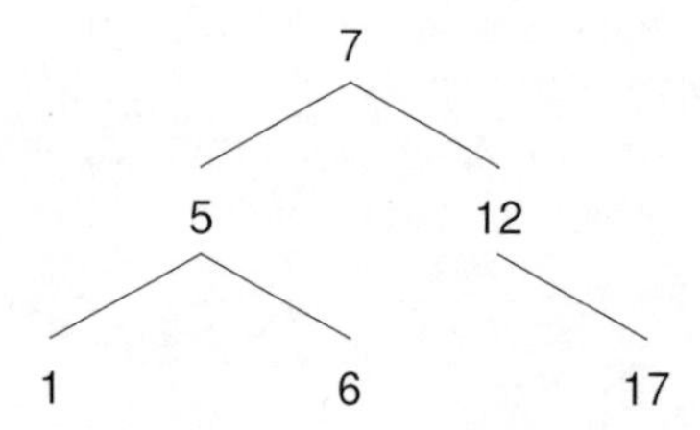

The top node has element value 7, and its left subtree is a tree containing the tree elements whose values are less than 7. The *null* subtrees are not shown. For example, the left subtree of the element whose value is 12 is *null*. Although there are six elements in the tree, we can reach any element from the top by following at most two branches. By contrast, with a list of six elements, we need five *cdr* operations to reach the last element.

depth The *depth* of a tree is the largest number of steps needed to reach any node in the tree starting from the root. The example tree has depth 2, since we can reach every node starting from the root of the tree in two or fewer steps. A tree of depth d can contain up to $2^{d+1}-1$ elements. One way to see this is from this recursive definition for the maximum number of nodes in a tree:

$$TreeNodes(d) = \begin{cases} 1 & : \ d=0 \\ TreeNodes(d-1) + 2 \times TreeLeaves(d-1) & : \ d>0 \end{cases}$$

A tree of depth zero has one node. Increasing the depth of a tree by one means we can add two nodes for each leaf node in the tree, so the total number of nodes in the new tree is the sum of the number of nodes in the original tree and twice the number of leaves in the original tree. The maximum number of leaves in a tree of depth d is 2^d since each level doubles the number of leaves. Hence, the second equation simplifies to

$$TreeNodes(d-1) + 2 \times 2^{d-1} = TreeNodes(d-1) + 2^d.$$

The value of $TreeNodes(d-1)$ is $2^{d-1} + 2^{d-2} + \ldots + 1 = 2^d - 1$. Adding 2^d and $2^d - 1$ gives $2^{d+1} - 1$ as the maximum number of nodes in a tree of depth d. Hence, a well-balanced tree containing n nodes has depth approximately $\log_2 n$. A tree is *well-balanced* if the left and right subtrees of all nodes in the contain nearly the same number of elements.

well-balanced

Procedures that are analogous to the *list-first-half*, *list-second-half*, and *list-append* procedures that had linear running times for the standard list representation can all be implemented with constant running times for the tree representation. For example, *tree-left* is analogous to *list-first-half* and *make-tree* is analogous to *list-append*.

The *tree-insert-one* procedure inserts an element in a sorted binary tree:

```
(define (tree-insert-one cf el tree)
  (if (null? tree) (make-tree null el null)
     (if (cf el (tree-element tree))
        (make-tree (tree-insert-one cf el (tree-left tree))
                   (tree-element tree)
                   (tree-right tree))
        (make-tree (tree-left tree)
                   (tree-element tree)
                   (tree-insert-one cf el (tree-right tree))))))
```

When the input tree is *null*, the new element is the top element of a new tree whose left and right subtrees are *null*. Otherwise, the procedure compares the element to insert with the element at the top node of the tree. If the comparison evaluates to true, the new element belongs in the left subtree. The result is a tree where the left tree is the result of inserting this element in the old left subtree, and the element and right subtree are the same as they were in the original tree. For the alternate case, the element is inserted in the right subtree, and the left subtree is unchanged.

In addition to the recursive call, *tree-insert-one* only applies constant time procedures. If the tree is well-balanced, each recursive application *halves* the size of the input tree so there are approximately $\log_2 n$ recursive calls. Hence, the running time to insert an element in a well-balanced tree using *tree-insert-one* is in $\Theta(\log n)$.

Using *tree-insert-one*, we define *list-to-sorted-tree*, a procedure that takes a comparison function and a list as its inputs, and outputs a sorted binary tree containing the elements in the input list. It inserts each element of the list in turn into the sorted tree:

```
(define (list-to-sorted-tree cf p)
  (if (null? p) null
     (tree-insert-one cf (car p) (list-to-sorted-tree cf (cdr p)))))
```

Assuming well-balanced trees as above (we revisit this assumption later), the expected running time of *list-to-sorted-tree* is in $\Theta(n \log n)$ where n is the size of the input list. There are n recursive applications of *list-to-sorted-tree* since each application uses *cdr* to reduce the size of the input list by one. Each application involves an application of *tree-insert-one* (as well as only constant time procedures), so the expected running time of each application is in $\Theta(\log n)$. Hence, the total running time for *list-to-sorted-tree* is in $\Theta(n \log n)$.

To use our *list-to-sorted-tree* procedure to perform sorting we need to extract a list of the elements in the tree in the correct order. The leftmost element in the tree should be the first element in the list. Starting from the top node, all elements in its left subtree should appear before the top element, and all the elements in its right subtree should follow it. The *tree-extract-elements* procedure does this:

```
(define (tree-extract-elements tree)
  (if (null? tree) null
     (list-append (tree-extract-elements (tree-left tree))
                  (cons (tree-element tree)
                        (tree-extract-elements (tree-right tree))))))
```

The total number of applications of *tree-extract-elements* is between n (the number of elements in the tree) and $3n$ since there can be up to two null trees for each leaf element (it could never actually be $3n$, but for our asymptotic analysis it is enough to know it is always less than some constant multiple of n). For each application, the body applies *list-append* where the first parameter is the elements extracted from the left subtree. The end result of all the *list-append* applications is the output list, containing the n elements in the input tree.

Hence, the total size of all the appended lists is at most n, and the running time for all the *list-append* applications is in $\Theta(n)$. Since this is the *total* time for all the *list-append* applications, not the time for *each* application of *tree-extract-elements*, the total running time for *tree-extract-elements* is the time for the recursive applications, in $\Theta(n)$, plus the time for the *list-append* applications, in $\Theta(n)$, which is in $\Theta(n)$.

Putting things together, we define *list-sort-tree*:

```
(define (list-sort-tree cf p)
  (tree-extract-elements (list-to-sorted-tree cf p)))
```

The total running time for *list-sort-tree* is the running time of the *list-to-sorted-tree* application plus the running time of the *tree-extract-elements* application. The running time of *list-sort-tree* is in $\Theta(n \log n)$ where n is the number of elements in the input list (in this case, the number of elements in *p*), and the running time of *tree-extract-elements* is in $\Theta(n)$ where n is the number of elements in its input list (which is the result of the *list-to-sorted* tree application, a list containing n elements where n is the number of elements in p).

Only the fastest-growing term contributes to the total asymptotic running time, so the expected total running time for an application of *list-sort-tree-insert* to a list containing n elements is in $\Theta(n \log n)$. This is substantially better than the previous sorting algorithms which had running times in $\Theta(n^2)$ since logarithms grow far slower than their input. For example, if n is one million, n^2 is over 50,000 times bigger than $n \log_2 n$; if n is one billion, n^2 is over 33 million times bigger than $n \log_2 n$ since $\log_2 1000000000$ is just under 30.

There is no general sorting procedure that has expected running time better than $\Theta(n \log n)$, so there is no algorithm that is asymptotically faster than *list-sort-tree* (in fact, it can be proven that no asymptotically faster sorting procedure exists). There are, however, sorting procedures that may have advantages such as how they use memory which may provide better absolute performance in some situations.

Unbalanced Trees. Our analysis assumes the left and right halves of the tree passed to *tree-insert-one* having approximately the same number of elements. If the input list is in random order, this assumption is likely to be valid: each element we insert is equally likely to go into the left or right half, so the halves contain approximately the same number of elements all the way down the tree. But, if the input list is not in random order this may not be the case.

For example, suppose the input list is already in sorted order. Then, each element that is inserted will be the rightmost node in the tree when it is inserted. For the previous example, this produces the unbalanced tree shown in Figure 8.1. This tree contains the same six elements as the earlier example, but because it is not well-balanced the number of branches that must be traversed to reach the deepest element is 5 instead of 2. Similarly, if the input list is in reverse sorted order, we will have an unbalanced tree where only the left branches are used.

In these pathological situations, the tree effectively becomes a list. The num-

Figure 8.1. Unbalanced trees.

ber of recursive applications of *tree-insert-one* needed to insert a new element will not be in $\Theta(\log n)$, but rather will be in $\Theta(n)$. Hence, the worst case running time for *list-sort-tree-insert* is in $\Theta(n^2)$ since the worst case time for *tree-insert-one* is in $\Theta(n)$ and there are $\Theta(n)$ applications of *tree-insert-one*. The *list-sort-tree-insert* procedure has expected running time in $\Theta(n \log n)$ for randomly distributed inputs, but has worst case running time in $\Theta(n^2)$.

Exercise 8.7. Define a procedure *binary-tree-size* that takes as input a binary tree and outputs the number of elements in the tree. Analyze the running time of your procedure.

Exercise 8.8. [★] Define a procedure *binary-tree-depth* that takes as input a binary tree and outputs the depth of the tree. The running time of your procedure should not grow faster than linearly with the number of nodes in the tree.

Exercise 8.9. [★★] Define a procedure *binary-tree-balance* that takes as input a sorted binary tree and the comparison function, and outputs a sorted binary tree containing the same elements as the input tree but in a well-balanced tree. The depth of the output tree should be no higher than $\log_2 n + 1$ where n is the number of elements in the input tree.

8.1.5 Quicksort

My first task was to implement a library subroutine for a new fast method of internal sorting just invented by Shell... My boss and tutor, Pat Shackleton, was very pleased with my completed program. I then said timidly that I thought I had invented a sorting method that would usually run faster than Shell sort, without taking much extra store. He bet me sixpence that I had not. Although my method was very difficult to explain, he finally agreed that I had won my bet.
Sir Tony Hoare, *The Emperor's Old Clothes*, 1980 Turing Award Lecture. (Shell sort is a $\Theta(n^2)$ sorting algorithm, somewhat similar to insertion sort.)

Although building and extracting elements from trees allows us to sort with expected time in $\Theta(n \log n)$, the constant time required to build all those trees and extract the elements from the final tree is high.

In fact, we can use the same approach to sort without needing to build trees. Instead, we keep the two sides of the tree as separate lists, and sort them recursively. The key is to divide the list into halves by *value*, instead of by *position*. The values in the first half of the list are all less than the values in the second half of the list, so the lists can be sorted separately.

The *list-quicksort* procedure uses *list-filter* (from Example 5.5) to divide the input list into sublists containing elements below and above the comparison element, and then recursively sorts those sublists:

```
(define (list-quicksort cf p)
  (if (null? p) null
      (list-append
       (list-quicksort cf
        (list-filter (lambda (el) (cf el (car p))) (cdr p)))
      (cons (car p)
            (list-quicksort cf
             (list-filter (lambda (el) (not (cf el (car p)))) (cdr p)))))))
```

This is the famous *quicksort* algorithm that was invented by Sir C. A. R. (Tony) Hoare while he was an exchange student at Moscow State University in 1959. He was there to study probability theory, but also got a job working on a project to translate Russian into English. The translation depended on looking up words in a dictionary. Since the dictionary was stored on a magnetic tape which could be read in order faster than if it was necessary to jump around, the translation could be done more quickly if the words to translate were sorted alphabetically. Hoare invented the quicksort algorithm for this purpose and it remains the most widely used sorting algorithm.

As with *list-sort-tree-insert*, the expected running time for a randomly arranged list is in $\Theta(n \log n)$ and the worst case running time is in $\Theta(n^2)$. In the expected cases, each recursive call halves the size of the input list (since if the list is randomly arranged we expect about half of the list elements are below the value of the first element), so there are approximately $\log n$ expected recursive calls.

Each call involves an application of *list-filter*, which has running time in $\Theta(m)$ where m is the length of the input list. At each call depth, the total length of the inputs to all the calls to *list-filter* is n since the original list is subdivided into 2^d sublists, which together include all of the elements in the original list. Hence, the total running time is in $\Theta(n \log n)$ in the expected cases where the input list is randomly arranged. As with *list-sort-tree-insert*, if the input list is not randomly rearranged it is possible that all elements end up in the same partition. Hence, the worst case running time of *list-quicksort* is still in $\Theta(n^2)$.

There are two ways of constructing a software design: one way is to make it so simple that there are obviously *no deficiencies, and the other way is to make it so complicated that there are no* obvious *deficiencies. The first method is far more difficult. It demands the same skill, devotion, insight, and even inspiration as the discovery of the simple physical laws which underlie the complex phenomena of nature.*
Sir Tony Hoare, *The Emperor's Old Clothes* (1980 Turing Award Lecture)

Exercise 8.10. Estimate the time it would take to sort a list of one million elements using *list-quicksort*.

Exercise 8.11. Both the *list-quicksort* and *list-sort-tree-insert* procedures have expected running times in $\Theta(n \log n)$. Experimentally compare their actual running times.

Exercise 8.12. What is the best case input for *list-quicksort*? Analyze the asymptotic running time for *list-quicksort* on best case inputs.

Exercise 8.13. [★] Instead of using binary trees, we could use ternary trees. A node in a ternary tree has two elements, a left element and a right element, where the left element must be before the right element according to the comparison function. Each node has three subtrees: *left*, containing elements before the left element; *middle*, containing elements between the left and right elements; and *right*, containing elements after the right element. Is it possible to sort faster using ternary trees?

8.2 Searching

In a broad sense, nearly all problems can be thought of as search problems. If we can define the space of possible solutions, we can search that space to find a correct solution. For example, to solve the pegboard puzzle (Exploration 5.2) we enumerate all possible sequences of moves and search that space to find a winning sequence. For most interesting problems, however, the search space is far too large to search through all possible solutions.

This section explores a few specific types of search problems. First, we consider the simple problem of finding an element in a list that satisfies some property. Then, we consider searching for an item in sorted data. Finally, we consider the more specific problem of efficiently searching for documents (such as web pages) that contain some target word.

8.2.1 Unstructured Search

Finding an item that satisfies an arbitrary property in unstructured data requires testing each element in turn until one that satisfies the property is found. Since we have no more information about the property or data, there is no way to more quickly find a satisfying element.

The *list-search* procedure takes as input a matching function and a list, and outputs the first element in the list that satisfies the matching function or false if there is no satisfying element:[1]

```
(define (list-search ef p)
  (if (null? p) false ; Not found
     (if (ef (car p)) (car p) (list-search ef (cdr p)))))
```

For example,

```
(list-search (lambda (el) (= 12 el)) (intsto 10)) ⇒ false
(list-search (lambda (el) (= 12 el)) (intsto 15)) ⇒ 12
(list-search (lambda (el) (> el 12)) (intsto 15)) ⇒ 13
```

Assuming the matching function has constant running time, the worst case running time of *list-search* is linear in the size of the input list. The worst case is when there is no satisfying element in the list. If the input list has length n, there are n recursive calls to *list-search*, each of which involves only constant time procedures.

Without imposing more structure on the input and comparison function, there is no more efficient search procedure. In the worst case, we always need to test every element in the input list before concluding that there is no element that satisfies the matching function.

8.2.2 Binary Search

If the data to search is structured, it may be possible to find an element that satisfies some property without examining all elements. Suppose the input data is a sorted binary tree, as introduced in Section 8.1.4. Then, with a single comparison we can determine if the element we are searching for would be in the left or right subtree. Instead of eliminating just one element with each application of the matching function as was the case with *list-search*, with a sorted binary tree a single application of the comparison function is enough to exclude approximately half the elements.

The *binary-tree-search* procedure takes a sorted binary tree and two procedures as its inputs. The first procedure determines when a satisfying element has been found (we call this the *ef* procedure, suggesting equality). The second procedure, *cf*, determines whether to search the left or right subtree. Since *cf* is used to traverse the tree, the input tree must be sorted by *cf*.

[1] If the input list contains *false* as an element, we do not know when the *list-search* result is false if it means the element is not in the list or the element whose value is *false* satisfies the property. An alternative would be to produce an error if no satisfying element is found, but this is more awkward when *list-search* is used by other procedures.

```
(define (binary-tree-search ef cf tree) ; requires: tree is sorted by cf
  (if (null? tree) false
    (if (ef (tree-element tree)) (tree-element tree)
      (if (cf (tree-element tree))
        (binary-tree-search ef cf (tree-left tree))
        (binary-tree-search ef cf (tree-right tree))))))
```

For example, we can search for a number in a sorted binary tree using = as the equality function and < as the comparison function:

```
(define (binary-tree-number-search tree target)
 (binary-tree-search (lambda (el) (= target el))
                     (lambda (el) (< target el))
                     tree))
```

To analyze the running time of *binary-tree-search*, we need to determine the number of recursive calls. Like our analysis of *list-sort-tree*, we assume the input tree is well-balanced. If not, all the elements could be in the right branch, for example, and *binary-tree-search* becomes like *list-search* in the pathological case.

If the tree is well-balanced, each recursive call approximately halves the number of elements in the input tree since it passed in either the left or right subtree. Hence, the number of calls needed to reach a *null* tree is in $\Theta(\log n)$ where n is the number of elements in the input tree. This is the depth of the tree: *binary-tree-search* traverses *one* path from the root through the tree until either reaching an element that satisfies the *ef* function, or reaching a *null* node.

Assuming the procedures passed as *ef* and *cf* have constant running time, the work for each call is constant except for the recursive call. Hence, the total running time for *binary-tree-search* is in $\Theta(\log n)$ where n is the number of elements in the input tree. This is a huge improvement over linear searching: with linear search, doubling the number of elements in the input doubles the search time; with binary search, doubling the input size only increases the search time by a constant.

8.2.3 Indexed Search

The limitation of binary search is we can only use is when the input data is already sorted. What if we want to search a collection of documents, such as finding all web pages that contain a given word? The web visible to search engines contains billions of web pages most of which contain hundreds or thousands of words. A linear search over such a vast corpus would be infeasible: supposing each word can be tested in 1 millisecond, the time to search 1 trillion words would be over 30 years!

Providing useful searches over large data sets like web documents requires finding a way to structure the data so it is not necessary to examine all documents to perform a search. One way to do this is to build an index that provides a mapping from words to the documents that contain them. Then, we can build the index once, store it in a sorted binary tree, and use it to perform all the searches. Once the index is built, the work required to perform one search is just the time it takes to look up the target word in the index. If the index is stored as a sorted binary tree, this is logarithmic in the number of distinct words.

Strings. We use the built-in String datatype to represent documents and target words. A String is similar to a List, but specialized for representing sequences of characters. A convenient way to make a String it to just use double quotes around a sequence of characters. For example, "abcd" evaluates to a String containing four characters.

The String datatype provides procedures for matching, ordering, and converting between Strings and Lists of characters:

string=?: String × String → Boolean
Outputs true if the input Strings have exactly the same sequence of characters, otherwise false.

string<?: String × String → Boolean
Outputs true if the first input String is lexicographically before the second input String, otherwise false.

string->list: String → List
Outputs a List containing the characters in the input String.

list->string: List → String
Outputs a String containing the characters in the input List.

One advantage of using Strings instead of Lists of characters is the built-in procedures for comparing Strings; we could write similar procedures for Lists of characters, but lexicographic ordering is somewhat tricky to get right, so it is better to use the built-in procedures.

Building the index. The entries in the index are Pairs of a word represented as a string, and a list of locations where that word appears. Each location is a Pair consisting of a document identifier (for web documents, this is the Uniform Resource Locator (URL) that is the address of the web page represented as a string) and a Number identifying the position within the document where the word appears (we label positions as the number of characters in the document before this location).

To build the index, we split each document into words and record the position of each word in the document. The first step is to define a procedure that takes as input a string representing an entire document, and produces a list of (*word . position*) pairs containing one element for each word in the document. We define a word as a sequence of alphabetic characters; non-alphabetic characters including spaces, numbers, and punctuation marks separate words and are not included in the index.

The *text-to-word-positions* procedure takes a string as input and outputs a list of word-position pairs corresponding to each word in the input. The inner procedure, *text-to-word-positions-iter*, takes three inputs: a list of the characters in the document, a list of the characters in the current word, and a number representing the position in the string where the current word starts; it outputs the list of (*word . position*) pairs. The value passed in as *w* can be *null*, meaning there is no current word. Otherwise, it is a list of the characters in the current word. A word starts when the first alphabetic character is found, and continues until either the first non-alphabetic character or the end of the document. We use the built-in *char-downcase* procedure to convert all letters to their lowercase form, so KING, King, and king all correspond to the same word.

```
(define (text-to-word-positions s)
  (define (text-to-word-positions-iter p w pos)
    (if (null? p)
       (if (null? w) null (list (cons (list->string w) pos)))
       (if (not (char-alphabetic? (car p))) ; finished word
          (if (null? w) ; no current word
             (text-to-word-positions-iter (cdr p) null (+ pos 1))
             (cons (cons (list->string w) pos)
                   (text-to-word-positions-iter (cdr p) null
                    (+ pos (list-length w) 1))))
          (text-to-word-positions-iter (cdr p)
           (list-append w (list (char-downcase (car p))))
           pos))))
  (text-to-word-positions-iter (string->list s) null 0))
```

The next step is to build an index from the list of word-position pairs. To enable fast searching, we store the index in a binary tree sorted by the target word. The *insert-into-index* procedure takes as input an index and a word-position pair and outputs an index consisting of the input index with the input word-position pair added.

The index is represented as a sorted binary tree where each element is a pair of a word and a list of the positions where that word appears. Each word should appear in the tree only once, so if the word-position pair to be added corresponds to a word that is already in the index, the position is added to the corresponding list of positions. Otherwise, a new entry is added to the index for the word with a list of positions containing the position as its only element.

```
(define (insert-into-index index wp)
  (if (null? index)
     (make-tree null (cons (car wp) (list (cdr wp))) null)
     (if (string=? (car wp) (car (tree-element index)))
        (make-tree (tree-left index)
                   (cons (car (tree-element index))
                         (list-append (cdr (tree-element index))
                                      (list (cdr wp))))
                   (tree-right index))
        (if (string<? (car wp) (car (tree-element index)))
           (make-tree (insert-into-index (tree-left index) wp)
                      (tree-element index)
                      (tree-right index))
           (make-tree (tree-left index)
                      (tree-element index)
                      (insert-into-index (tree-right index) wp))))))
```

To insert all the (*word* . *position*) pairs in a list into the index, we use *insert-into-index* to add each pair, passing the resulting index into the next recursive call:

```
(define (insert-all-wps index wps)
  (if (null? wps) index
     (insert-all-wps (insert-into-index index (car wps)) (cdr wps))))
```

To add all the words in a document to the index we use *text-to-word-positions* to obtain the list of word-position pairs. Since we want to include the document identity in the positions, we use *list-map* to add the *url* (a string that identifies the document location) to the position of each word. Then, we use *insert-all-wps* to add all the word-position pairs in this document to the index. The *index-document* procedure takes a document identifier and its text as a string, and produces an index of all words in the document.

```
(define (index-document url text)
  (insert-all-wps
   null
   (list-map (lambda (wp) (cons (car wp) (cons url (cdr wp))))
             (text-to-word-positions text))))
```

We leave analyzing the running time of *index-document* as an exercise. The important point, though, is that it only has to be done once for a given set of documents. Once the index is built, we can use it to answer any number of search queries without needing to reconstruct the index.

Merging indexes. Our goal is to produce an index for a set of documents, not just a single document. So, we need a way to take two indexes produced by *index-document* and combine them into a single index. We use this repeatedly to create an index of any number of documents. To merge two indexes, we combine their word occurrences. If a word occurs in both documents, the word should appear in the merged index with a position list that includes all the positions in both indexes. If the word occurs in only one of the documents, that word and its position list should be included in the merged index.

```
(define (merge-indexes d1 d2)
  (define (merge-elements p1 p2)
    (if (null? p1) p2
        (if (null? p2) p1
            (if (string=? (car (car p1)) (car (car p2)))
                (cons (cons (car (car p1))
                            (list-append (cdr (car p1)) (cdr (car p2))))
                      (merge-elements (cdr p1) (cdr p2)))
                (if (string<? (car (car p1)) (car (car p2)))
                    (cons (car p1) (merge-elements (cdr p1) p2))
                    (cons (car p2) (merge-elements p1 (cdr p2))))))))
  (list-to-sorted-tree
   (lambda (e1 e2) (string<? (car e1) (car e2)))
   (merge-elements (tree-extract-elements d1)
                   (tree-extract-elements d2))))
```

To merge the indexes, we first use *tree-extract-elements* to convert the tree representations to lists. The inner *merge-elements* procedure takes the two lists of word-position pairs and outputs a single list.

Since the lists are sorted by the target word, we can perform the merge efficiently. If the first words in both lists are the same, we produce a word-position pair that appends the position lists for the two entries. If they are different, we use *string<?* to determine which of the words belongs first, and include that element in the merged list. This way, the two lists are kept synchronized, so there is no need to search the lists to see if the same word appears in both lists.

Obtaining documents. To build a useful index for searching, we need some documents to index. The web provides a useful collection of freely available documents. To read documents from the web, we use library procedures provided by DrRacket.

This expression loads the libraries for managing URLs and getting files from the network: (*require* (*lib* "url.ss" "net")). One procedure this library defines is *string->url*, which takes a string as input and produces a representation of that string as a URL. A Uniform Resource Locator (URL) is a standard way to identify a document on the network. The address bar in most web browsers displays the URL of the current web page.

The full grammar for URLs is quite complex (see Exercise 2.14), but we will use simple web page addresses of the form:[2]

URL	::⇒	**http://** *Domain OptPath*
Domain	::⇒	*Name SubDomains*
SubDomains	::⇒	**.** *Domain*
SubDomains	::⇒	ϵ
OptPath	::⇒	Path
OptPath	::⇒	ϵ
Path	::⇒	**/** *Name OptPath*

An example of a URL is http://www.whitehouse.gov/index.html. The http indicates the HyperText Transfer Protocol, which prescribes how the web client (browser) and server communicate with each other. The domain name is www.whitehouse.gov, and the path name is /index.html (which is the default page for most web servers).

The library also defines the *get-pure-port* procedure that takes as input a URL and produces a port for reading the document at that location. The *read-char* procedure takes as input a port, and outputs the first character in that port. It also has a side effect: it advances the port to the next character. We can use *read-char* repeatedly to read each character in the web page of the port. When the end of the file is reached, the next application of *read-char* outputs a special marker representing the end of the file. The procedure *eof-object?* evaluates to true when applied to this marker, and false for all other inputs.

The *read-all-chars* procedure takes a port as its input, and produces a list containing all the characters in the document associated with the port:

```
(define (read-all-chars port)
  (let ((c (read-char port)))
    (if (eof-object? c) null
       (cons c (read-all-chars port)))))
```

Using these procedures, we define *web-get*, a procedure that takes as input a string that represents the URL of some web page, and outputs a string representing the contents of that page.

```
(define (web-get url)
  (list->string (read-all-chars (get-pure-port (string->url url)))))
```

[2]We use *Name* to represent sequences of characters in the domain and path names, although the actual rules for valid names for each of these are different.

To make it easy to build an index of a set of web pages, we define the *index-pages* procedure that takes as input a list of web pages and outputs an index of the words in those pages. It recurses through the list of pages, indexing each document, and merging that index with the result of indexing the rest of the pages in the list.

```
(define (index-pages p)
  (if (null? p) null
     (merge-indexes (index-document (car p) (web-get (car p)))
                    (index-pages (cdr p)))))
```

We can use this to create an index of any set of web pages. For example, here we use Jeremy Hylton's collection of the complete works of William Shakespeare (http://shakespeare.mit.edu) to define *shakespeare-index* as an index of the words used in all of Shakespeare's plays.

```
(define shakespeare-index
  (index-pages
   (list-map
    (lambda (play)
     (string-append "http://shakespeare.mit.edu/" play "/full.html"))
     ;; List of plays following the site's naming conventions.
    (list "allswell" "asyoulikeit" "comedy_errors" "cymbeline" "lll"
     "measure" "merry_wives" "merchant" "midsummer" "much_ado"
     "pericles" "taming_shrew" "tempest" "troilus_cressida" "twelfth_night"
     "two_gentlemen" "winters_tale" "1henryiv" "2henryiv" "henryv"
     "1henryvi" "2henryvi" "3henryvi" "henryviii" "john" "richardii"
     "richardiii" "cleopatra" "coriolanus" "hamlet" "julius_caesar" "lear"
     "macbeth" "othello" "romeo_juliet" "timon" "titus"))))
```

Building the index takes about two and a half hours on my laptop. It contains 22949 distinct words and over 1.6 million word occurrences. Much of the time spent building the index is in constructing new lists and trees for every change, which can be avoided by using the mutable data types we cover in the next chapter. The key idea, though, is that the index only needs to be built once. Once the documents have been indexed, we can use the index to quickly perform any search.

Searching. Using an index, searching for pages that use a given word is easy and efficient. Since the index is a sorted binary tree, we use *binary-tree-search* to search for a word in the index:

```
(define (search-in-index index word)
  (binary-tree-search
   (lambda (el) (string=? word (car el))) ; first element of (word . position)
   (lambda (el) (string<? word (car el)))
   index))
```

As analyzed in the previous section, the expected running time of *binary-tree-search* is in $\Theta(\log n)$ where n is the number of nodes in the input tree.[3] The body of *search-in-index* applies *binary-tree-search* to the index. The number of nodes in the index is the number of distinct words in the indexed documents.

[3]Because of the way *merge-indexes* is defined, we do not actually get this expected running time. See Exercise 8.17.

So, the running time of *search-in-index* scales logarithmically with the number of distinct words in the indexed documents. Note that the number and size of the documents does not matter! This is why a search engine such as Google can respond to a query quickly even though its index contains many billions of documents.

One issue we should be concerned with is the running time of the procedures passed into *binary-tree-search*. Our analysis of *binary-tree-search* assumes the equality and comparison functions are constant time procedures. Here, the procedures as *string=?* and *string<?*, which both have worst case running times that are linear in the length of the input string. As used here, one of the inputs is the target word. So, the amount of work for each *binary-tree-search* recursive call is in $\Theta(w)$ where w is the length of *word*. Thus, the overall running time of *search-in-index* is in $\Theta(w \log d)$ where w is the length of *word* and d is the number of words in the *index*. If we assume all words are of some maximum length, though, the w term disappears as a constant factor (that is, we are assuming $w < C$ for some constant C. Thus, the overall running time is in $\Theta(\log d)$.

Here are some examples:

```
> (search-in-index shakespeare-index "mathematics")
("mathematics"
 ("http://shakespeare.mit.edu/taming_shrew/full.html" . 26917)
 ("http://shakespeare.mit.edu/taming_shrew/full.html" . 75069)
 ("http://shakespeare.mit.edu/taming_shrew/full.html" . 77341))
> (search-in-index shakespeare-index "procedure")
false
```

The mathematics and the metaphysics, Fall to them as you find your stomach serves you; No profit grows where is no pleasure ta'en: In brief, sir, study what you most affect.
William Shakespeare, *The Taming of the Shrew*

Our *search-in-index* and *index-pages* procedures form the beginnings of a search engine service. A useful web search engine needs at least two more capabilities: a way to automate the process of finding documents to index, and a way to rank the documents that contain the target word by the likelihood they are useful. The exploration at the end of this section addresses these capabilities.

Histogram. We can also use our index to analyze Shakespeare's writing. The *index-histogram* procedure produces a list of the words in an index sorted by how frequently they appear:

```
(define (index-histogram index)
  (list-quicksort
   (lambda (e1 e2) (> (cdr e1) (cdr e2)))
   (list-map (lambda (el) (cons (car el) (length (cdr el))))
             (tree-extract-elements index))))
```

The expression,

```
(list-filter (lambda (entry) (> string-length (car entry) 5))
             (index-histogram shakespeare-index))
```

evaluates to a list of Shakespeare's favorite 6-letter and longer words along with the number of times they appear in the corpus (the first two entries are from their use in the page formatting):

```
(("blockquote" . 63345) ("speech" . 31099)
 ("should" . 1557) ("father" . 1086) ("exeunt" . 1061)
 ("master" . 861) ("before" . 826) ("mistress" . 787)
 ... ("brother" . 623)
 ... ("daughter" . 452)
 ... ("mother" . 418)
 ... ("mustardseed" . 13)
 ... ("excrement" . 5)
 ... ("zwaggered" . 1))
```

Exercise 8.14. Define a procedure for finding the longest word in a document. Analyze the running time of your procedure.

Exercise 8.15. Produce a list of the words in Shakespeare's plays sorted by their length.

Exercise 8.16. [★] Analyze the running time required to build the index.

a. Analyze the running time of the *text-to-word-positions* procedure. Use n to represent the number of characters in the input string, and w to represent the number of distinct words. Be careful to clearly state all assumptions on which your analysis relies.

b. Analyze the running time of the *insert-into-index* procedure.

c. Analyze the running time of the *index-document* procedure.

d. Analyze the running time of the *merge-indexes* procedure.

e. Analyze the overall running time of the *index-pages* procedure. Your result should describe how the running time is impacted by the number of documents to index, the size of each document, and the number of distinct words.

Exercise 8.17. [★] The *search-in-index* procedure does not actually have the expected running time in $\Theta(\log w)$ (where w is the number of distinct words in the index) for the Shakespeare index because of the way it is built using *merge-indexes*. The problem has to do with the running time of the binary tree on pathological inputs. Explain why the input to *list-to-sorted-tree* in the *merge-indexes* procedure leads to a binary tree where the running time for searching is in $\Theta(w)$. Modify the *merge-indexes* definition to avoid this problem and ensure that searches on the resulting index run in $\Theta(\log w)$.

Exercise 8.18. [★★] The site http://www.speechwars.com provides an interesting way to view political speeches by looking at how the frequency of the use of different words changes over time. Use the *index-histogram* procedure to build a historical histogram program that takes as input a list of indexes ordered by time, and a target word, and output a list showing the number of occurrences of the target word in each of the indexes. You could use your program to analyze how Shakespeare's word use is different in tragedies and comedies or to compare Shakespeare's vocabulary to Jefferson's.

Exploration 8.1: Searching the Web

In addition to fast indexed search, web search engines have to solve two problems: (1) find documents to index, and (2) identify the most important documents that contain a particular search term.

For our Shakespeare index example, we manually found a list of interesting documents to index. This approach does not scale well to indexing the World Wide Web where there are trillions of documents and new ones are created all the time. For this, we need a *web crawler*.

web crawler

A web crawler finds documents on the web. Typical web crawlers start with a set of seed URLs, and then find more documents to index by following the links on those pages. This proceeds recursively: the links on each newly discovered page are added to the set of URLs for the crawler to index. To develop a web crawler, we need a way to extract the links on a given web page, and to manage the set of pages to index.

a. [★] Define a procedure *extract-links* that takes as input a string representing the text of a web page and outputs a list of all the pages linked to from this page. Linked pages can be found by searching for anchor tags on the web page. An anchor tag has the form:[4] <a href=target>. (The *text-to-word-positions* procedure may be a helpful starting point for defining *extract-links*.)

b. Define a procedure *crawl-page* that takes as input an index and a string representing a URL. As output, it produces a pair consisting of an index (that is the result of adding all words from the page at the input URL to the input index) and a list of URLs representing all pages linked to by the crawled page.

c. [★★] Define a procedure *crawl-web* that takes as input a list of seed URLs and a Number indicating the maximum depth of the crawl. It should output an index of all the words on the web pages at the locations given by the seed URLs and any page that can be reached from these seed URLs by following no more than the maximum depth number of links.

For a web search engine to be useful, we don't want to just get a list of all the pages that contain some target word, we want the list to be sorted according to which of those pages are most likely to be interesting. Selecting the best pages for a given query is a challenging and important problem, and the ability to do this well is one of the main things that distinguishes web search engines. Many factors are used to rank pages including an analysis of the text on the page itself, whether the target word is part of a title, and how recently the page was updated.

The rank assigned to a document is calculated from the ranks of documents citing it. In addition, the rank of a document is calculated from a constant representing the probability that a browser through the database will randomly jump to the document. The method is particularly useful in enhancing the performance of search engine results for hypermedia databases, such as the world wide web, whose documents have a large variation in quality. United States Patent #6,285,999, September 2001. (Inventor: Lawrence Page, Assignee: Stanford University)

The best ways of ranking pages also consider the pages that link to the ranked page. If many pages link to a given page, it is more likely that the given page is useful. This property can also be defined recursively: a page is highly ranked if there are many highly-ranked pages that link to it.

The ranking system used by Google is based on this formula:

$$R(u) = \sum_{v \in L_u} \frac{R(v)}{L(v)}$$

[4]Not all links match this structure exactly, so this may miss some of the links on a page.

where L_u is the set of web pages that contain links to the target page u and $L(v)$ is the number of links on the page v (thus, the value of a link from a page containing many links is less than the value of a link from a page containing only a few links). The value $R(u)$ gives a measure of the ranking of the page identified by u, where higher values indicate more valuable pages.

The problem with this formula is that is is circular: there is no base case, and no way to order the web pages to compute the correct rank of each page in turn, since the rank of each page depends on the rank of the pages that link to it.

relaxation One way to approximate equations like this one is to use *relaxation*. Relaxation obtains an approximate solution to some systems of equations by repeatedly evaluating the equations. To estimate the page ranks for a set of web pages, we initially assume every page has rank 1 and evaluate $R(u)$ for all the pages (using the value of 1 as the rank for every other page). Then, re-evaluate the $R(u)$ values using the resulting ranks. A relaxation keeps repeating until the values change by less than some threshold amount, but there is no guarantee how quickly this will happen. For the page ranking evaluation, it may be enough to decide on some fixed number of iterations.

d. [★★] Define a procedure, *web-link-graph*, that takes as input a set of URLs and produces as output a graph of the linking structure of those documents. The linking structure can be represented as a List where each element of the List is a pair of a URL and a list of all the URLs that include a link to that URL. The *extract-links* procedure from the previous exploration will be useful for determining the link targets of a given URL.

e. [★] Define a procedure that takes as input the output of *web-link-graph* and outputs a preliminary ranking of each page that measures the number of other pages that link to that page.

f. [★★] Refine your page ranking procedure to weight links from highly-ranked pages more heavily in a page's rank by using a algorithm.

g. [★★★★] Come up with a cool name, set up your search engine as a web service, and attract more than 0.001% of all web searches to your site.

8.3 Summary

The focus of Part II has been on predicting properties of procedures, in particular how their running time scales with the size of their input. This involved many encounters with the three powerful ideas introduced in Section 1.4: recursive definitions, universality, and abstraction. The simple Turing Machine model is a useful abstraction for modeling nearly all conceivable computing machines, and the few simple operations it defines are enough for a universal computer. Actual machines use the digital abstraction to allow a continuous range of voltages to represent just two values. The asymptotic operators used to describe running times are also a kind of abstraction—they allow us to represent the set of infinitely many different functions with a compact notation.

In Part III, we will see many more recursive definitions, and extend the notion of recursive definitions to the language interpreter itself. We change the language evaluation rules themselves, and see how different evaluation rules enable different ways of expressing computations.

Mutation

Faced with the choice between changing one's mind and proving that there is no need to do so, almost everyone gets busy on the proof.
John Kenneth Galbraith

The subset of Scheme we have used until this chapter provides no means to change the value associated with a name. This enabled very simple evaluation rules for names, as well as allowing the substitution model of evaluation. Since the value associated with a name was always the value it was defined as, no complex evaluation rules are needed to determine the value associated with a name.

This chapter introduces special forms known as *mutators* that allow programs to change the value in a given place. Introducing mutation does not change the computations we can express—every computation that can be expressed using mutation could also be expressed using the only purely functional subset of Scheme from Chapter 3. It does, however, make it possible to express certain computations more efficiently and clearly than could be done without it. Adding mutation is not free, however; reasoning about the value of expressions becomes much more complex.

mutators

9.1 Assignment

The **set!** (pronounced "set-bang!") special form associates a new value with an already defined name. The exclamation point at the end of **set!** follows a naming convention to indicate that an operation may mutate state. A set expression is also known as an *assignment*. It *assigns* a value to a variable.

assignment

The grammar rule for assignment is:

Expression ::⇒ *Assignment*
Assignment ::⇒ (**set!** *Name Expression*)

The evaluation rule for an assignment is:

Evaluation Rule 7: Assignment. To evaluate an assignment, evaluate the expression, and replace the value associated with the name with the value of the expression. An assignment has no value.

Assignments do not produce output values, but are used for their side effects. They change the value of some state (namely, the value associated with the name in the set expression), but do not produce an output.

Here is an example use of **set!**:

```
> (define num 200)
> num
200
> (set! num 150)
> (set! num 1120)
> num
1120
```

Begin expression. Since assignments do not evaluate to a value, they are often used inside a begin expression. A begin expression is a special form that evaluates a sequence of expressions in order and evaluates to the value of the last expression.

The grammar rule for the begin expression is:

Expression ::⇒ *BeginExpression*
BeginExpression ::⇒ (**begin** *MoreExpressions Expression*)

The evaluation rule is:

Evaluation Rule 8: Begin. To evaluate a begin expression,

(**begin** $Expression_1$ $Expression_2$ ... $Expression_k$)

evaluate each subexpression in order from left to right. The value of the begin expression is the value of the last subexpression, $Expression_k$.

The values of all the subexpressions except the last one are ignored; these subexpressions are only evaluated for their side effects.

The begin expression must be a special form. It is not possible to define a procedure that behaves identically to a begin expression since the application rule does not specify the order in which the operand subexpressions are evaluated.

The definition syntax for procedures includes a hidden begin expression.

(**define** (*Name Parameters*) *MoreExpressions Expression*)

is an abbreviation for:

(**define** *Name*
  (**lambda** (*Parameters*) (**begin** *MoreExpressions Expression*)))

The let expression introduced in Section 8.1.1 also includes a hidden begin expression.

(**let** (($Name_1$ $Expression_1$) ($Name_2$ $Expression_2$)
    ··· ($Name_k$ $Expression_k$))
  MoreExpressions Expression)

is equivalent to the application expression:

((**lambda** ($Name_1$ $Name_2$ ... $Name_k$)
   (**begin** *MoreExpressions Expression*))
 $Expression_1$ $Expression_2$ ... $Expression_k$)

9.2 Impact of Mutation

Introducing assignment presents many complications for our programming model. It invalidates the substitution model of evaluation introduced in Section 3.6.2 and found satisfactory until this point. All the procedures we can define without using mutation behave almost like mathematical functions—every time they are applied to the same inputs they produce the same output.[1] Assignments allow us to define non-functional procedures that produce different results for different applications even with the same inputs.

Example 9.1: Counter

Consider the *update-counter!* procedure:

```
(define (update-counter!)
  (set! counter (+ counter 1))
  counter)
```

To use *update-counter!*, we must first define the *counter* variable it uses:

```
(define counter 0)
```

Every time (*update-counter!*) is evaluated the value associated with the name *counter* is increased by one and the result is the new value of counter. Because of the hidden begin expression in the definition, the (**set!** *counter* (+ *counter* 1)) is always evaluated first, followed by *counter* which is the last expression in the begin expression so its value is the value of the procedure. Thus, the value of (*update-counter!*) is 1 the first time it is evaluated, 2 the second time, and so on.

The substitution model of evaluation doesn't make any sense for this evaluation: the value of *counter* changes during the course of the evaluation. Even though (*update-counter!*) is the same expression, every time it is evaluated it evaluates to a different value.

Mutation also means some expressions have undetermined values. Consider evaluating the expression (+ *counter* (*update-counter!*)). The evaluation rule for the application expression does not specify the order in which the operand subexpressions are evaluated. But, the value of the name expression *counter* depends on whether it is evaluated before or after the application of *update-counter!* is evaluated!

The meaning of the expression is ambiguous since it depends on the order in which the subexpressions are evaluated. If the second subexpression, *counter*, is evaluated before the third subexpression, (*update-counter!*), the value of the expression is 1 the first time it is evaluated, and 3 the second time it is evaluated. Alternately, but still following the evaluation rules correctly, the third subexpression could be evaluated before the second subexpression. With this ordering, the value of the expression is 2 the first time it is evaluated, and 4 the second time it is evaluated.

[1] Observant readers should notice that we have already used a few procedures that are not functions including the printing procedures from Section 4.5.1, and *random* and *read-char* from the previous chapter.

9.2.1 Names, Places, Frames, and Environments

Because assignments can change the value associated with a name, the order in which expressions are evaluated now matters. As a result, we need to revisit several of our other evaluation rules and change the way we think about processes.

place

Since the value associated with a name can now change, instead of associating a value directly with a name we use a name as a way to identify a *place*. A place has a name and holds the value associated with that name. With mutation, we can change the value in a place; this changes the value associated with the place's name. A *frame* is a collection of places.

frame

environment

An *environment* is a pair consisting of a frame and a pointer to a parent environment. A special environment known as the *global environment* has no parent environment. The global environment exists when the interpreter starts, and is maintained for the lifetime of the interpreter. Initially, the global environment contains the built-in procedures. Names defined in the interactions buffer are placed in the global environment. Other environments are created and destroyed as a program is evaluated. Figure 9.1 shows some example environments, frames, and places.

Every environment has a parent environment except for the global environment. All other environments descend from the global environment. Hence, if we start with any environment, and continue to follow its parent pointers we always eventually reach the global environment.

The key change to our evaluation model is that whereas before we could evaluate expressions without any notion of *where* they are evaluated, once we introduce mutation, we need to consider the environment in which an expression is evaluated. An environment captures the current state of the interpreter. The value of an expression depends on both the expression itself, and on the environment in which it is evaluated.

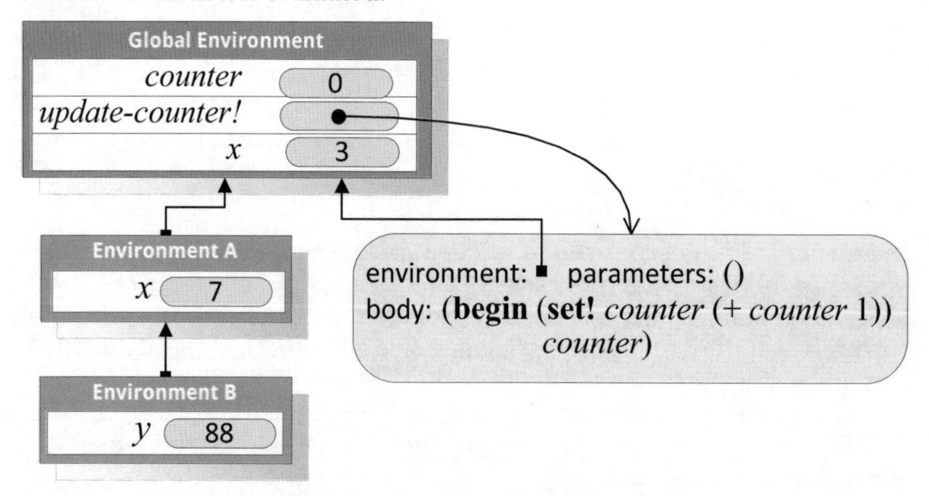

Figure 9.1. Sample environments.

The global environment contains a frame with three names. Each name has an associated place that contains the value associated with that name. The value associated with *counter* is the currently 0. The value associated with *set-counter!* is the procedure we defined in Example 9.1. A procedure is characterized by its parameters, body code, and a pointer to the environment in which it will be evaluated.

9.2.2 Evaluation Rules with State

Introducing mutation requires us to revise the evaluation rule for names, the definition rule, and the application rule for constructed procedures. All of these rules must be adapted to be more precise about how values are associated with names by using places and environments.

Names. The new evaluation rule for a name expression is:

> **Stateful Evaluation Rule 2: Names.** To evaluate a name expression, search the evaluation environment's frame for a place with a name that matches the name in the expression. If such a place exists, the value of the name expression is the value in that place. Otherwise, the value of the name expression is the result of evaluating the name expression in the parent environment. If the evaluation environment has no parent, the name is not defined and the name expression evaluates to an error.

For example, to evaluate the value of the name expression *x* in Environment B in Figure 9.1, we first look in the frame of Environment B for a place named *x*. Since there is no place named *x* in that frame, we follow the parent pointer to Environment A, and evaluate the value of the name expression in Environment A. Environment A's frame contains a place named *x* that contains the value 7, so the value of evaluating *x* in Environment B is 7.

The value of the same expression in the Global Environment is 3 since that is the value in the place named *x* in the Global Environment's frame.

To evaluate the value of *y* in Environment A, we first look in the frame in Environment A for a place named *y*. Since no *y* place exists, evaluation continues by evaluating the expression in the parent environment, which is the Global Environment. The Global Environments frame does not contain a place named *y*, and the global environment has no parent, so the name is undefined and the evaluation results in an error.

Definition. The revised evaluation rule for a definition is:

> **Stateful Definition Rule.** A definition creates a new place with the definition's name in the frame associated with the evaluation environment. The value in the place is value of the definition's expression. If there is already a place with the name in the current frame, the definition replaces the old place with a new place and value.

The rule for redefinitions means we could use **define** in some situations to mean something similar to **set!**. The meaning is different, though, since an assignment finds the place associated with the name and puts a new value in that place. Evaluating an assignment follows the Stateful Evaluation Rule 2 to find the place associated with a name. Hence, (**define** *Name Expression*) has a different meaning from (**set!** *Name Expression*) when there is no place named *Name* in the current execution environment. To avoid this confusion, only use **define** for the first definition of a name and always use **set!** when the intent is to change the value associated with a name.

Application. The final rule that must change because of mutation is the application rule for constructed procedures. Instead of using substitution, the new application rule creates a new environment with a frame containing places named for the parameters.

> **Stateful Application Rule 2: Constructed Procedures.** To apply a constructed procedure:
>
> 1. Construct a new environment, whose parent is the environment of the applied procedure.
> 2. For each procedure parameter, create a place in the frame of the new environment with the name of the parameter. Evaluate each operand expression in the environment or the application and initialize the value in each place to the value of the corresponding operand expression.
> 3. Evaluate the body of the procedure in the newly created environment. The resulting value is the value of the application.

Consider evaluating the application expression (*bigger* 3 4) where *bigger* is the procedure from Example 3.3: (**define** (*bigger a b*) (**if** (> *a b*) *a b*))).

Evaluating an application of *bigger* involves following the Stateful Application Rule 2. First, create a new environment. Since *bigger* was defined in the global environment, its environment pointer points to the global environment. Hence, the parent environment for the new environment is the global environment.

Next, create places in the new environment's frame named for the procedure parameters, *a* and *b*. The value in the place associated with *a* is 3, the value of the first operand expression. The value in the place associated with *b* is 4.

The final step is to evaluate the body expression, (**if** (> *a b*) *a b*), in the newly created environment. Figure 9.2 shows the environment where the body expression is evaluated. The values of *a* and *b* are found in the application environment.

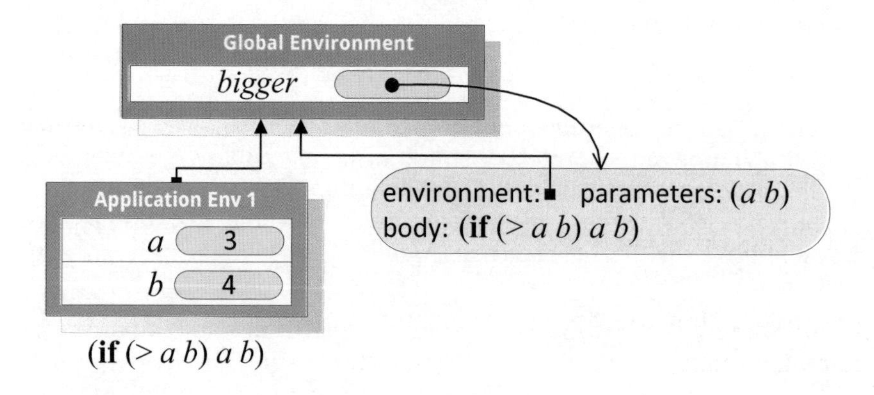

Figure 9.2. Environment created to evaluate (*bigger* 3 4).

The new application rule becomes more interesting when we consider procedures that create new procedures. For example, *make-adder* takes a number as input and produces as output a procedure:

(**define** (*make-adder v*) (**lambda** (*n*) (+ *n v*)))

The environment that results from evaluating (**define** *inc* (*make-adder* 1)) is shown in Figure 9.3. The name *inc* has a value that is the procedure resulting from the application of (*make-adder* 1). To evaluate the application, we follow the application rule above and create a new environment containing a frame with the parameter name, *inc*, and its associated operand value, 1.

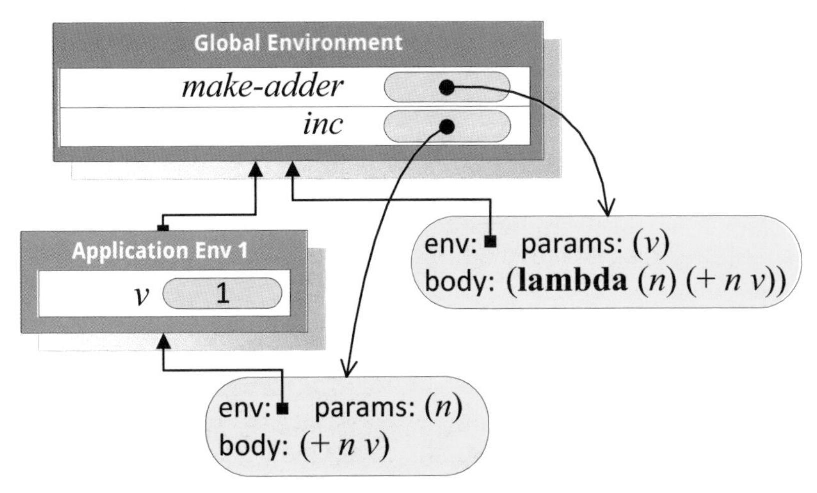

Figure 9.3. Environment after evaluating (define *inc* (*make-adder* 1)).

The result of the application is the value of evaluating its body in this new environment. Since the body is a lambda expression, it evaluates to a procedure. That procedure was created in the execution environment that was created to evaluate the application of *make-adder*, hence, its environment pointer points to the application environment which contains a place named *inc* holding the value 1.

Next, consider evaluating (*inc* 149). Figure 9.4 illustrates the environment for evaluating the body of the *inc* procedure. The evaluation creates a new environment with a frame containing the place n and its associated value 149. We evaluate the body of the procedure, $(+\ n\ v)$, in that environment. The value of n is found in the execution environment. The value of v is not found there, so evaluation continues by looking in the parent environment. It contains a place v containing the value 1.

Exercise 9.1. Devise a Scheme expression that could have four possible values, depending on the order in which application subexpressions are evaluated.

Exercise 9.2. Draw the environment that results after evaluating:

```
> (define alpha 0)
> (define beta 1)
> (define update-beta! (lambda () (set! beta (+ alpha 1)))
> (set! alpha 3)
> (update-beta!)
> (set! alpha 4)
```

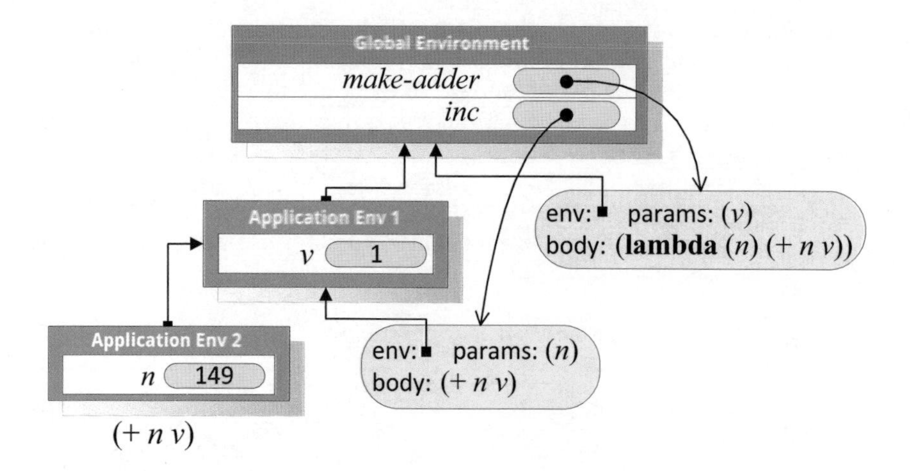

Figure 9.4. Environment for evaluating the body of (*inc* 149).

Exercise 9.3. Draw the environment that results after evaluating the following expressions, and explain what the value of the final expression is. (Hint: first, rewrite the let expression as an application.)

> (**define** (*make-applier proc*) (**lambda** (*x*) (*proc x*)))
> (**define** *p* (*make-applier* (**lambda** (*x*) (**let** ((*x* 2)) *x*))))
> (*p* 4)

9.3 Mutable Pairs and Lists

immutable The Pair datatype introduced in Chapter 5 is *immutable*. This means that once a Pair is created, the values in its cells cannot be changed.[2]

The MutablePair datatype is a mutable pair. A MutablePair is constructed using *mcons*, which is similar to *cons* but produces a MutablePair. The parts of a MutablePair can be extracted using the *mcar* and *mcdr* procedures, which behave analogously to the *car* and *cdr* procedures. A MutablePair is a distinct datatype from a Pair; it is an error to apply *car* to a MutablePair, or to apply *mcar* to an immutable Pair.

The MutablePair datatype also provides two procedures that change the values in the cells of a MutablePair:

set-mcar!: MutablePair $\times$ Value $\rightarrow$ Void
  Replaces the value in the first cell of the MutablePair with the value of the second input.

set-mcdr!: MutablePair $\times$ Value $\rightarrow$ Void
  Replaces the value in the second cell of the MutablePair with the value of the second input.

[2]The mutability of standard Pairs is quite a controversial issue. In most Scheme implementations and the standard definition of Scheme, a standard *cons* pair is mutable. But, as we will see later in the section, mutable pairs cause lots of problems. So, the designers of DrRacket decided for Version 4.0 to make the standard Pair datatype immutable and to provide a MutablePair datatype for use when mutation is needed.

The Void result type indicates that *set-mcar!* and *set-mcdr!* produce no output.

Here are some interactions using a MutablePair:

```
> (define pair (mcons 1 2))
> (set-mcar! pair 3)
> pair
(3 . 2)
> (set-mcdr! pair 4)
> pair
(3 . 4)
```

The *set-mcdr!* procedure allows us to create a pair where the second cell of the pair is itself: (*set-mcdr! pair pair*). This produces the rather frightening object shown in Figure 9.5. Every time we apply *mcdr* to *pair*, we get the same pair as

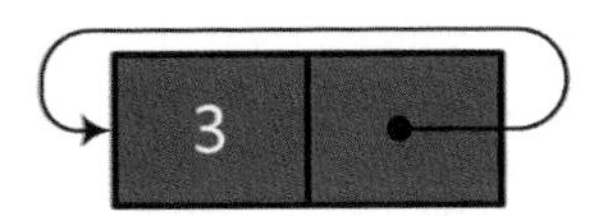

Figure 9.5. Mutable pair created by evaluating (*set-mcdr! pair pair*).

the output. Hence, the value of (*mcar* (*mcdr* (*mcdr* (*mcdr pair*)))) is 3.

We can also create objects that combine mutable and immutable Pairs. For example, (**define** *mstruct* (*cons* (*mcons* 1 2) 3)) defines *mstruct* as an immutable Pair containing a MutablePair in its first cell. Since the outer Pair is immutable, we cannot change the objects in its cells. Thus, the second cell of *mstruct* always contains the value 3. We can, however, change the values in the cells of the mutable pair in its first cell. For example, (*set-mcar!* (*car mstruct*) 7) replaces the value in the first cell of the MutablePair in the first cell of *mstruct*.

Mutable Lists. As we used immutable Pairs to build immutable Lists, we can use MutablePairs to construct MutableLists. A MutableList is either null or a MutablePair whose second cell contains a MutableList.

The MutableList type is defined by a library. To use it, evaluate the following expression: (*require racket/mpair*). All of the examples in this chapter assume this expression has been evaluated. This library defines the *mlist* procedure that is similar to the *list* procedure, but produces a MutableList instead of an immutable List. For example, (*mlist* 1 2 3) produces the structure shown in Figure 9.6. Each node in the list is a MutablePair, so we can use the *set-mcar!* and

Figure 9.6. MutableList created by evaluating (*mlist* 1 2 3).

set-mcdr! procedures to change the values in the cells.

```
> (define m1 (mlist 1 2 3))
> (set-mcar! (mcdr m1) 5)
> (set-mcar! (mcdr (mcdr m1)) 0)
> m1
{1 5 0} ; DrRacket denotes MutableLists using curly brackets.
```

Many of the list procedures from Chapter 5 can be directly translated to work on mutable lists. For example, we can define *mlist-length* as:

```
(define (mlist-length m)
  (if (null? m) 0 (+ 1 (mlist-length (mcdr m)))))
```

As shown in Exercise 9.4, though, we need to be careful when using *mcdr* to recurse through a MutableList since structures created with MutablePairs can include circular pointers.

Exercise 9.4. What is the value of (*mlist-length pair*) for the pair shown in Figure 9.5?

Exercise 9.5. [★] Define a *mpair-circular?* procedure that takes a MutablePair as its input and outputs true when the input contains a cycle and false otherwise.

9.4 Imperative Programming

imperative programming

Mutation enables a style of programming known as *imperative programming*. Whereas *functional programming* is concerned with defining procedures that can be composed to solve a problem, imperative programming is primarily concerned with modifying state in ways that lead to a state that provides a solution to a problem.

The main operation in function programming is application. A functional program applies a series of procedures, passing the outputs of one application as the inputs to the next procedure application. With imperative programming, the primary operation is assignment (performed by **set!**, *set-mcar!*, and *set-mcdr!* in Scheme; but typically by an assignment operator, often := or =, in languages designed for imperative programming such as Pascal, Algol60, Java, and Python).

The next subsection presents imperative-style versions of some of the procedures we have seen in previous chapters for manipulating lists. The following subsection introduces some imperative control structures.

9.4.1 List Mutators

All the procedures for changing the value of a list in Section 5.4.3 actually do not change any values; instead they construct new lists. When our goal is only to change some elements in an existing list, this wastes memory constructing a new list and may require more running time than a procedure that modifies the input list instead. Here, we revisit some of the procedures from Section 5.4.3, but instead of producing new lists with the desired property these procedures modify the input list.

Example 9.2: Mapping

The *list-map* procedure (from Example 5.4) produces a new list that is the result of applying the same procedure to every element in the input list.

```
(define (list-map f p)
  (if (null? p) null (cons (f (car p)) (list-map f (cdr p)))))
```

Whereas the functional *list-map* procedure uses *cons* to build up the output list, the imperative *mlist-map!* procedure uses *set-car!* to mutate the input list's elements:

```
(define (mlist-map! f p)
  (if (null? p) (void)
    (begin (set-mcar! p (f (mcar p)))
           (mlist-map! f (mcdr p)))))
```

The base case uses (*void*) to evaluate to no value. Unlike *list-map* which evaluates to a List, *mlist-map!* is evaluated for its side effects and produces no output.

Assuming the procedure passed as *f* has constant running time, the running time of the *mlist-map!* procedure is in $\Theta(n)$ where n is the number of elements in the input list. There will be n recursive applications of *mlist-map!* since each one passes in a list one element shorter than the input list, and each application requires constant time. This is asymptotically the same as the *list-map* procedure, but we would expect the actual running time to be faster since there is no need to construct a new list.

The memory consumed is asymptotically different. The *list-map* procedure allocates n new *cons* cells, so it requires memory in $\Theta(n)$ where n is the number of elements in the input list. The *mlist-map!* procedure is tail recursive (so no stack needs to be maintained) and does not allocate any new *cons* cells, so it requires constant memory.

Example 9.3: Filtering

The *list-filter* procedure takes as inputs a test procedure and a list and outputs a list containing the elements of the input list for which applying the test procedure evaluates to a true value. In Example 5.5, we defined *list-filter* as:

```
(define (list-filter test p)
  (if (null? p) null
    (if (test (car p)) (cons (car p) (list-filter test (cdr p)))
      (list-filter test (cdr p)))))
```

An imperative version of *list-filter* removes the unsatisfying elements from a mutable list. We define *mlist-filter!* using *set-mcdr!* to skip over elements that should not be included in the filtered list:

```
(define (mlist-filter! test p)
  (if (null? p) null
    (begin (set-mcdr! p (mlist-filter! test (mcdr p)))
           (if (test (mcar p)) p (mcdr p)))))
```

Assuming the test procedure has constant running time, the running time of the *mlist-filter!* procedure is linear in the length of the input list. As with *mlist-map!*, the space used by *mlist-filter!* is constant, which is better than the $\Theta(n)$ space used by *list-filter*.

Unlike *mlist-map!*, *mlist-filter!* outputs a value. This is needed when the first element is not in the list. Consider this example:

```
> (define a (mlist 1 2 3 1 4))
> (mlist-filter! (lambda (x) (> x 1)) a)
{2 3 4}
```

```
> a
{1 2 3 4}
```

The value of *a* still includes the initial 1. There is no way for the *mlist-filter!* procedure to remove the first element of the list: the *set-mcar!* and *set-mcdr!* procedures only enable us to change what the mutable pair's components contain.

To avoid this, *mlist-filter!* should be used with **set!** to assign the variable to the resulting mutable list:

```
(set! a (mlist-filter! (lambda (x) (> x 1)) a))
```

Example 9.4: Append

The *list-append* procedure takes as input two lists and produces a list consisting of the elements of the first list followed by the elements of the second list. An imperative version of this procedure instead mutates the first list to contain the elements of both lists.

```
(define (mlist-append! p q)
  (if (null? p) (error "Cannot append to an empty list")
    (if (null? (mcdr p)) (set-mcdr! p q)
      (mlist-append! (mcdr p) q))))
```

The *mlist-append!* procedure produces an error when the first input is *null* — this is necessary since if the input is *null* there is no pair to modify.[3]

Like *list-append*, the running time of the *mlist-append!* procedure is in $\Theta(n)$ where n is the number of elements in the first input list. The *list-append* procedure copies the first input list, so its memory use is in $\Theta(n)$ where n is the number of elements in the first input list. The memory use of *mlist-append!* is constant: it does not create any new cons cells to append the lists.

Aliasing. Adding mutation makes it possible to define many procedures more efficiently and compactly, but introduces many new potential pitfalls in producing reliable programs. Since our evaluation model now depends on the environment in which an expression is evaluated, it becomes much harder to reason about code by itself.

aliasing

One challenge introduced by mutation is *aliasing*. There may be different ways to refer to the same object. This was true before mutation also, but didn't matter since the value of an object never changed. Once object values can change, however, aliasing can lead to surprising behaviors.

For example,

```
> (define m1 (mlist 1 2 3))
> (define m2 (mlist 4 5 6))
> (mlist-append! m1 m2)
> (set! m1 (mlist-filter! (lambda (el) (= (modulo el 2) 0)) m1))
```

[3]The *mappend!* library procedure in DrRacket takes a different approach: when the first input is null it produces the value of the second list as output in this case. This has unexpected behavior when an expression like (*append! a b*) is evaluated where the value of *a* is *null* since the value of *a* is not modified.

The value of *m2* was defined as {4 5 6}, and no expressions since then explicitly modified *m2*. But, the value of *m2* has still changed! It changed because after evaluating (*mlist-append! m1 m2*) the *m1* object shares cells with *m2*. Thus, when the *mlist-filter!* application changes the value of *m1*, it also changes the value of *m2* to {4 6}.

The built-in procedure *eq?* takes as input any two objects and outputs a Boolean. The result is true if and only if the inputs are the same object. For example, (*eq?* 3 3) evaluates to true but (*eq?* (*mcons* 1 2) (*mcons* 1 2)) evaluates to false. Even though the input pairs have the same value, they are different objects—mutating one of the pairs does not effect the value of the other pair.

For the earlier *mlist-append!* example, (*eq? m1 m2*) evaluates to false since *m1* and *m2* do not refer to the same object. But, (*eq?* (*mcdr m1*) *m2*) evaluates to true since the second cell of *m1* points to the same object as *m2*. Evaluating (*set-mcar! m2* 3) changes the value of both *m1* and *m2* since the modified cell is common to both structures.

Exercise 9.6. Define an imperative-style procedure, *mlist-inc!* that takes as input a MutableList of Numbers and modifies the list by adding one to the value of each element in the list.

Exercise 9.7. [★] Define a procedure *mlist-truncate!* that takes as input a MutableList and modifies the list by removing the last element in the list. Specify carefully the requirements for the input list to your procedure.

Exercise 9.8. [★] Define a procedure *mlist-make-circular!* that takes as input a MutableList and modifies the list to be a circular list containing all the elements in the original list. For example, (*mlist-make-circular!* (*mlist* 3)) should produce the same structure as the circular pair shown in Figure 9.5.

If you steal property, you must report its fair market value in your income in the year you steal it unless in the same year, you return it to its rightful owner.
Your Federal Income Tax, IRS Publication 17, 2009.

Exercise 9.9. [★] Define an imperative-style procedure, *mlist-reverse!*, that reverses the elements of a list. Is it possible to implement a *mlist-reverse!* procedure that is asymptotically faster than the *list-reverse* procedure from Example 5.4?

Exercise 9.10. [★★] Define a procedure *mlist-aliases?* that takes as input two mutable lists and outputs true if and only if there are any mcons cells shared between the two lists.

9.4.2 Imperative Control Structures

The imperative style of programming makes progress by using assignments to manipulate state. In many cases, solving a problem requires repeated operations. With functional programming, this is done using recursive definitions. We make progress towards a base case by passing in different values for the operands with each recursive application. With imperative programming, we can make progress by changing state repeatedly without needing to pass in different operands.

while loop A common control structure in imperative programming is a *while loop*. A while loop has a test condition and a body. The test condition is a predicate. If it evaluates to true, the while loop body is executed. Then, the test condition is evaluated again. The while loop continues to execute until the test condition evaluates to false.

We can define *while* as a procedure that takes as input two procedures, a test procedure and a body procedure, each of which take no parameters. Even though the test and body procedures take no parameters, they need to be procedures instead of expressions, since every iteration of the loop should re-evaluate the test and body expressions of the passed procedures.

```
(define (while test body)
  (if (test)
     (begin (body) (while test body))
     (void))) ; no result value
```

We can use the *while* procedure to implement Fibonacci similarly to the *fast-fibo* procedure:

```
(define (fibo-while n)
  (let ((a 1) (b 1))
    (while (lambda () (> n 2))
           (lambda () (set! b (+ a b))
                      (set! a (- b a))
                      (set! n (- n 1))))
    b))
```

The final value of *b* is the result of the *fibo-while* procedure. In each iteration, the body procedure is applied, updating the values of *a* and *b* to the next Fibonacci numbers.

The value assigned to *a* is computed as (− *b a*) instead of *b*. The reason for this is the previous assignment expression has already changed the value of *b*, by adding *a* to it. Since the next value of *a* should be the old value of *b*, we can find the necessary value by subtracting *a*. The fact that the value of a variable can change depending on when it is used often makes imperative programming trickier than functional programming.

An alternative approach, which would save the need to do subtraction, is to store the old value in a temporary value:

```
(lambda ()
  (let ((oldb b))
    (set! b (+ a b))
    (set! a oldb)
    (set! n (- n 1))))
```

Many programming languages designed to support imperative programming provide control constructs similar to the *while* procedure defined above. For example, here is a version of the procedure in the Python programming language:

```
def fibonacci (n):
  a = 1
  b = 1
```

```
while n > 2:
  a, b = b, a + b
  n = n − 1
return b
```

We will use Python starting in Chapter 11, although you can probably guess what most of this procedure means without knowing Python.

The most interesting statement is the double assignment: *a*, *b* = *b*, *a* + *b*. This assigns the new value of *a* to the old value of *b*, and the new value of *b* to the sum of the old values of *a* and *b*. Without the double assignment operator, it would be necessary to store the old value of *b* in a new variable so it can be assigned to *a* after updating *b* to the new value.

Exercise 9.11. Define the *mlist-map!* example from the previous section using *while*.

Exercise 9.12. Another common imperative programming structure is a *repeat-until* loop. Define a *repeat-until* procedure that takes two inputs, a body procedure and a test procedure. The procedure should evaluate the body procedure repeatedly, until the test procedure evaluates to a true value. For example, using *repeat-until* we could define *factorial* as:

repeat-until

```
(define (factorial n)
  (let ((fact 1))
    (repeat-until
     (lambda () (set! fact (* fact n)) (set! n (− n 1)))
     (lambda () (< n 1)))
    fact))
```

Exercise 9.13. [★★] Improve the efficiency of the indexing procedures from Section 8.2.3 by using mutation. Start by defining a mutable binary tree abstraction, and then use this and the MutableList data type to implement an imperative-style *insert-into-index!* procedure that mutates the input index by adding a new word-position pair to it. Then, define an efficient *merge-index!* procedure that takes two mutable indexes as its inputs and modifies the first index to incorporate all word occurrences in the second index. Analyze the impact of your changes on the running time of indexing a collection of documents.

9.5 Summary

Adding the ability to change the value associated with a name complicates our evaluation rules, but enables simpler and more efficient solutions to many problems. Mutation allows us to efficiently manipulate larger data structures since it is not necessary to copy the data structure to make changes to it.

Once we add assignment to our language, the order in which things happen affects the value of some expressions. Instead of evaluating expressions using substitution, we now need to always evaluate an expression in a particular execution environment.

The problem with mutation is that it makes it much tougher to reason about the meaning of an expression. In the next chapter, we introduce a new kind of abstraction that packages procedures with the state they manipulate. This helps manage some of the complexity resulting from mutation by limiting the places where data may be accessed and modified.

10

Objects

It was amazing to me, and it is still amazing, that people could not imagine what the psychological difference would be to have an interactive terminal. You can talk about it on a blackboard until you are blue in the face, and people would say, "Oh, yes, but why do you need that?"... We used to try to think of all these analogies, like describing it in terms of the difference between mailing a letter to your mother and getting on the telephone. To this day I can still remember people only realizing when they saw a real demo, say, "Hey, it talks back. Wow! You just type that and you got an answer."

Fernando Corbató (who worked on Whirlwind in the 1950s)
Charles Babbage Institute interview, 1989

So far, we have seen two main approaches for solving problems:

Functional programming
Break a problem into a group of simpler procedures that can be composed to solve the problem (introduced in Chapter 4).

Data-centric programming
Model the data the problem involves, and develop procedures to manipulate that data (introduced in Chapter 5, and extended to imperative programming with mutation in the previous chapter).

All computational problems involve both data and procedures. All procedures act on some form of data; without data they can have no meaningful inputs and outputs. Any data-focused design must involve some procedures to perform computations using that data.

This chapter introduces a new problem-solving approach known as *object-oriented programming*. By packaging procedures and data together, object-oriented programming overcomes a weakness of both previous approaches: the data and the procedures that manipulate it are separate.

object-oriented programming

Unlike many programming languages, Scheme does not provide special built-in support for objects.[1] We build an object system ourselves, taking advantage of the stateful evaluation rules. By building an object system from simple components, we provide a clearer and deeper understanding of how object systems work. In Chapter 11, we see how Python provides language support for object-oriented programming.

The next section introduces techniques for programming with objects that combine state with procedures that manipulate that state. Section 10.2 describes

[1] This refers to the standard Scheme language, not the many extended Scheme languages provided by DrRacket. The MzScheme language does provide additional constructs for supporting objects, but we do not cover them in this book.

inheritance *inheritance*, a powerful technique for programming with objects by implementing new objects that add or modify the behaviors of previously implemented objects. Section 10.3 provides some historical background on the development of object-oriented programming.

10.1 Packaging Procedures and State

Recall our counter from Example 9.1:

```
(define (update-counter!) (set! counter (+ counter 1)) counter)
```

Every time an application of *update-counter!* is evaluated, we expect to obtain a value one larger than the previous application. This only works, however, if there are no other evaluations that modify the *counter* variable. Hence, we can only have one counter: there is only one *counter* place in the global environment. If we want to have a second counter, we would need to define a new variable (such as *counter2*, and implement a new procedure, *update-counter2!*, that is identical to *update-counter!*, but manipulates *counter2* instead. For each new counter, we would need a new variable and a new procedure.

10.1.1 Encapsulation

It would be more useful to package the counter variable with the procedure that manipulates it. Then we could create as many counters as we want, each with its own counter variable to manipulate.

The Stateful Application Rule (from Section 9.2.2) suggests a way to do this: evaluating an application creates a new environment, so a counter variable defined an the application environment is only visible through body of the created procedure.

The *make-counter* procedure creates a counter object that packages the *count* variable with the procedure that increases its value:

```
(define (make-counter)
  ((lambda (count)
     (lambda () (set! count (+ 1 count)) count))
   0))
```

Each application of *make-counter* produces a new object that is a procedure with its own associated *count* variable. Protecting state so it can only be manip-
encapsulation ulated in controlled ways is known as *encapsulation*.

The *count* place is encapsulated within the counter object. Whereas the previous counter used the global environment to store the counter in a way that could be manipulated by other expressions, this version encapsulates the counter variable so the only way to manipulate the counter value is through the counter object.

An equivalent *make-counter* definition uses a let expression to make the initialization of the *count* variable clearer:

```
(define (make-counter)
  (let ((count 0))
    (lambda () (set! count (+ 1 count)) count)))
```

Figure 10.1 depicts the environment after creating two counter objects and applying one of them.

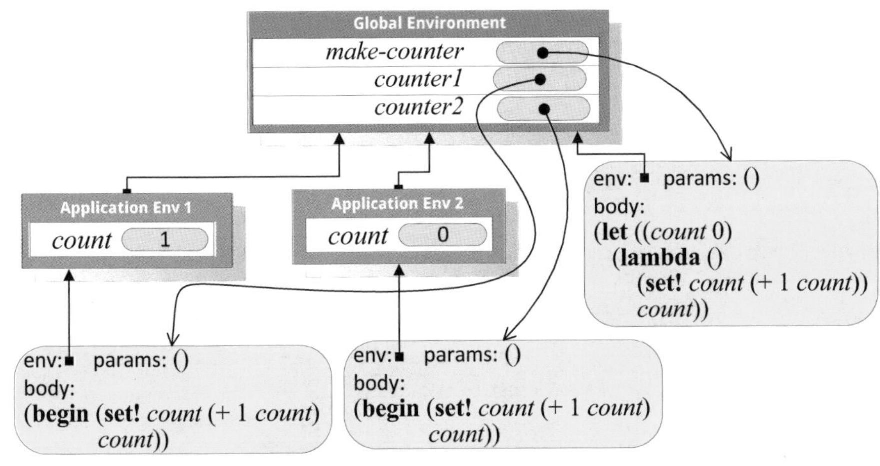

Figure 10.1. Environment produced by evaluating:
(**define** *counter1* (*make-counter*))
(**define** *counter2* (*make-counter*))
(*counter1*)

10.1.2 Messages

The object produced by *make-counter* is limited to only one behavior: every time it is applied the associated count variable is increased by one and the new value is output. To produce more useful objects, we need a way to combine state with multiple behaviors.

For example, we might want a counter that can also return the current count and reset the count. We do this by adding a *message* parameter to the procedure produced by *make-counter*:

```
(define (make-counter)
  (let ((count 0))
    (lambda (message)
      (if (eq? message 'get-count) count
        (if (eq? message 'reset!) (set! count 0)
          (if (eq? message 'next!) (set! count (+ 1 count))
            (error "Unrecognized message")))))))
```

Like the earlier *make-counter*, this procedure produces a procedure with an environment containing a frame with a place named *count*. The produced procedure takes a *message* parameter and selects different behavior depending on the input message.

The *message* parameter is a Symbol. A Symbol is a sequence of characters preceded by a quote character such as 'next!. Two Symbols are equal, as determined by the *eq?* procedure, if their sequences of characters are identical. The running time of the *eq?* procedure on symbol type inputs is constant; it does not increase with the length of the symbols since the symbols can be represented internally as small numbers and compared quickly using number equality. This makes symbols a more efficient way of selecting object behaviors than Strings, and a more memorable way to select behaviors than using Numbers.

Here are some sample interactions using the counter object:

```
> (define counter (make-counter))
> (counter 'next!)
> (counter 'get-count)
1
> (counter 'previous!)
Unrecognized message
```

Conditional expressions. For objects with many behaviors, the nested if expressions can get quite cumbersome. Scheme provides a compact conditional expression for combining many if expressions into one smaller expression:

Expression	::⇒	*CondExpression*
CondExpression	::⇒	(**cond** *CondClauseList*)
CondClauseList	::⇒	*CondClause CondClauseList*
CondClauseList	::⇒	ϵ
CondClause	::⇒	($Expression_{predicate}$ $Expression_{consequent}$)

The evaluation rule for a conditional expression can be defined as a transformation into an if expression:

Evaluation Rule 9: Conditional. The conditional expression (**cond**) has no value. All other conditional expressions are of the form (**cond** ($Expression_{p1}$ $Expression_{c1}$) *Rest*) where *Rest* is a list of conditional clauses. The value of such a conditional expression is the value of the if expression:

(**if** $Expression_{p1}$ $Expression_{c1}$ (**cond** *Rest*))

This evaluation rule is recursive since the transformed expression still includes a conditional expression, but uses the empty conditional with no value as its base case.

The conditional expression can be used to define *make-counter* more clearly than the nested if expressions:

```
(define (make-counter)
  (let ((count 0))
    (lambda (message)
      (cond ((eq? message 'get-count) count)
            ((eq? message 'reset!)   (set! count 0))
            ((eq? message 'next!)    (set! count (+ 1 count)))
            (true (error "Unrecognized message"))))))
```

For linguistic convenience, Scheme provides a special syntax **else** for use in conditional expressions. When used as the predicate in the last conditional clause it means the same thing as *true*. So, we could write the last clause equivalently as (**else** (*error* "Unrecognized message")).

Sending messages. A more natural way to interact with objects is to define a generic procedure that takes an object and a message as its parameters, and send the message to the object.

The *ask* procedure is a simple procedure that does this:

```
(define (ask object message) (object message))
```

It applies the *object* input to the *message* input. So, (*ask counter* 'next!) is equivalent to (*counter* 'next!), but looks more like passing a message to an object than applying a procedure. Later, we will develop more complex versions of the *ask* procedure to provide a more powerful object model.

Messages with parameters. Sometimes it is useful to have behaviors that take additional parameters. For example, we may want to support a message *adjust!* that increases the counter value by an input value.

To support such behaviors, we generalize the behaviors so that the result of applying the message dispatching procedure is itself a procedure. The procedures for *reset!*, *next!*, and *get-count* take no parameters; the procedure for *adjust!* takes one parameter.

```
(define (make-adjustable-counter)
  (let ((count 0))
    (lambda (message)
      (cond ((eq? message 'get-count) (lambda () count))
            ((eq? message 'reset!) (lambda () (set! count 0)))
            ((eq? message 'next!) (lambda () (set! count (+ 1 count))))
            ((eq? message 'adjust!)
             (lambda (val) (set! count (+ count val))))
            (else (error "Unrecognized message"))))))
```

We also need to also change the *ask* procedure to pass in the extra arguments. So far, all the procedures we have defined take a fixed number of operands. To allow *ask* to work for procedures that take a variable number of arguments, we use a special definition construct:

Definition ::⇒ (**define** (***Name*** Parameters . $Name_{Rest}$) *Expression*)

The name following the dot is bound to all the remaining operands combined into a list. This means the defined procedure can be applied to n or more operands where n is the number of names in *Parameters*. If there are only n operand expressions, the value bound to $Name_{Rest}$ is null. If there are $n+k$ operand expressions, the value bound to $Name_{Rest}$ is a list containing the values of the last k operand expressions.

To apply the procedure we use the built-in *apply* procedure which takes two inputs, a Procedure and a List. It applies the procedure to the values in the list, extracting them from the list as each operand in order.

```
(define (ask object message . args)
  (apply (object message) args))
```

We can use the new *ask* procedure with two or more parameters to invoke methods with any number of arguments (e.g., > (*ask counter* 'adjust! 5)).

10.1.3 Object Terminology

An *object* is an entity that packages state and procedures. *object*

The state variables that are part of an object are called *instance variables*. The *instance variables* instance variables are stored in places that are part of the application environment for the object. This means they are encapsulated with the object and can only be accessed through the object. An object produced by (*make-counter*) defines a single instance variable, *count*.

methods The procedures that are part of an object are called *methods*. Methods may provide information about the state of an object (we call these *observers*) or modify the state of an object (we call these *mutators*). An object produced by (*make-counter*) provides three methods: *reset!* (a mutator), *next!* (a mutator), and *get-count* (an observer).

invoke An object is manipulated using the object's methods. We *invoke* a method on an object by sending the object a message. This is analogous to applying a procedure.

class A *class* is a kind of object. Classes are similar to data types. They define a set of possible values and operations (methods in the object terminology) for manipulating those values. We also need procedures for creating new objects, such as the *make-counter* procedure above. We call these *constructors*. By convention, we call the constructor for a class *make-<class>* where *<class>* is the name of the class. Hence, an instance of the *counter* class is the result produced when the *make-counter* procedure is applied.

constructors

Exercise 10.1. Modify the *make-counter* definition to add a *previous!* method that decrements the counter value by one.

Exercise 10.2. [$\star$] Define a *variable-counter* object that provides these methods:

make-variable-counter: Number → VariableCounter
Creates a *variable-counter* object with an initial counter value of 0 and an initial increment value given by the parameter.

set-increment!: Number → Void
Sets the increment amount for this counter to the input value.

next!: Void → Void
Adds the increment amount to the value of the counter.

get-count: Void → Number
Outputs the current value of the counter.

Here are some sample interactions using a *variable-counter* object:

```
> (define vcounter (make-variable-counter 1))
> (ask vcounter 'next!)
> (ask vcounter 'set-increment! 2)
> (ask vcounter 'next!)
> (ask vcounter 'get-count)
3
```

10.2 Inheritance

Objects are particularly well-suited to programs that involve modeling real or imaginary worlds such as graphical user interfaces (modeling windows, files, and folders on a desktop), simulations (modeling physical objects in the real world and their interactions), and games (modeling creatures and things in an imagined world).

Objects in the real world (or most simulated worlds) are complex. Suppose we are implementing a game that simulates a typical university. It might include many different kinds of objects including places (which are stationary and may contain other objects), things, and people. There are many different kinds of people, such as students and professors. All objects in our game have a name and a location; some objects also have methods for talking and moving. We could define classes independently for all of the object types, but this would involve a lot of duplicate effort. It would also make it hard to add a new behavior to all of the objects in the game without modifying many different procedures.

The solution is to define more specialized kinds of objects using the definitions of other objects. For example, a *student* is a kind of *person*. A *student* has all the behaviors of a normal *person*, as well as some behaviors particular to a *student* such as choosing a major and graduating. To implement a *student* class, we want to reuse methods from the *person* class without needing to duplicate them in the *student* implementation. We call the more specialized class (in this case the *student* class) the *subclass* and say *student* is a subclass of *person*. The reused class is known as the *superclass*, so *person* is the superclass of *student*. A class can have many subclasses but only one superclass.[2]

subclass
superclass

Figure 10.2 illustrates some inheritance relationships for a university simulator. The arrows point from subclasses to their superclass. A class may be both a subclass to another class, and a superclass to a different class. For example, *person* is a subclass of *movable-object*, but a superclass of *student* and *professor*.

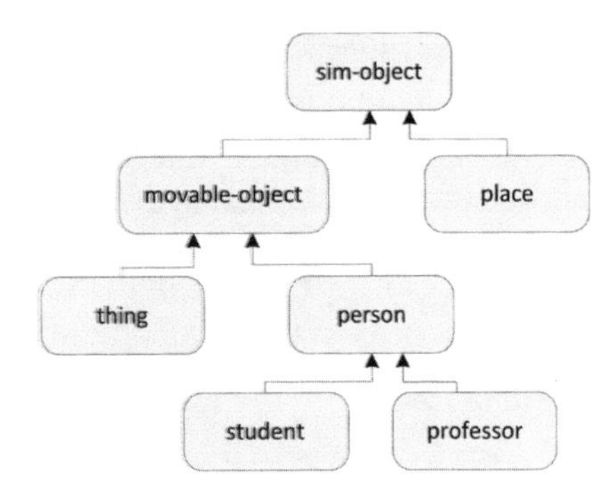

Figure 10.2. Inheritance hierarchy.

Our goal is to be able to reuse superclass methods in subclasses. When a method is invoked in a subclass, if the subclass does not provide a definition of the method, then the definition of the method in the superclass is used. This can continue up the superclass chain. For instance, *student* is a subclass of *person*, which is a subclass of *movable-object*, which is a subclass of *sim-object* (simulation object), which is the superclass of all classes in the simulator.

[2]Some object systems (such as the one provided by the C++ programming language) allow a class to have more than one superclass. This can be confusing, though. If a class has two superclasses and both define methods with the same name, it may be ambiguous which of the methods is used when it is invoked on an object of the subclass. In our object system, a class may have only one superclass.

Hence, if the *sim-object* class defines a *get-name* method, when the *get-name* method is invoked on a *student* object, the implementation of *get-name* in the *sim-object* class will be used (as long as neither *person* nor *movable-object* defines its own *get-name* method).

inherits When one class implementation uses the methods from another class we say the subclass *inherits* from the superclass. Inheritance is a powerful way to obtain many different objects with a small amount of code.

10.2.1 Implementing Subclasses

To implement inheritance we change class definitions so that if a requested method is not defined by the subclass, the method defined by its superclass will be used.

The *make-sub-object* procedure does this. It takes two inputs, a superclass object and the object dispatching procedure of the subclass, and produces an instance of the subclass which is a procedure that takes a message as input and outputs the method corresponding to that message. If the method is defined by the subclass, the result will be the subclass method. If the method is not defined by the subclass, it will be the superclass method.

```
(define (make-sub-object super subproc)
  (lambda (message)
    (let ((method (subproc message)))
      (if method method (super message)))))
```

When an object produced by (*make-sub-object obj proc*) is applied to a message, it first applies the subclass dispatch procedure to the message to find an appropriate method if one is defined. If no method is defined by the subclass implementation, it evaluates to (*super message*), the method associated with the *message* in the superclass.

References to self. It is useful to add an extra parameter to all methods so the object on which the method was invoked is visible. Otherwise, the object will lose its special behaviors as it is moves up the superclasses. We call this the *self* object (in some languages it is called the *this* object instead). To support this, we modify the *ask* procedure to pass in the object parameter to the method:

```
(define (ask object message . args)
  (apply (object message) object args))
```

All methods now take the *self* object as their first parameter, and may take additional parameters. So, the *counter* constructor is defined as:

```
(define (make-counter)
  (let ((count 0))
    (lambda (message)
      (cond
       ((eq? message 'get-count) (lambda (self) count))
       ((eq? message 'reset!) (lambda (self) (set! count 0)))
       ((eq? message 'next!) (lambda (self) (set! count (+ 1 count))))
       (else (error "Unrecognized message"))))))
```

Subclassing counter. Since subclass objects cannot see the instance variables of their superclass objects directly, if we want to provide a versatile counter class we need to also provide a *set-count!* method for setting the value of the counter to an arbitrary value. For reasons that will become clear later, we should use *set-count!* everywhere the value of the *count* variable is changed instead of setting it directly:

```
(define (make-counter)
  (let ((count 0))
    (lambda (message)
      (cond
       ((eq? message 'get-count) (lambda (self) count))
       ((eq? message 'set-count!) (lambda (self val) (set! count val)))
       ((eq? message 'reset!) (lambda (self) (ask self 'set-count! 0)))
       ((eq? message 'next!)
        (lambda (self) (ask self 'set-count! (+ 1 (ask self 'current)))))
       (else (error "Unrecognized message"))))))
```

Previously, we defined *make-adjustable-counter* by repeating all the code from *make-counter* and adding an *adjust!* method. With inheritance, we can define *make-adjustable-counter* as a subclass of *make-counter* without repeating any code:

```
(define (make-adjustable-counter)
  (make-sub-object
   (make-counter)
   (lambda (message)
     (cond
      ((eq? message 'adjust!)
       (lambda (self val)
         (ask self 'set-count! (+ (ask self 'get-count) val))))
      (else false)))))
```

We use *make-sub-object* to create an object that inherits the behaviors from one class, and extends those behaviors by defining new methods in the subclass implementation.

The new *adjust!* method takes one Number parameter (in addition to the *self* object that is passed to every method) and adds that number to the current counter value. It cannot use (**set!** *count* (+ *count val*)) directly, though, since the *count* variable is defined in the application environment of its superclass object and is not visible within *adjustable-counter*. Hence, it accesses the counter using the *set-count!* and *get-count* methods provided by the superclass.

Suppose we create an *adjustable-counter* object:

```
(define acounter (make-adjustable-counter))
```

Consider what happens when (*ask acounter* 'adjust! 3) is evaluated. The *acounter* object is the result of the application of *make-sub-object* which is the procedure,

```
(lambda (message)
  (let ((method (subproc message)))
    (if method method (super message))))
```

where *super* is the *counter* object resulting from evaluating (*make-counter*) and *subproc* is the procedure created by the lambda expression in *make-adjustable-*

counter. The body of *ask* evaluates (*object message*) to find the method associated with the input message, in this case 'adjust!. The *acounter* object takes the *message* input and evaluates the let expression:

```
(let ((method (subproc message))) ...)
```

The result of applying *subproc* to *message* is the *adjust!* procedure defined by *make-adjustable-counter*:

```
(lambda (self val)
  (ask self 'set-count! (+ (ask self 'get-count) val)))
```

Since this is not false, the predicate of the if expression is non-false and the value of the consequent expression, *method*, is the result of the procedure application. The *ask* procedure uses *apply* to apply this procedure to the *object* and *args* parameters. The *object* is the *acounter* object, and the *args* is the list of the extra parameters, in this case (3).

Thus, the *adjust!* method is applied to the *acounter* object and 3. The body of the *adjust!* method uses *ask* to invoke the *set-count!* method on the *self* object. As with the first invocation, the body of *ask* evaluates (*object message*) to find the method. In this case, the subclass implementation provides no *set-count!* method so the result of (*subproc message*) in the application of the subclass object is false. Hence, the alternate expression is evaluated: (*super message*). This evaluates to the method associated with the *set-count!* message in the superclass. The *ask* body will apply this method to the *self* object, setting the value of the counter to the new value.

We can define new classes by defining subclasses of previously defined classes. For example, *reversible-counter* inherits from *adjustable-counter*:

```
(define (make-reversible-counter)
  (make-subobject
   (make-adjustable-counter)
   (lambda (message)
     (cond
      ((eq? message 'previous!) (lambda (self) (ask self 'adjust! -1)))
      (else false)))))
```

The *reversible-counter* object defines the *previous!* method which provides a new behavior. If the message to a *adjustable-counter* object is not *previous!*, the method from its superclass, *adjustable-counter* is used. Within the *previous!* method we use *ask* to invoke the *adjust!* method on the *self* object. Since the subclass implementation does not provide an *adjust!* method, this results in the superclass method being applied.

10.2.2 Overriding Methods

In addition to adding new methods, subclasses can replace the definitions of methods defined in the superclass. When a subclass replaces a method defined by its superclass, then the subclass method *overrides* the superclass method. When the method is invoked on a subclass object, the new method will be used.

overrides

For example, we can define a subclass of *reversible-counter* that is not allowed to have negative counter values. If the counter would reach a negative number, instead of setting the counter to the new value, it produces an error message and maintains the counter at zero. We do this by overriding the *set-count!* method, replacing the superclass implementation of the method with a new implementation.

```
(define (make-positive-counter)
  (make-subobject
   (make-reversible-counter)
   (lambda (message)
     (cond
      ((eq? message 'set-count!)
       (lambda (self val) (if (< val 0) (error "Negative count")
                                          ...)))
      (else false)))))
```

What should go in place of the ...? When the value to set the count to is not negative, what should happen is the count is set as it would be by the superclass *set-count!* method. In the *positive-counter* code though, there is no way to access the *count* variable since it is in the superclass procedure's application environment. There is also no way to invoke the superclass' *set-count!* method since it has been overridden by *positive-counter*.

The solution is to provide a way for the subclass object to obtain its superclass object. We can do this by adding a *get-super* method to the object produced by *make-sub-object*:

```
(define (make-sub-object super subproc)
  (lambda (message)
    (if (eq? message 'get-super)
        (lambda (self) super)
        (let ((method (subproc message)))
          (if method method (super message))))))
```

Thus, when an object produced by *make-sub-object* is passed the *get-super* message it returns a method that produces the *super* object. The rest of the procedure is the same as before, so for every other message it behaves like the earlier *make-sub-object* procedure.

With the *get-super* method we can define the *set-count!* method for *positive-counter*, replacing the ... with:

```
(ask (ask self 'get-super) 'set-count! val))
```

Figure 10.3 shows the subclasses that inherit from *counter* and the methods they define or override.

Consider these sample interactions with a *positive-counter* object:

```
> (define poscount (make-positive-counter))
> (ask poscount 'next!)
> (ask poscount 'previous!)
> (ask poscount 'previous!)
Negative count
> (ask poscount 'get-count)
0
```

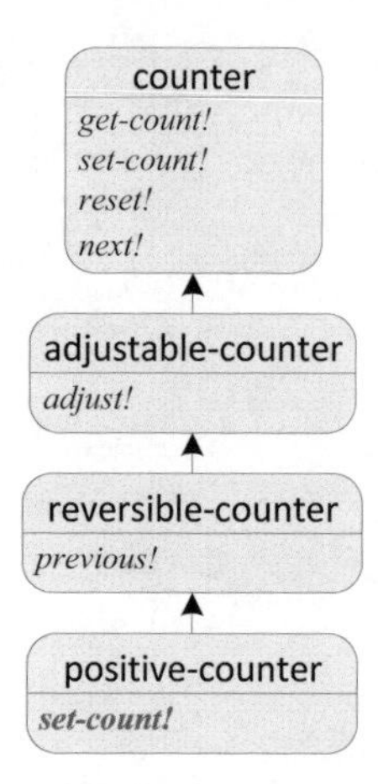

Figure 10.3. Counter class hierarchy.

For the first *ask* application, the *next!* method is invoked on a *positive-counter* object. Since the *positive-counter* class does not define a *next!* method, the message is sent to the superclass, *reversible-counter*. The *reversible-counter* implementation also does not define a *next!* method, so the message is passed up to its superclass, *adjustable-counter*. This class also does not define a *next!* method, so the message is passed up to its superclass, *counter*. The *counter* class defines a *next!* method, so that method is used.

For the next *ask*, the *previous!* method is invoked. Since the *positive-counter* class does not define a *previous!* method, the message is sent to the superclass. The superclass, *reversible-counter*, defines a *previous!* method. Its implementation involves an invocation of the *adjust!* method: (*ask self* 'adjust! −1). This invocation is done on the *self* object, which is an instance of the *positive-counter* class. Hence, the *adjust!* method is found from the *positive-counter* class implementation. This is the method that overrides the *adjust!* method defined by the *adjustable-counter* class. Hence, the second invocation of *previous!* produces the "Negative count" error and does not adjust the count to −1.

dynamic dispatch

The property this object system has where the method invoked depends on the object is known as *dynamic dispatch*. The method used for an invocation depends on the *self* object. In this case, for example, it means that when we inspect the implementation of the *previous!* method in the *reversible-counter* class by itself it is not possible to determine what procedure will be applied for the method invocation, (*ask self* 'adjust! −1). It depends on the actual *self* object: if it is a *positive-counter* object, the *adjust!* method defined by *positive-counter* is used; if it is a *reversible-counter* object, the *adjust!* method defined by *adjustable-counter* class (the superclass of *reversible-counter*) is used.

Dynamic dispatch provides for a great deal of expressiveness. It enables us to use the same code to produce many different behaviors by overriding methods in subclasses. This is very useful, but also very dangerous — it makes it impossible to reason about what a given procedure does, without knowing about all possible subclasses. For example, we cannot make any claims about what the *previous!* method in *reversible-counter* actually does without knowing what the *adjust!* method does in all subclasses of *reversible-counter*.

The value of encapsulation and inheritance increases as programs get more complex. Programming with objects allows a programmer to manage complexity by hiding the details of *how* objects are implemented from *what* those objects represent and do.

Exercise 10.3. Define a *countdown* class that simulates a rocket launch countdown: it starts at some initial value, and counts down to zero, at which point the rocket is launched. Can you implement *countdown* as a subclass of *counter*?

Exercise 10.4. Define the *variable-counter* object from Exercise 10.2 as a subclass of *counter*.

Exercise 10.5. Define a new subclass of *parameterizable-counter* where the increment for each *next!* method application is a parameter to the constructor procedure. For example, (*make-parameterizable-counter* 0.1) would produce a counter object whose counter has value 0.1 after one invocation of the *next!* method.

10.3 Object-Oriented Programming

Object-oriented programming is a style of programming where programs are broken down into objects that can be combined to solve a problem or model a simulated world. The notion of designing programs around object manipulations goes back at least to Ada (see the quote at the end if Chapter 6), but started in earnest in the early 1960s.

During World War II, the US Navy began to consider the possibility of building a airplane simulator for training pilots and aiding aircraft designers. At the time, pilots trained in mechanical simulators that were custom designed for particular airplanes. The Navy wanted a simulator that could be used for multiple airplanes and could accurately model the aerodynamics of different airplanes.

Project Whirlwind was started at MIT to build the simulator. The initial plans called for an analog computer which would need to be manually reconfigured to change the aerodynamics model to a different airplane. Jay Forrester learned about emerging projects to build digital computers, including ENIAC which became operational in 1946, and realized that building a programmable digital computer would enable a much more flexible and powerful simulator, as well as a machine that could be used for many other purposes.

Before Whirlwind, all digital computers operated as batch processors where a programmer creates a program (typically described using a stack of punch cards) and submits it to the computer. A computer operator would set up the computer to run the program, after which it would run and (hopefully) produce a result. A flight simulator, though, requires direct interaction between a human user and the computer.

The first Whirlwind computer was designed in 1947 and operational by 1950. It was the first interactive programmable digital computer. Producing a machine that could perform the complex computations needed for a flight simulator fast enough to be used interactively required much faster and more reliable memory that was possible with available technologies based on storing electrostatic charges in vacuum tubes. Jay Forrester invented a much faster memory based known as magnetic-core memory. Magnetic-core memory stores a bit using magnetic polarity.

The interactiveness of the Whirlwind computer opened up many new possibilities for computing. Shortly after the first Whirlwind computer, Ken Olson led an effort to build a version of the computer using transistors. The successor to this machine became the TX-2, and Ken Olsen went on to found Digital Equipment Corporation (DEC) which pioneered the widespread use of moderately priced computers in science and industry. DEC was very successful in the 1970s and 1980s, but suffered a long decline before eventually being bought by Compaq.

Ivan Sutherland, then a graduate student at MIT, had an opportunity to use the TX-2 machine. He developed a program called *Sketchpad* that was the first program to have an interactive graphical interface. Sketchpad allowed users to draw and manipulate objects on the screen using a light pen. It was designed around objects and operations on those objects:[3]

> *In the process of making the Sketchpad system operate, a few very general functions were developed which make no reference at all to the specific types of entities on which they operate. These general functions give the Sketchpad system the ability to operate on a wide range of problems. The motivation for making the functions as general as possible came from the desire to get as much result as possible from the programming effort involved... Each of the general functions implemented in the Sketchpad system abstracts, in some sense, some common property of pictures independent of the specific subject matter of the pictures themselves.*

Components in Sketchpad

Sketchpad was a great influence on Douglas Engelbart who developed a research program around a vision of using computers interactively to enhance human intellect. In what has become known as "the mother of all demos", Engelbart and his colleagues demonstrated a networked, graphical, interactive computing system to the general public for the first time in 1968. With Bill English, Engelbard also invented the computer mouse.

Sketchpad also influenced Alan Kay in developing object-oriented programming. The first language to include support for objects was the Simula programming language, developed in Norway in the 1960s by Kristen Nygaard and Ole Johan Dahl. Simula was designed as a language for implementing simulations. It provided mechanisms for packaging data and procedures, and for implementing subclasses using inheritance.

In 1966, Alan Kay entered graduate school at the University of Utah, where Ivan Sutherland was then a professor. Here's how he describes his first assignment:[4]

> *Head whirling, I found my desk. On it was a pile of tapes and listings, and a note: "This is the Algol for the 1108. It doesn't work. Please make it work." The latest graduate student gets the latest dirty task. The documentation was incomprehensible. Supposedly, this was the Case-Western Reserve 1107 Algol—but it had been doctored to make a language called Simula; the documentation read like Norwegian transliterated into English,*

[3]Ivan Sutherland, *Sketchpad: a Man-Machine Graphical Communication System*, 1963
[4]Alan Kay, *The Early History of Smalltalk*, 1993

> *which in fact it was. There were uses of words like activity and process that didn't seem to coincide with normal English usage. Finally, another graduate student and I unrolled the program listing 80 feet down the hall and crawled over it yelling discoveries to each other. The weirdest part was the storage allocator, which did not obey a stack discipline as was usual for Algol. A few days later, that provided the clue. What Simula was allocating were structures very much like the instances of Sketchpad. There were descriptions that acted like masters and they could create instances, each of which was an independent entity. ...*
>
> *This was the big hit, and I've not been the same since... For the first time I thought of the whole as the entire computer and wondered why anyone would want to divide it up into weaker things called data structures and procedures. Why not divide it up into little computers, as time sharing was starting to? But not in dozens. Why not thousands of them, each simulating a useful structure?*

Alan Kay

Alan Kay went on to design the language Smalltalk, which became the first widely used object-oriented language. Smalltalk was developed as part of a project at XEROX's Palo Alto Research Center to develop a hand-held computer that could be used as a learning environment by children.

In Smalltalk, *everything* is an object, and all computation is done by sending messages to objects. For example, in Smalltalk one computes (+ 1 2) by sending the message + 2 to the object 1. Here is Smalltalk code for implementing a counter object:

Don't worry about what anybody else is going to do. The best way to predict the future is to invent it. Really smart people with reasonable funding can do just about anything that doesn't violate too many of Newton's Laws!
Alan Kay

```
class name counter
  instance variable names count
  new count <- 0
  next count <- count + 1
  current ^ count
```

The *new* method is a constructor analogous to *make-counter*. The *count* instance variable stores the current value of the counter, and the *next* method updates the counter value by sending the message + 1 to the *count* object.

Nearly all widely-used languages today provide built-in support for some form of object-oriented programming. For example, here is how a counter object could be defined in Python:

```
class counter:
  def __init__(self): self._count = 0
  def rest(self): self._count = 0
  def next(self): self._count = self._count + 1
  def current(self): return self._count
```

The constructor is named *__init__*. Similarly to the object system we developed for Scheme, each method takes the *self* object as its parameter.

10.4 Summary

An object is an entity that packages state with procedures that manipulate that state. By packaging state and procedures together, we can encapsulate state in ways that enable more elegant and robust programs.

Inheritance allows an implementation of one class to reuse or override methods in another class, known as its superclass. Programming using objects and inheritance enables a style of problem solving known as object-oriented programming in which we solve problems by modeling problem instances using objects.

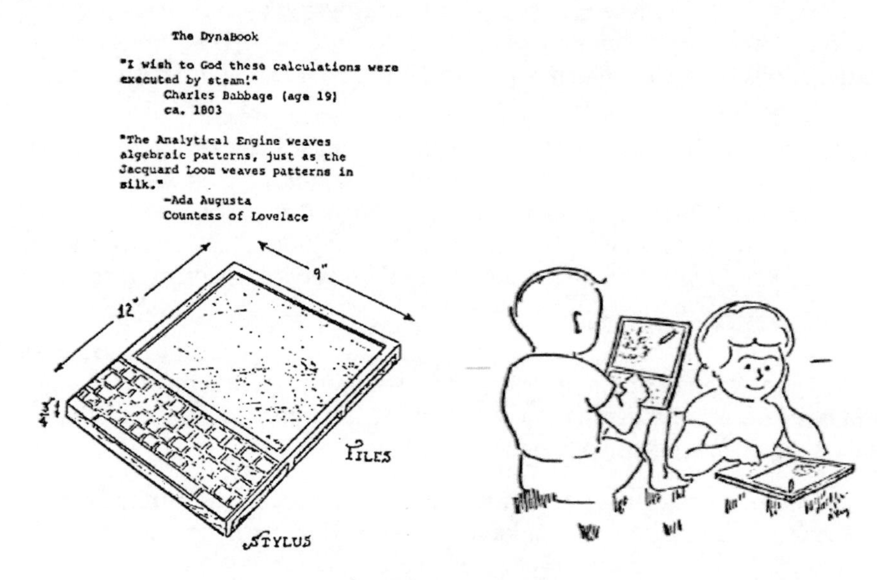

Dynabook Images

From Alan Kay, *A Personal Computer for Children of All Ages,* 1972.

11

Interpreters

"When I use a word," Humpty Dumpty said, in a rather scornful tone, "it means just what I choose it to mean - nothing more nor less."

"The question is," said Alice, "whether you can make words mean so many different things."

Lewis Carroll, *Through the Looking Glass*

The tools we use have a profound (and devious!) influence on our thinking habits, and, therefore, on our thinking abilities.

Edsger Dijkstra, *How do we tell truths that might hurt?*

Languages are powerful tools for thinking. Different languages encourage different ways of thinking and lead to different thoughts. Hence, inventing new languages is a powerful way for solving problems. We can solve a problem by designing a language in which it is easy to express a solution and implementing an interpreter for that language.

interpreter

An *interpreter* is just a program. As input, it takes a specification of a program in some language. As output, it produces the output of the input program. Implementing an interpreter further blurs the line between *data* and *programs*, that we first crossed in Chapter 3 by passing procedures as parameters and returning new procedures as results. Programs are just data input for the interpreter program. The interpreter determines the meaning of the program.

To implement an interpreter for a given target language we need to:

parser

1. Implement a *parser* that takes as input a string representation of a program in the target language and produces a structural parse of the input program. The parser should break the input string into its language components, and form a parse tree data structure that represents the input text in a structural way. Section 11.2 describes our parser implementation.

evaluator

2. Implement an *evaluator* that takes as input a structural parse of an input program, and evaluates that program. The evaluator should implement the target language's evaluation rules. Section 11.3 describes our evaluator.

Our target language is a simple subset of Scheme we call *Charme*.[1] The Charme language is very simple, yet is powerful enough to express all computations (that is, it is a universal programming language). Its evaluation rules are a subset of

[1]The original name of Scheme was "Schemer", a successor to the languages "Planner" and "Conniver". Because the computer on which "Schemer" was implemented only allowed six-letter file names, its name was shortened to "Scheme". In that spirit, we name our snake-charming language, "Charmer" and shorten it to Charme. Depending on the programmer's state of mind, the language name can be pronounced either "charm" or "char me".

the stateful evaluation rules for Scheme. The full grammar and evaluation rules for Charme are given in Section 11.3. The evaluator implements those evaluation rules.

Section 11.4 illustrates how changing the evaluation rules of our interpreter opens up new ways of programming.

11.1 Python

We could implement a Charme interpreter using Scheme or any other universal programming language, but implement it using the programming language Python. Python is a popular programming language initially designed by Guido van Rossum in 1991.[2] Python is freely available from http://www.python.org.

We use Python instead of Scheme to implement our Charme interpreter for a few reasons. The first reason is pedagogical: it is instructive to learn new languages. As Dijkstra's quote at the beginning of this chapter observes, the languages we use have a profound effect on how we think. This is true for natural languages, but also true for programming languages. Different languages make different styles of programming more convenient, and it is important for every programmer to be familiar with several different styles of programming. All of the major concepts we have covered so far apply to Python nearly identically to how they apply to Scheme, but seeing them in the context of a different language should make it clearer what the fundamental concepts are and what are artifacts of a particular programming language.

Another reason for using Python is that it provides some features that enhance expressiveness that are not available in Scheme. These include built-in support for objects and imperative control structures. Python is also well-supported by most web servers (including Apache), and is widely used to develop dynamic web applications.

The grammar for Python is quite different from the Scheme grammar, so Python programs look very different from Scheme programs. The evaluation rules, however, are quite similar to the evaluation rules for Scheme. This chapter does not describe the entire Python language, but introduces the grammar rules and evaluation rules for the most important Python constructs as we use them to implement the Charme interpreter.

Like Scheme, Python is a *universal programming language*. Both languages can express *all* mechanical computations. For any computation we can express in Scheme, there is a Python program that defines the same computation. Conversely, every Python program has an equivalent Scheme program.

One piece of evidence that every Scheme program has an equivalent Python program is the interpreter we develop in this chapter. Since we can implement an interpreter for a Scheme-like language in Python, we know we can express every computation that can be expressed by a program in that language with an equivalent Python program: the Charme interpreter with the Charme program as its input.

Tokenizing. We introduce Python using one of the procedures in our inter-

[2] The name *Python* alludes to Monty Python's Flying Circus.

preter implementation. We divide the job of parsing into two procedures that are combined to solve the problem of transforming an input string into a list describing the input program's structure. The first part is the *tokenizer*. It takes as input a string representing a Charme program, and outputs a list of the tokens in that string.

tokenizer

A *token* is an indivisible syntactic unit. For example, the Charme expression, (**define** *square* (**lambda** (*x*) (* *x x*))), contains 15 tokens: (, define, square, (, lambda, (, x,), (, *, x, x,),), and). Tokens are separated by whitespace (spaces, tabs, and newlines). Punctuation marks such as the left and right parentheses are tokens by themselves.

token

The *tokenize* procedure below takes as input a string *s* in the Charme target language, and produces as output a list of the tokens in *s*. We describe the Python language constructs it uses next.

```
def tokenize(s):  #                # starts a comment until the end of the line
  current = '' #          initialize current to the empty string (two single quotes)
  tokens = [] #                          initialize tokens to the empty list
  for c in s: #                          for each character, c, in the string s
    if c.isspace(): #                                    if c is a whitespace
      if len(current) > 0: #                     if the current token is non-empty
        tokens.append(current) #                                add it to the list
        current = '' #                          reset current token to empty string
    elif c in '()': #                             otherwise, if c is a parenthesis
      if len(current) > 0: #                                 end the current token
        tokens.append(current) #                         add it to the tokens list
        current = '' #                    and reset current to the empty string
      tokens.append(c) #                    add the parenthesis to the token list
    else: #                                  otherwise (it is an alphanumeric)
      current = current + c #              add the character to the current token
  # end of the for loop                                       reached the end of s
  if len(current) > 0: #                                     if there is a current token
    tokens.append(current) #                                 add it to the token list
  return tokens #                                    the result is the list of tokens
```

11.1.1 Python Programs

Whereas Scheme programs are composed of expressions and definitions, Python programs are mostly sequences of statements. Unlike expressions, a statement has no value. The emphasis on statements impacts the style of programming used with Python. It is more imperative than that used with Scheme: instead of composing expressions in ways that pass the result of one expression as an operand to the next expression, Python procedures consist mostly of statements, each of which alters the state in some way towards reaching the goal state. Nevertheless, it is possible (but not recommended) to program in Scheme using an imperative style (emphasizing assignments), and it is possible (but not recommended) to program in Python using a functional style (emphasizing procedure applications and eschewing statements).

Defining a procedure in Python is similar to defining a procedure in Scheme, except the syntax is different:

ProcedureDefinition ::⇒ **def** ***Name*** **(** *Parameters* **)** **:** *Block*
Parameters ::⇒ ϵ
Parameters ::⇒ *SomeParameters*
SomeParameters ::⇒ ***Name***
SomeParameters ::⇒ ***Name*** **,** *SomeParameters*

Block ::⇒ *Statement*
Block ::⇒ <**newline**> *indented*(*Statements*)
Statements ::⇒ *Statement* <**newline**> *MoreStatements*
MoreStatements ::⇒ *Statement* <**newline**> *MoreStatements*
MoreStatements ::⇒ ϵ

Unlike in Scheme, whitespace (such as new lines) has meaning in Python. Statements cannot be separated into multiple lines, and only one statement may appear on a single line. Indentation within a line also matters. Instead of using parentheses to provide code structure, Python uses the indentation to group statements into blocks. The Python interpreter reports an error if the indentation does not match the logical structure of the code.

Since whitespace matters in Python, we include newlines (<**newline**>) and indentation in our grammar. We use *indented*(*elements*) to indicate that the *elements* are indented. For example, the rule for *Block* is a newline, followed by one or more statements. The statements are all indented one level inside the block's indentation. The block ends when the indenting returns to the outer level.

The evaluation rule for a procedure definition is similar to the rule for evaluating a procedure definition in Scheme.

> **Python Procedure Definition.** The procedure definition,
>
> **def** ***Name*** (*Parameters*)**:** *Block*
>
> defines ***Name*** as a procedure that takes as inputs the *Parameters* and has the body expression *Block*.

The procedure definition, **def** *tokenize*(*s*): ..., defines a procedure named *tokenize* that takes a single parameter, *s*.

Assignment. The body of the procedure uses several different types of Python statements. Following Python's more imperative style, five of the statements in *tokenize* are assignment statements including the first two statements. For example, the assignment statement, *tokens* = [] assigns the value [] (the empty list) to the name *tokens*.

The grammar for the assignment statement is:

Statement ::⇒ *AssignmentStatement*
AssignmentStatement ::⇒ *Target* = *Expression*
Target ::⇒ ***Name***

For now, we use only a *Name* as the left side of an assignment, but since other constructs can appear on the left side of an assignment statement, we introduce the nonterminal *Target* for which additional rules can be defined to encompass other possible assignees. Anything that can hold a value (such as an element of a list) can be the target of an assignment.

The evaluation rule for an assignment statement is similar to Scheme's evaluation rule for assignments: the meaning of $x = e$ in Python is similar to the meaning of (**set!** x e) in Scheme, except that in Python the target *Name* need not exist before the assignment. In Scheme, it is an error to evaluate (**set!** x 7) where the name x has not been previously defined; in Python, if x is not already defined, evaluating $x = 7$ creates a new place named x with its value initialized to 7.

> **Python Evaluation Rule: Assignment.** To evaluate an assignment statement, evaluate the expression, and assign the value of the expression to the place identified by the target. If no such place exists, create a new place with that name.

Arithmetic and Comparison Expressions. Python supports many different kinds of expressions for performing arithmetic and comparisons. Since Python does not use parentheses to group expressions, the grammar provides the grouping by breaking down expressions in several steps. This defines an order of *precedence* for parsing expressions.

precedence

For example, consider the expression $3 + 4 * 5$. In Scheme, the expressions (+ 3 (∗ 4 5)) and (∗ (+ 3 4) 5) are clearly different and the parentheses group the subexpressions. The Python expression, $3 + 4 * 5$, means (+ 3 (∗ 4 5)) and evaluates to 23.

Supporting precedence makes the Python grammar rules more complex since they must deal with ∗ and + differently, but it makes the meaning of Python expressions match our familiar mathematical interpretation, without needing to clutter expressions with parentheses. This is done is by defining the grammar rules so an *AddExpression* can contain a *MultExpression* as one of its subexpressions, but a *MultExpression* cannot contain an *AddExpression*. This makes the multiplication operator have *higher precedence* than the addition operator. If an expression contains both + and ∗ operators, the ∗ operator is grouped with its operands first. The replacement rules that happen first have lower precedence, since their components must be built from the remaining pieces.

Here are the grammar rules for Python expressions for comparison, multiplication, and addition expressions:

Expression ::⇒ *CompExpr*
CompExpr ::⇒ *CompExpr Comparator CompExpr*
Comparator ::⇒ $< \mid > \mid == \mid <= \mid >=$
CompExpr ::⇒ *AddExpression*

AddExpression ::⇒ *AddExpression* + *MultExpression*
AddExpression ::⇒ *AddExpression* - *MultExpression*
AddExpression ::⇒ *MultExpression*

MultExpression ::⇒ *MultExpression* * *PrimaryExpression*
MultExpression ::⇒ *PrimaryExpression*

PrimaryExpression ::⇒ *Literal*
PrimaryExpression ::⇒ ***Name***
PrimaryExpression ::⇒ (*Expression*)

The last rule allows expressions to be grouped explicitly using parentheses. For example, $(3 + 4) * 5$ is parsed as the *PrimaryExpression*, $(3 + 4)$, times 5, so evaluates to 35; without the parentheses, $3 + 4 * 5$ is parsed as 3 plus the *MultExpression*, $4 * 5$, so evaluates to 23.

A *PrimaryExpression* can be a *Literal*, such as a number. Numbers in Python are similar (but not identical) to numbers in Scheme.

A *PrimaryExpression* can also be a name, similar to names in Scheme. The evaluation rule for a name in Python is similar to the stateful rule for evaluating a name in Scheme[3].

Exercise 11.1. Draw the parse tree for each of the following Python expressions and provide the value of each expression.

a. $1 + 2 + 3 * 4$

b. $3 > 2 + 2$

c. $3 * 6 >= 15 == 12$

d. $(3 * 6 >= 15) ==$ True

Exercise 11.2. Do comparison expressions have higher or lower precedence than addition expressions? Explain why using the grammar rules.

11.1.2 Data Types

Python provides many built-in data types. We describe three of the most useful data types here: lists, strings, and dictionaries.

Lists. Python provides a list datatype similar to lists in Scheme, except instead of building lists from simpler parts (that is, using *cons* pairs in Scheme), the Python list type is a built-in datatype. The other important difference is that Python lists are mutable like *mlist* from Section 9.3.

Lists are denoted in Python using square brackets. For example, [] denotes an empty list and [1, 2] denotes a list containing two elements. The elements in a list can be of any type (including other lists).

Elements can be selected from a list using the list subscript expression:

PrimaryExpression ::⇒ *SubscriptExpression*
SubscriptExpression ::⇒ *PrimaryExpression* [*Expression*]

A subscript expression evaluates to the element indexed by value of the inner expression from the list. For example,

```
≫ a = [1, 2, 3]
≫ a[0]          ⇒ 1
≫ a[1+1]        ⇒ 3
≫ a[3]          ⇒ IndexError: list index out of range
```

[3]There are some subtle differences and complexities (see Section 4.1 of the Python Reference Manual), however, which we do not go into here.

The expression *p*[0] in Python is analogous to (*car p*) in Scheme.

The subscript expression has constant running time; unlike indexing Scheme lists, the time required does not depend on the length of the list even if the selection index is the end of the list. The reason for this is that Python stores lists internally differently from how Scheme stores as chains of pairs. The elements of a Python list are stored as a block in memory, so the location of the kth element can be calculated directly by adding k times the size of one element to the location of the start of the list.

A subscript expression can also select a range of elements from the list:

$$\begin{array}{ll} \textit{SubscriptExpression} ::\Rightarrow & \textit{PrimaryExpression} \; [\; \textit{Bound}_{Low} : \textit{Bound}_{High} \;] \\ \textit{Bound} ::\Rightarrow & \textit{Expression} \mid \epsilon \end{array}$$

Subscript expressions with ranges evaluate to a list containing the elements between the low bound and the high bound. If the low bound is missing, the low bound is the beginning of the list. If the high bound is missing, the high bound is the end of the list. For example,

```
≫ a = [1, 2, 3]
≫ a[:1]          ⇒ [1]
≫ a[1:]          ⇒ [2, 3]
≫ a[4−2:3]       ⇒ [3]
≫ a[:]           ⇒ [1, 2, 3]
```

The expression *p*[1:] in Python is analogous to (*cdr p*) in Scheme.

Python lists are mutable (the value of a list can change after it is created). We can use list subscripts as the targets for an assignment expression:

$$\textit{Target} ::\Rightarrow \textit{SubscriptExpression}$$

Assignments using ranges as targets can add elements to the list as well as changing the values of existing elements:

```
≫ a = [1, 2, 3]
≫ a[0] = 7
≫ a              ⇒ [7, 2, 3]
≫ a[1:4] = [4, 5, 6]
≫ a              ⇒ [7, 4, 5, 6]
≫ a[1:] = [6]
≫ a              ⇒ [7, 6]
```

In the *tokenize* procedure, we use *tokens* = [] to initialize *tokens* to an empty list, and use *tokens.append*(*current*) to append an element to the *tokens* list. The Python *append* procedure is similar to the *mlist-append!* procedure (except it works on the empty list, where there is no way in Scheme to modify the null input list).

Strings. The other datatype used in *tokenize* is the string datatype, named *str* in Python. As in Scheme, a String is a sequence of characters. Unlike Scheme strings which are mutable, the Python *str* datatype is immutable. Once a string is created its value cannot change. This means all the string methods that seem to change the string values actually return new strings (for example, *capitalize*() returns a copy of the string with its first letter capitalized).

Strings can be enclosed in single quotes (e.g., 'hello'), double quotes (e.g., "*hello*"), and triple-double quotes (e.g., " " "*hello*" " "; a string inside triple quotes can span multiple lines). In our example program, we use the assignment expression, *current* = '' (two single quotes), to initialize the value of *current* to the empty string. The input, *s*, is a string object.

The addition operator can be used to concatenate two strings. In *tokenize*, we use *current* = *current* + *c* to update the value of *current* to include a new character. Since strings are immutable there is no string method analogous to the list *append* method. Instead, appending a character to a string involves creating a new string object.

Dictionaries. A dictionary is a lookup-table where values are associated with keys. The keys can be any immutable type (strings and numbers are commonly used as keys); the values can be of any type. We did not use the dictionary type in *tokenize*, but it is very useful for implementing frames in the evaluator.

A dictionary is denoted using curly brackets. The empty dictionary is {}. We add a key-value pair to the dictionary using an assignment where the left side is a subscript expression that specifies the key and the right side is the value assigned to that key. For example,

```
birthyear = {}
birthyear['Euclid'] = '300BC'
birthyear['Ada'] = 1815
birthyear['Alan Turing'] = 1912
birthyear['Alan Kay'] = 1940
```

defines *birthyear* as a dictionary containing four entries. The keys are all strings; the values are numbers, except for Euclid's entry which is a string.

We can obtain the value associated with a key in the dictionary using a subscript expression. For example, *birthyear*['Alan Turing'] evaluates to 1912. We can replace the value associated with a key using the same syntax as adding a key-value pair to the dictionary. The statement,

```
birthyear['Euclid'] = −300
```

replaces the value of *birthyear*['Euclid'] with the number −300.

The dictionary type also provides a method *has_key* that takes one input and produces a Boolean indicating if the dictionary object contains the input value as a key. For the *birthyear* dictionary,

```
≫ birthyear.has_key('John Backus')  ⇒ False
≫ birthyear.has_key('Ada')          ⇒ True
```

The dictionary type lookup and update operations have approximately constant running time: the time it takes to lookup the value associated with a key does not scale as the size of the dictionary increases. This is done by computing a number based on the key that determines where the associated value would be stored (if that key is in the dictionary). The number is used to index into a structure similar to a Python list (so it has constant time to retrieve any element). Mapping keys to appropriate numbers to avoid many keys mapping to the same location in the list is a difficult problem, but one the Python dictionary object does well for most sets of keys.

11.1.3 Applications and Invocations

The grammar rules for expressions that apply procedures are:

PrimaryExpression ::⇒ *CallExpression*
CallExpression ::⇒ *PrimaryExpression* (*ArgumentList*)
ArgumentList ::⇒ *SomeArguments*
ArgumentList ::⇒ ϵ
SomeArguments ::⇒ *Expression*
SomeArguments ::⇒ *Expression* , *SomeArguments*

In Python, nearly every data value (including lists and strings) is an object. This means the way we manipulate data is to invoke methods on objects. To invoke a method we use the same rules, but the *PrimaryExpression* of the *CallExpression* specifies an object and method:

PrimaryExpression ::⇒ *AttributeReference*
AttributeReference ::⇒ *PrimaryExpression* . ***Name***

The name *AttributeReference* is used since the same syntax is used for accessing the internal state of objects as well.

The *tokenize* procedure includes five method applications, four of which are *tokens.append(current)*. The object reference is *tokens*, the list of tokens in the input. The list *append* method takes one parameter and adds that value to the end of the list.

The other method invocation is *c.isspace()* where *c* is a string consisting of one character in the input. The *isspace* method for the string datatype returns true if the input string is non-empty and all characters in the string are whitespace (either spaces, tabs, or newlines).

The *tokenize* procedure also uses the built-in function *len* which takes as input an object of a collection datatype such as a list or a string, and outputs the number of elements in the collection. It is a procedure, not a method; the input object is passed in as a parameter. In *tokenize*, we use *len(current)* to find the number of characters in the current token.

11.1.4 Control Statements

Python provides control statements for making decisions, looping, and for returning from a procedure.

If statement. Python's if statement is similar to the conditional expression in Scheme:

$$\begin{array}{lll} \textit{Statement} & ::\Rightarrow & \text{IfStatement} \\ \textit{IfStatement} & ::\Rightarrow & \textbf{if } \textit{Expression}_{\textit{Predicate}} \textbf{ : } \textit{Block Elifs OptElse} \\ \textit{Elifs} & ::\Rightarrow & \epsilon \\ \textit{Elifs} & ::\Rightarrow & \textbf{elif } \textit{Expression}_{\textit{Predicate}} \textbf{ : } \textit{Block Elifs} \\ \textit{OptElse} & ::\Rightarrow & \epsilon \\ \textit{OptElse} & ::\Rightarrow & \textbf{else : } \textit{Block} \end{array}$$

Unlike in Scheme, there is no need to have an alternate clause since the Python if statement does not need to produce a value. The evaluation rule is similar to Scheme's conditional expression:

> **Python Evaluation Rule: If.** First, evaluate the $\textit{Expression}_{\textit{Predicate}}$. If it evaluates to a true value, the consequent *Block* is evaluated, and none of the rest of the *IfStatement* is evaluated. Otherwise, each of the *elif* predicates is evaluated in order. If one evaluates to a true value, its *Block* is evaluated and none of the rest of the *IfStatement* is evaluated. If none of the *elif* predicates evaluates to a true value, the **else** *Block* is evaluated if there is one.

The main if statement in *tokenize* is:

```
if c.isspace(): ...
elif c in '()': ...
else: current = current + c
```

The first if predicate tests if the current character is a space. If so, the end of the current token has been reached. The consequent *Block* is itself an *IfStatement*:

```
if len(current) > 0:
  tokens.append(current)
  current = ''
```

If the current token has at least one character, it is appended to the list of tokens in the input string and the current token is reset to the empty string. This *IfStatement* has no *elif* or *else* clauses, so if the predicate is false, there is nothing to do.

For statement. A **for** statement provides a way of iterating through a set of values, carrying out a body block for each value.

$$\begin{array}{lll} \textit{Statement} & ::\Rightarrow & \text{ForStatement} \\ \textit{ForStatement} & ::\Rightarrow & \textbf{for } \textit{Target} \textbf{ in } \textit{Expression} \textbf{ : } \textit{Block} \end{array}$$

Its evaluation rule is:

> **Python Evaluation Rule: For.** First evaluate the *Expression* which must produce a value that is a collection. Then, for each value in the collection assign the *Target* to that value and evaluate the *Block*.

Other than the first two initializations, and the final two statements, the bulk of the *tokenize* procedure is contained in a **for** statement. The for statement in *tokenize* header is **for** *c* **in** *s*: .... The string *s* is the input string, a collection of characters. So, the loop will repeat once for each character in *s*, and the value of *c* is each character in the input string (represented as a singleton string), in turn.

Return statement. In Scheme, the body of a procedure is an expression and the value of that expression is the result of evaluating an application of the procedure. In Python, the body of a procedure is a block of one or more statements. Statements have no value, so there is no obvious way to decide what the result of a procedure application should be. Python's solution is to use a *return statement.*

The grammar for the return statement is:

Statement ::⇒ ReturnStatement
ReturnStatement ::⇒ **return** *Expression*

A return statement finishes execution of a procedure, returning the value of the *Expression* to the caller as the result. The last statement of the *tokenize* procedure is: **return** *tokens.* It returns the value of the *tokens* list to the caller.

11.2 Parser

The parser takes as input a Charme program string, and produces as output a nested list that encodes the structure of the input program. The first step is to break the input string into tokens; this is done by the *tokenize* procedure defined in the previous section.

The next step is to take the list of tokens and produce a data structure that encodes the structure of the input program. Since the Charme language is built from simple parenthesized expressions, we can represent the parsed program as a list. But, unlike the list returned by *tokenize* which is a flat list containing the tokens in order, the list returned by *parse* is a structured list that may have lists (and lists of lists, etc.) as elements.

Charme's syntax is very simple, so the parser can be implemented by just breaking an expression into its components using the parentheses and whitespace. The parser needs to balance the open and close parentheses that enclose expressions. For example, if the input string is

(**define** *square* (**lambda** (*x*) (∗ *x x*)))

the output of *tokenizer* is the list:

```
['(', 'define', 'square', '(', 'lambda', '(', 'x', ')', '(', '*', 'x', 'x', ')', ')', ')']
```

The parser structures the tokens according to the program structure, producing a parse tree that encodes the structure of the input program. The parenthesis provide the program structure, so are removed from the parse tree. For the example, the resulting parse tree is:

```
['define',
 'square',
 [ 'lambda',
   ['x'],
   ['*', 'x', 'x'] ] ]
```

Here is the definition of *parse*:

```
def parse(s):
  def parse_tokens(tokens, inner):
    res = []
    while len(tokens) > 0:
      current = tokens.pop(0)
      if current == '(':
        res.append (parse_tokens(tokens, True))
      elif current == ')':
        if inner: return res
        else:
          error('Unmatched close paren: ' + s)
          return None
      else:
        res.append(current)

    if inner:
      error ('Unmatched open paren: ' + s)
      return None
    else:
      return res

  return parse_tokens(tokenize(s), False)
```

The input to *parse* is a string in the target language. The output is a list of the parenthesized expressions in the input. Here are some examples:

```
≫ parse('150')             ⇒ ['150']
≫ parse('(+ 1 2)')         ⇒ [['+', '1', '2']]
≫ parse('(+ 1 (* 2 3))')   ⇒ [['+', '1', ['*', '2', '3']]]
≫ parse('(define square (lambda (x) (* x x)))')
                           ⇒ [['define', 'square', ['lambda', ['x'], ['*', 'x', 'x']]]]
≫ parse('(+ 1 2) (+ 3 4)') ⇒ [['+', '1', '2'], ['+', '3', '4']]
```

The parentheses are no longer included as tokens in the result, but their presence in the input string determines the structure of the result.

recursive descent

The *parse* procedure implements a *recursive descent* parser. The main *parse* procedure defines the *parse_tokens* helper procedure and returns the result of calling it with inputs that are the result of tokenizing the input string and the Boolean literal False: **return** *parse_tokens*(*tokenize*(*s*), False).

The *parse_tokens* procedure takes two inputs: *tokens*, a list of tokens (that results from the *tokenize* procedure); and *inner*, a Boolean that indicates whether the parser is inside a parenthesized expression. The value of *inner* is False for the initial call since the parser starts outside a parenthesized expression. All of the recursive calls result from encountering a '(', so the value passed as *inner* is True for all the recursive calls.

The body of the *parse_tokens* procedure initializes *res* to an empty list that is used to store the result. Then, the **while** statement iterates as long as the token list contains at least one element.

The first statement of the **while** statement block assigns *tokens.pop*(0) to *current*. The *pop* method of the list takes a parameter that selects an element from the list. The selected element is returned as the result. The *pop* method also mutates the list object by removing the selected element. So, *tokens.pop*(0) returns the first element of the *tokens* list and removes that element from the list. This is essential to the parser making progress: every time the *tokens.pop*(0) expression is evaluated the number of elements in the token list is reduced by one.

If the *current* token is an open parenthesis, *parse_tokens* is called recursively to parse the inner expression (that is, all the tokens until the matching close parenthesis). The result is a list of tokens, which is appended to the result. If the *current* token is a close parenthesis, the behavior depends on whether or not the parser is parsing an inner expression. If it is inside an expression (that is, an open parenthesis has been encountered with no matching close parenthesis yet), the close parenthesis closes the inner expression, and the result is returned. If it is not in an inner expression, the close parenthesis has no matching open parenthesis so a parse error is reported.

The **else** clause deals with all other tokens by appending them to the list.

The final if statement checks that the parser is not in an inner context when the input is finished. This would mean there was an open parenthesis without a corresponding close, so an error is reported. Otherwise, the list representing the parse tree is returned.

11.3 Evaluator

The evaluator takes a list representing the parse tree of a Charme expression or definition and an environment, and outputs the result of evaluating the expression in the input environment. The evaluator implements the evaluation rules for the target language.

The core of the evaluator is the procedure *meval*:

```
def meval(expr, env):
  if is_primitive(expr): return eval_primitive(expr)
  elif is_if(expr): return eval_if(expr, env)
  elif is_definition(expr): eval_definition(expr, env)
  elif is_name(expr): return eval_name(expr, env)
  elif is_lambda(expr): return eval_lambda(expr, env)
  elif is_application(expr): return eval_application(expr, env)
  else: error ('Unknown expression type: ' + str(expr))
```

The if statement matches the input expression with one of the expression types (or the definition) in the Charme language, and returns the result of applying the corresponding evaluation procedure (if the input is a definition, no value is returned since definitions do not produce an output value). We next consider each evaluation rule in turn.

11.3.1 Primitives

Charme supports two kinds of primitives: natural numbers and primitive procedures. If the expression is a number, it is a string of digits. The *is_number* procedure evaluates to True if and only if its input is a number:

```
def is_primitive(expr):
    return is_number(expr) or is_primitive_procedure(expr)

def is_number(expr):
    return isinstance(expr, str) and expr.isdigit()
```

Here, we use the built-in function *isinstance* to check if *expr* is of type *str*. The and expression in Python evaluates similarly to the Scheme **and** special form: the left operand is evaluated first; if it evaluates to a false value, the value of the and expression is that false value. If it evaluates to a true value, the right operand is evaluated, and the value of the and expression is the value of its right operand. This evaluation rule means it is safe to use *expr.isdigit*() in the right operand, since it is only evaluated if the left operand evaluated to a true value, which means *expr* is a string.

Primitive procedures are defined using Python procedures. We define the procedure *is_primitive_procedure* using *callable*, a procedure that returns true only for callable objects such as procedures and methods:

```
def is_primitive_procedure(expr):
    return callable(expr)
```

The evaluation rule for a primitive is identical to the Scheme rule:

> **Charme Evaluation Rule 1: Primitives.** A primitive expression evaluates to its pre-defined value.

We need to implement the *pre-defined* values in our Charme interpreter.

To evaluate a number primitive, we need to convert the string representation to a number of type *int*. The *int*(*s*) constructor takes a string as its input and outputs the corresponding integer:

```
def eval_primitive(expr):
    if is_number(expr): return int(expr)
    else: return expr
```

The **else** clause means that all other primitives (in Charme, this is only primitive procedures and Boolean constants) self-evaluate: the value of evaluating a primitive is itself.

For the primitive procedures, we need to define Python procedures that implement the primitive procedure. For example, here is the *primitive_plus* procedure that is associated with the + primitive procedure:

```
def primitive_plus (operands):
    if (len(operands) == 0): return 0
    else: return operands[0] + primitive_plus (operands[1:])
```

The input is a list of operands. Since a procedure is applied only after all subexpressions are evaluated, there is no need to evaluate the operands: they are already the evaluated values. For numbers, the values are Python integers, so we can use the Python + operator to add them. To provide the same behavior as the Scheme primitive + procedure, we define our Charme primitive + procedure to evaluate to 0 when there are no operands, and otherwise to recursively add all of the operand values.

The other primitive procedures are defined similarly:

```
def primitive_times (operands):
  if (len(operands) == 0): return 1
  else: return operands[0] * primitive_times (operands[1:])

def primitive_minus (operands):
  if (len(operands) == 1): return -1 * operands[0]
  elif len(operands) == 2: return operands[0] - operands[1]
  else:
    eval_error('- expects 1 or 2 operands, given %s: %s'
               % (len(operands), str(operands)))

def primitive_equals (operands):
  check_operands (operands, 2, '=')
  return operands[0] == operands[1]

def primitive_lessthan (operands):
  check_operands (operands, 2, '<')
  return operands[0] < operands[1]
```

The *check_operands* procedure reports an error if a primitive procedure is applied to the wrong number of operands:

```
def check_operands(operands, num, prim):
  if (len(operands) != num):
    eval_error('Primitive %s expected %s operands, given %s: %s'
               % (prim, num, len(operands), str(operands)))
```

11.3.2 If Expressions

Charme provides an if expression special form with a syntax and evaluation rule identical to the Scheme if expression. The grammar rule for an if expression is:

IfExpression ::⇒ (**if** $Expression_{\text{Predicate}}$
$Expression_{\text{Consequent}}$
$Expression_{\text{Alternate}}$)

The expression object representing an if expression should be a list containing three elements, with the first element matching the keyword if.

All special forms have this property: they are represented by lists where the first element is a keyword that identifies the special form.

The *is_special_form* procedure takes an expression and a keyword and outputs a Boolean. The result is True if the expression is a special form matching the keyword:

```
def is_special_form(expr, keyword):
  return isinstance(expr, list) and len(expr) > 0 and expr[0] == keyword
```

We can use this to recognize different special forms by passing in different keywords. We recognize an if expression by the if token at the beginning of the expression:

```
def is_if(expr):
    return is_special_form(expr, 'if')
```

The evaluation rule for an if expression is:[4]

> **Charme Evaluation Rule 5: If.** To evaluate an if expression in the current environment, (a) evaluate the predicate expression in the current environment; then, (b) if the value of the predicate expression is a false value then the value of the if expression is the value of the alternate expression in the current environment; otherwise, the value of the if expression is the value of the consequent expression in the current environment.

This procedure implements the if evaluation rule:

```
def eval_if(expr,env):
    if meval(expr[1], env) != False: return meval(expr[2],env)
    else: return meval(expr[3],env)
```

11.3.3 Definitions and Names

To evaluate definitions and names we need to represent environments. A definition adds a name to a frame, and a name expression evaluates to the value associated with a name.

We use a Python class to represent an environment. As in Chapter 10, a class packages state and procedures that manipulate that state. In Scheme, we needed to use a message-accepting procedure to do this. Python provides the class construct to support it directly. We define the *Environment* class for representing an environment. It has internal state for representing the parent (itself an *Environment* or None, Python's equivalent to *null* for the global environment's parent), and for the frame.

The dictionary datatype provides a convenient way to implement a frame. The *__init__* procedure constructs a new object. It initializes the frame of the new environment to the empty dictionary using *self._frame* = {}.

The *add_variable* method either defines a new variable or updates the value associated with a variable. With the dictionary datatype, we can do this with a simple assignment statement.

The *lookup_variable* method first checks if the frame associated with this environment has a key associated with the input *name*. If it does, the value associated with that key is the value of the variable and that value is returned. Otherwise, if the environment has a parent, the value associated with the name is the value of looking up the variable in the parent environment. This directly follows from the stateful Scheme evaluation rule for name expressions. The **else** clause

[4]We number the Charme evaluation rules using the numbers we used for the analogous Scheme evaluation rules, but present them in a different order.

addresses the situation where the name is not found and there is no parent environment (since we have already reached the global environment) by reporting an evaluation error indicating an undefined name.

```
class Environment:
  def __init__(self, parent):
    self._parent = parent
    self._frame = {}

  def add_variable(self, name, value):
    self._frame[name] = value

  def lookup_variable(self, name):
    if self._frame.has_key(name): return self._frame[name]
    elif (self._parent): return self._parent.lookup_variable(name)
    else: eval_error('Undefined name: %s' % (name))
```

Using the *Environment* class, the evaluation rules for definitions and name expressions are straightforward.

```
def is_definition(expr): return is_special_form(expr, 'define')
def eval_definition(expr, env):
  name = expr[1]
  value = meval(expr[2], env)
  env.add_variable(name, value)

def is_name(expr): return isinstance(expr, str)
def eval_name(expr, env):
  return env.lookup_variable(expr)
```

11.3.4 Procedures

The result of evaluating a lambda expression is a procedure. Hence, to define the evaluation rule for lambda expressions we need to define a class for representing user-defined procedures. It needs to record the parameters, procedure body, and defining environment:

```
class Procedure:
  def __init__(self, params, body, env):
    self._params = params
    self._body = body
    self._env = env
  def getParams(self): return self._params
  def getBody(self): return self._body
  def getEnvironment(self): return self._env
```

The evaluation rule for lambda expressions creates a *Procedure* object:

```
def is_lambda(expr): return is_special_form(expr, 'lambda')

def eval_lambda(expr,env):
  return Procedure(expr[1], expr[2], env)
```

11.3.5 Application

Evaluation and application are defined recursively. To perform an application, we need to evaluate all the subexpressions of the application expression, and then apply the result of evaluating the first subexpression to the values of the other subexpressions.

```
def is_application(expr): # requires: all special forms checked first
    return isinstance(expr, list)

def eval_application(expr, env):
    subexprs = expr
    subexprvals = map (lambda sexpr: meval(sexpr, env), subexprs)
    return mapply(subexprvals[0], subexprvals[1:])
```

The *eval_application* procedure uses the built-in *map* procedure, which is similar to *list-map* from Chapter 5. The first parameter to *map* is a procedure constructed using a lambda expression (similar in meaning, but not in syntax, to Scheme's lambda expression); the second parameter is the list of subexpressions.

The *mapply* procedure implements the application rules. If the procedure is a primitive, it "just does it": it applies the primitive procedure to its operands.

To apply a constructed procedure (represented by a *Procedure*), follow the stateful application rule for applying constructed procedures:

> **Charme Application Rule 2: Constructed Procedures.** To apply a constructed procedure:
>
> 1. Construct a new environment, whose parent is the environment of the applied procedure.
> 2. For each procedure parameter, create a place in the frame of the new environment with the name of the parameter. Evaluate each operand expression in the environment or the application and initialize the value in each place to the value of the corresponding operand expression.
> 3. Evaluate the body of the procedure in the newly created environment. The resulting value is the value of the application.

The *mapply* procedure implements the application rules for primitive and constructed procedures:

```
def mapply(proc, operands):
    if (is_primitive_procedure(proc)): return proc(operands)
    elif isinstance(proc, Procedure):
        params = proc.getParams()
        newenv = Environment(proc.getEnvironment())
        if len(params) != len(operands):
            eval_error ('Parameter length mismatch: %s given operands %s'
                        % (str(proc), str(operands)))
        for i in range(0, len(params)):
            newenv.add_variable(params[i], operands[i])
        return meval(proc.getBody(), newenv)
    else: eval_error('Application of non-procedure: %s' % (proc))
```

11.3.6 Finishing the Interpreter

To finish the interpreter, we define the *evalLoop* procedure that sets up the global environment and provides an interactive interface to the interpreter. The evaluation loop reads a string from the user using the Python built-in procedure *raw_input*. It uses *parse* to convert that string into a structured list representation. Then, it uses a for loop to iterate through the expressions. It evaluates each expression using *meval* and the result is printed.

To initialize the global environment, we create an environment with no parent and place variables in it corresponding to the primitives in Charme.

```
def evalLoop():
    genv = Environment(None)
    genv.add_variable('true', True)
    genv.add_variable('false', False)
    genv.add_variable('+', primitive_plus)
    genv.add_variable('-', primitive_minus)
    genv.add_variable('*', primitive_times)
    genv.add_variable('=', primitive_equals)
    genv.add_variable('<', primitive_lessthan)
    while True:
        inv = raw_input('Charme> ')
        if inv == 'quit': break
        for expr in parse(inv):
            print str(meval(expr, genv))
```

Here are some sample interactions with our Charme interpreter:

```
>> evalLoop()
Charme> (+ 2 2)
4
Charme> (define fibo
           (lambda (n)
             (if (= n 1) 1
               (if (= n 2) 1
                 (+ (fibo (- n 1)) (fibo (- n 2)))))))
None
Charme> (fibo 10)
55
```

11.4 Lazy Evaluation

Once we have an interpreter, we can change the meaning of our language by changing the evaluation rules. This enables a new problem-solving strategy: if the solution to a problem cannot be expressed easily in an existing language, define and implement an interpreter for a new language in which the problem can be solved more easily.

This section explores a variation on Charme we call *LazyCharme*. LazyCharme changes the application evaluation rule so that operand expressions are not evaluated until their values are needed. This is known as *lazy evaluation*. Lazy evaluation enables many procedures which would otherwise be awkward to express to be defined concisely. Since both Charme and LazyCharme are universal

lazy evaluation

programming languages they can express the same set of computations: all of the procedures we define that take advantage of lazy evaluation could be defined with eager evaluation (for example, by first defining a lazy interpreter as we do here).

11.4.1 Lazy Interpreter

The Charme interpreter as well as the standard Scheme language evaluate application expressions *eagerly*: all operand subexpressions are evaluated whether or not their values are needed. This is known as *eager evaluation*. Eager evaluation means that any expression that does not always evaluate all of its subexpressions must be a special form. For example, there is no way to define a procedure that behaves like the if special form.

eager evaluation

Much of my work has come from being lazy.
John Backus

With lazy evaluation, an expression is evaluated only when its value is needed. Lazy evaluation changes the evaluation rule for applications of constructed procedures. Instead of evaluating all operand expressions, lazy evaluation delays evaluation of an operand expression until the value of the parameter is needed. To keep track of what is needed to perform the evaluation when and if it is needed, a special object known as a *thunk* is created and stored in the place associated with the parameter name. By delaying evaluation of operand expressions until their value is needed, we can enable programs to define procedures that conditionally evaluate their operands like the if special form.

thunk

We will encourage you to develop the three great virtues of a programmer: Laziness, Impatience, and Hubris.
Larry Wall, *Programming Perl*

The lazy rule for applying constructed procedures is:

Lazy Application Rule 2: Constructed Procedures. To apply a constructed procedure:

1. Construct a new environment, whose parent is the environment of the applied procedure.
2. For each procedure parameter, create a place in the frame of the new environment with the name of the parameter. **Put a *thunk* in that place, which is an object that can be used later to evaluate the value of the corresponding operand expression if and when its value is needed.**
3. Evaluate the body of the procedure in the newly created environment. The resulting value is the value of the application.

The rule is identical to the Stateful Application Rule except for the bolded part of step 2. To implement lazy evaluation we modify the interpreter to implement the lazy application rule. We start by defining a Python class for representing thunks and then modify the interpreter to support lazy evaluation.

Making Thunks. A thunk keeps track of an expression whose evaluation is delayed until it is needed. Once the evaluation is performed, the resulting value is saved so the expression does not need to be re-evaluated the next time the value is needed. Thus, a thunk is in one of two possible states: *unevaluated* and *evaluated*.

The *Thunk* class implements thunks:

```
class Thunk:
  def __init__(self, expr, env):
    self._expr = expr
```

```
        self._env = env
        self._evaluated = False
    def value(self):
        if not self._evaluated:
            self._value = force_eval(self._expr, self._env)
            self._evaluated = True
        return self._value
```

A *Thunk* object keeps track of the expression in the *_expr* instance variable. Since the value of the expression may be needed when the evaluator is evaluating an expression in some other environment, it also keeps track of the environment in which the thunk expression should be evaluated in the *_env* instance variable.

The *_evaluated* instance variable is a Boolean that records whether or not the thunk expression has been evaluated. Initially this value is False. After the expression is evaluated, *_evaluated* is True and the *_value* instance variable keeps track of the resulting value.

The *value* method uses *force_eval* (defined later) to obtain the evaluated value of the thunk expression and stores that result in *_value*.

The *is_thunk* procedure returns True only when its parameter is a thunk:

```
def is_thunk(expr): return isinstance(expr, Thunk)
```

Changing the evaluator. To implement lazy evaluation, we change the evaluator so there are two different evaluation procedures: *meval* is the standard evaluation procedure (which leaves thunks in their unevaluated state), and *force_eval* is the evaluation procedure that forces thunks to be evaluated to values. The interpreter uses *meval* when the actual expression value may not be needed, and *force_eval* to force evaluation of thunks when the value of an expression is needed.

In the *meval* procedure, a thunk evaluates to itself. We add a new **elif** clause for thunk objects to the *meval* procedure:

```
elif is_thunk(expr):    return expr
```

The *force_eval* procedure first uses *meval* to evaluate the expression normally. If the result is a thunk, it uses the *Thunk.value* method to force evaluation of the thunk expression. That method uses *force_eval* to find the value of the thunk expression, so any thunks inside the expression will be recursively evaluated.

```
def force_eval(expr, env):
    val = meval(expr, env)
    if is_thunk(val): return val.value()
    else: return val
```

Next, we change the application rule to perform delayed evaluation and change a few other places in the interpreter to use *force_eval* instead of *meval* to obtain the actual values when they are needed.

We change *eval_application* to delay evaluation of the operands by creating *Thunk* objects representing each operand:

```
def eval_application(expr, env):
  ops = map (lambda sexpr: Thunk(sexpr, env), expr[1:])
  return mapply(force_eval(expr[0], env), ops)
```

Only the first subexpression must be evaluated to obtain the procedure to apply. Hence, *eval_application* uses *force_eval* to obtain the value of the first subexpression, but makes Thunk objects for the operand expressions.

Modern methods of production have given us the possibility of ease and security for all; we have chosen, instead, to have overwork for some and starvation for others. Hitherto we have continued to be as energetic as we were before there were machines; in this we have been foolish, but there is no reason to go on being foolish forever.
Bertrand Russell, *In Praise of Idleness*, 1932

To apply a primitive, we need the actual values of its operands, so must force evaluation of any thunks in the operands. Hence, the definition for *mapply* forces evaluation of the operands to a primitive procedure:

```
def mapply(proc, operands):
  def dethunk(expr):
    if is_thunk(expr): return expr.value()
    else: return expr

  if (is_primitive_procedure(proc)):
    ops = map (dethunk, operands)
    return proc(ops)
  elif isinstance(proc, Procedure):
    ... # same as in Charme interpreter
```

To evaluate an if expression, it is necessary to know the actual value of the predicate expressions. We change the *eval_if* procedure to use *force_eval* when evaluating the predicate expression:

```
def eval_if(expr,env):
  if force_eval(expr[1], env) != False: return meval(expr[2],env)
  else: return meval(expr[3],env)
```

This forces the predicate to evaluate to a value so its actual value can be used to determine how the rest of the if expression evaluates; the evaluations of the consequent and alternate expressions are left as *meval*s since it is not necessary to force them to be evaluated yet.

The final change to the interpreter is to force evaluation when the result is displayed to the user in the *evalLoop* procedure by replacing the call to *meval* with *force_eval*.

11.4.2 Lazy Programming

Lazy evaluation enables programming constructs that are not possible with eager evaluation. For example, with lazy evaluation we can define a procedure that behaves like the if expression special form. We first define *true* and *false* as procedures that take two parameters and output the first or second parameter:

```
(define true (lambda (a b) a))
(define false (lambda (a b) b))
```

Then, this definition defines a procedure with behavior similar to the **if** special form:

```
(define ifp (lambda (p c a) (p c a)))
```

With eager evaluation, this would not work since all operands would be evaluated; with lazy evaluation, only the operand that corresponds to the appropriate consequent or alternate expression is evaluated.

Lazy evaluation also enables programs to deal with seemingly infinite data structures. This is possible since only those values of the apparently infinite data structure that are used need to be created.

Suppose we define procedures similar to the Scheme procedures for manipulating pairs:

```
(define cons (lambda (a b) (lambda (p) (if p a b))))
(define car (lambda (p) (p true)))
(define cdr (lambda (p) (p false)))
(define null false)
(define null? (lambda (x) (= x false)))
```

These behave similarly to the corresponding Scheme procedures, except in LazyCharme their operands are evaluated lazily. This means, we can define an infinite list:

```
(define ints-from (lambda (n) (cons n (ints-from (+ n 1)))))
```

With eager evaluation, (*ints-from* 1) would never finish evaluating; it has no base case for stopping the recursive applications. In LazyCharme, however, the operands to the *cons* application in the body of *ints-from* are not evaluated until they are needed. Hence, (*ints-from* 1) terminates and produces a seemingly infinite list, but only the evaluations that are needed are performed:

```
LazyCharme> (car (ints-from 1))
1
LazyCharme> (car (cdr (cdr (cdr (ints-from 1)))))
4
```

Some evaluations fail to terminate even with lazy evaluation. For example, assume the standard definition of *list-length*:

```
(define list-length
    (lambda (lst) (if (null? lst) 0 (+ 1 (list-length (cdr lst))))))
```

An evaluation of (*length* (*ints-from* 1)) never terminates. Every time an application of *list-length* is evaluated, it applies *cdr* to the input list, which causes *ints-from* to evaluate another *cons*, increasing the length of the list by one. The actual length of the list is infinite, so the application of *list-length* does not terminate.

Lists with delayed evaluation can be used in useful programs. Reconsider the Fibonacci sequence from Chapter 7. Using lazy evaluation, we can define a list that is the infinitely long Fibonacci sequence:[5]

```
(define fibo-gen (lambda (a b) (cons a (fibo-gen b (+ a b)))))
(define fibos (fibo-gen 0 1))
```

[5]This example is based on Abelson and Sussman, *Structure and Interpretation of Computer Programs*, Section 3.5.2, which also presents several other examples of interesting programs constructed using delayed evaluation.

The nth Fibonacci number is the nth element of *fibos*:

```
(define fibo
  (lambda (n)
    (list-get-element fibos n)))
```

where *list-get-element* is defined as it was defined in Chapter 5.

Another strategy for defining the Fibonacci sequence is to first define a procedure that merges two (possibly infinite) lists, and then define the Fibonacci sequence recursively. The *merge-lists* procedure combines elements in two lists using an input procedure.

```
(define merge-lists
  (lambda (lst1 lst2 proc)
    (if (null? lst1) null
      (if (null? lst2) null
        (cons (proc (car lst1) (car lst2))
              (merge-lists (cdr lst1) (cdr lst2) proc))))))
```

We can define the Fibonacci sequence as the combination of two sequences, starting with the 0 and 1 base cases, combined using addition where the second sequence is offset by one position:

```
(define fibos (cons 0 (cons 1 (merge-lists fibos (cdr fibos) +))))
```

The sequence is defined to start with 0 and 1 as the first two elements. The following elements are the result of merging *fibos* and (*cdr fibos*) using the + procedure. This definition relies heavily on lazy evaluation; otherwise, the evaluation of (*merge-lists fibos* (*cdr fibos*) +) would never terminate: the input lists are effectively infinite.

Exercise 11.3. Define the sequence of factorials as an infinite list using delayed evaluation.

Exercise 11.4. Describe the infinite list defined by each of the following definitions. (Check your answers by evaluating the expressions in LazyCharme.)

a. (**define** *p* (*cons* 1 (*merge-lists p p* +)))

b. (**define** *t* (*cons* 1 (*merge-lists t* (*merge-lists t t* +) +)))

c. (**define** *twos* (*cons* 2 *twos*))

d. (**define** *doubles* (*merge-lists* (*ints-from* 1) *twos* *))

Eratosthenes

Exercise 11.5. [★★] A simple procedure known as the *Sieve of Eratosthenes* for finding prime numbers was created by Eratosthenes, an ancient Greek mathematician and astronomer. The procedure imagines starting with an (infinite) list of all the integers starting from 2. Then, it repeats the following two steps forever:

1. Circle the first number that is not crossed off; it is prime.
2. Cross off all numbers that are multiples of the circled number.

To carry out the procedure in practice, of course, the initial list of numbers must be finite, otherwise it would take forever to cross off all the multiples of 2. But, with delayed evaluation, we can implement the Sieve procedure on an effectively infinite list.

Implement the sieve procedure using lists with lazy evaluation. You may find the *list-filter* and *merge-lists* procedures useful, but will probably find it necessary to define some additional procedures.

11.5 Summary

Languages are tools for thinking, as well as means to express executable programs. A programming language is defined by its grammar and evaluation rules. To implement a language, we need to implement a parser that carries out the grammar rules and an evaluator that implements the evaluation rules.

We can produce new languages by changing the evaluation rules of an interpreter. Changing the evaluation rules changes what programs mean, and enables new approaches to solving problems.

xkcd

12 Computability

However unapproachable these problems may seem to us and however helpless we stand before them, we have, nevertheless, the firm conviction that their solution must follow by a finite number of purely logical processes...This conviction of the solvability of every mathematical problem is a powerful incentive to the worker. We hear within us the perpetual call: There is the problem. Seek its solution. You can find it by pure reason; for in mathematics there is no ignorabimus.
David Hilbert, 1900

In this chapter we consider the question of what problems can and cannot be solved by mechanical computation. This is the question of *computability*: a problem is *computable* if it can be solved by some algorithm; a problem that is *noncomputable* cannot be solved by any algorithm.

computability

Section 12.1 considers first the analogous question for declarative knowledge: are there true statements that cannot be proven by *any* proof? Section 12.2 introduces the *Halting Problem*, a problem that cannot be solved by any algorithm. Section 12.3 sketches Alan Turing's proof that the Halting Problem is noncomputable. Section 12.4 discusses how to show other problems are noncomputable.

12.1 Mechanizing Reasoning

Humans have been attempting to mechanize reasoning for thousands of years. Aristotle's *Organon* developed rules of inference known as *syllogisms* to codify logical deductions in approximately 350 BC.

syllogisms

Euclid went beyond Aristotle by developing a formal axiomatic system. An *axiomatic system* is a formal system consisting of a set of *axioms* and a set of *inference rules.* The goal of an axiomatic system is to codify knowledge in some domain.

axiomatic system

The axiomatic system Euclid developed in *The Elements* concerned constructions that could be drawn using just a straightedge and a compass.

Euclid started with five axioms (more commonly known as *postulates*); an example axiom is: *A straight line segment can be drawn joining any two points.* In addition to the postulates, Euclid states five *common notions,* which could be considered inference rules. An example of a common notion is: *The whole is greater than the part.*

Starting from the axioms and common notions, along with a set of definitions (e.g., defining a *circle*), Euclid proved 468 propositions mostly about geometry *proposition* and number theory. A *proposition* is a statement that is stated precisely enough to be either true or false. Euclid's first proposition is: given any line, an equilateral triangle can be constructed whose edges are the length of that line.

proof A *proof* of a proposition in an axiomatic system is a sequence of steps that ends with the proposition. Each step must follow from the axioms using the inference rules. Most of Euclid's proofs are constructive: propositions state that a thing with a particular property exists, and proofs show steps for constructing something with the stated property. The steps start from the postulates and follow the inference rules to prove that the constructed thing resulting at the end satisfies the requirements of the proposition.

consistent A *consistent* axiomatic system is one that can never derive contradictory statements by starting from the axioms and following the inference rules. If a system can generate both A and *not* A for any proposition A, the system is inconsistent. If the system cannot generate any contradictory pairs of statements it is consistent.

complete A *complete* axiomatic system can derive all true statements by starting from the axioms and following the inference rules. This means if a given proposition is true, some proof for that proposition can be found in the system. Since we do not have a clear definition of *true* (if we defined true as something that can be derived in the system, all axiomatic systems would automatically be complete by definition), we state this more clearly by saying that the system can decide any proposition. This means, for any proposition P, a complete axiomatic system would be able to derive either P or *not* P. A system that cannot decide all statements in the system is *incomplete*. An ideal axiomatic system would be complete and consistent: it would derive all true statements and no false statements.

The completeness of a system depends on the set of possible propositions. Euclid's system is consistent but not complete for the set of propositions about geometry. There are statements that concern simple properties in geometry (a famous example is *any angle can be divided into three equal sub-angles*) that cannot be derived in the system; trisecting an angle requires more powerful tools than the straightedge and compass provided by Euclid's postulates.

Figure 12.1 depicts two axiomatic systems. The one on the left one *incomplete*: there are some propositions that can be stated in the system that are true for which no valid proof exists in the system. The one on the right is *inconsistent*: it is possible to construct valid proofs of both P and *not* P starting from the axioms and following the inference rules. Once a single contradictory proposition can be proven the system becomes completely useless. The contradictory propositions amount to a proof that $true = false$, so once a single pair of contradictory propositions can be proven every other false proposition can also be proven in the system. Hence, only consistent systems are interesting and we focus on whether it is possible for them to also be complete.

Russell's Paradox. Towards the end of the 19th century, many mathematicians sought to systematize mathematics by developing a consistent axiomatic system that is complete for some area of mathematics. One notable attempt was Gottlob Frege's *Grundgestze der Arithmetik* (1893) which attempted to develop an axiomatic system for all of mathematics built from simple logic.

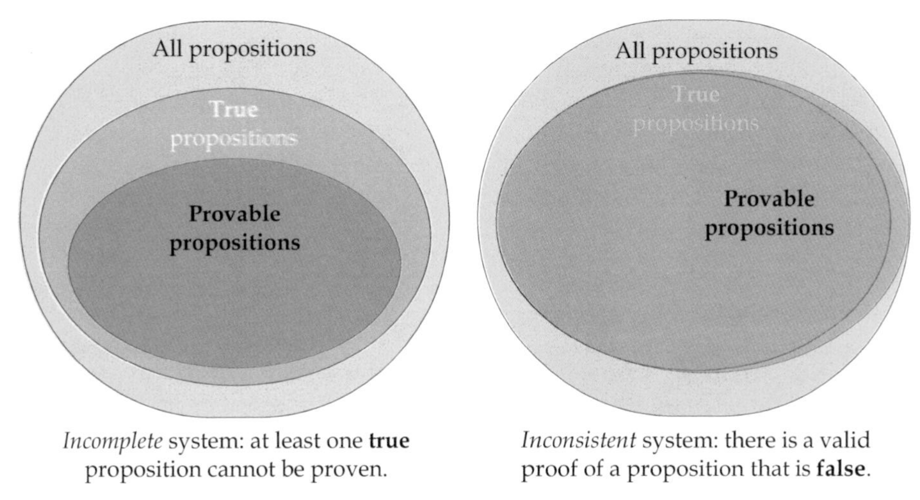

Incomplete system: at least one **true** proposition cannot be proven.

Inconsistent system: there is a valid proof of a proposition that is **false**.

Figure 12.1. Incomplete and inconsistent axiomatic systems.

Bertrand Russell discovered a problem with Frege's system, which is now known as *Russell's paradox*. Suppose R is defined as the set containing all sets that do not contain themselves as members. For example, the set of all prime numbers does not contain itself as a member, so it is a member of R. On the other hand, the set of all entities that are not prime numbers is a member of R. This set contains all sets, since a set is not a prime number, so it must contain itself.

Russell's paradox

The paradoxical question is: *is the set R a member of R?* There are two possible answers to consider but neither makes sense:

Yes: R is a member of R
: We defined the set R as the set of all sets that do not contain themselves as member. Hence, R cannot be a member of itself, and the statement that R is a member of R must be false.

No: R is not a member of R
: If R is not a member of R, then R does not contain itself and, by definition, must be a member of set R. This is a contradiction, so the statement that R is not a member of R must be false.

The question is a perfectly clear and precise binary question, but neither the "yes" nor the "no" answer makes any sense. Symbolically, we summarize the paradox: for any set s, $s \in R$ if and only if $s \notin s$. Selecting $s = R$ leads to the contradiction: $R \in R$ if and only if $R \notin R$.

Whitehead and Russell attempted to resolve this paradox by constructing their system to make it impossible to define the set R. Their solution was to introduce types. Each set has an associated type, and a set cannot contain members of its own type. The set types are defined recursively:

- A *type zero set* is a set that contains only non-set objects.
- A *type-n set* can only contain sets of type $n - 1$ and below.

This definition avoids the paradox: the definition of R must now define R as a set of type k set containing all sets of type $k - 1$ and below that do not contain themselves as members. Since R is a type k set, it cannot contain itself, since it cannot contain any type k sets.

Principia Mathematica

In 1913, Whitehead and Russell published *Principia Mathematica*, a bold attempt to mechanize mathematical reasoning that stretched to over 2000 pages. Whitehead and Russell attempted to derive all true mathematical statements about numbers and sets starting from a set of axioms and formal inference rules. They employed the type restriction to eliminate the particular paradox caused by set inclusion, but it does not eliminate all self-referential paradoxes.

For example, consider this paradox named for the Cretan philosopher Epimenides who was purported to have said "All Cretans are liars". If the statement is true, than Epimenides, a Cretan, is not a liar and the statement that all Cretans are liars is false. Another version is the self-referential sentence: *this statement is false.* If the statement is true, then it is true that the statement is false (a contradiction). If the statement is false, then it is a true statement (also a contradiction). It was not clear until Gödel, however, if such statements could be stated in the *Principia Mathematica* system.

12.1.1 Gödel's Incompleteness Theorem

Gödel with Einstein, 1950
Princeton, Institute for Advanced Study Archives

Kurt Gödel was born in Brno (then in Austria-Hungary, now in the Czech Republic) in 1906. Gödel proved that the axiomatic system in *Principia Mathematica* could not be complete and consistent. More generally, Gödel showed that *no* powerful axiomatic system could be both complete and consistent: no matter what the axiomatic system is, if it is powerful enough to express a notion of proof, it must also be the case that there exist statements that can be expressed in the system but cannot be proven either true or false within the system.

Gödel's proof used construction: to prove that *Principia Mathematica* contains statements which cannot be proven either true or false, it is enough to find one such statement. The statement Gödel found:

> G_{PM}: Statement G_{PM} does not have any proof in the system of *Principia Mathematica*.

Similarly to Russel's Paradox, this statement leads to a contradiction. It makes no sense for G_{PM} to be either true or false:

Statement G_{PM} is provable in the system.
: If G_{PM} is proven, then it means G_{PM} does have a proof, but G_{PM} stated that G_{PM} has no proof. The system is inconsistent: it can be used to prove a statement that is not true.

Statement G_{PM} is not provable in the system.
: Since G_{PM} cannot be proven in the system, G_{PM} is a true statement. The system is incomplete: we have a true statement that is not provable in the system.

The proof generalizes to *any* axiomatic system, powerful enough to express a corresponding statement G:

> G: Statement G does not have any proof in the system.

For the proof to be valid, it is necessary to show that statement G can be expressed in the system.

To express G formally, we need to consider what it means for a statement to not have any proof in the system. A proof of the statement G is a sequence of steps, T_0, T_1, T_2, ..., T_N. Each step is the set of all statements that have been proven true so far. Initially, T_0 is the set of axioms in the system. To be a proof of G, T_N must contain G. To be a valid proof, each step should be producible from the previous step by applying one of the inference rules to statements from the previous step.

To express statement G an axiomatic system needs to be powerful enough to express the notion that a valid proof does not exist. Gödel showed that such a statement could be constructed using the *Principia Mathematica* system, and using any system powerful enough to be able to express interesting properties. That is, in order for an axiomatic system to be complete and consistent, it must be so weak that it is not possible to express *this statement has no proof* in the system.

12.2 The Halting Problem

Gödel established that no interesting and consistent axiomatic system is capable of proving all true statements in the system. Now we consider the analogous question for computing: *are there problems for which no algorithm exists?*

Recall these definitions form Chapters 1 and 4:

problem: A description of an input and a desired output.

procedure: A specification of a series of actions.

algorithm: A procedure that is guaranteed to always terminate.

A procedure solves a problem if that procedure produces a correct output for every possible input. If that procedure always terminates, it is an algorithm. So, the question can be stated as: *are there problems for which no procedure exists that produces the correct output for every possible problem instance in a finite amount of time?*

A problem is *computable* if there exists an algorithm that solves the problem. It is important to remember that in order for an algorithm to be a solution for a problem P, it must always terminate (otherwise it is not an algorithm) and must always produce the correct output for *all* possible inputs to P. If no such algorithm exists, the problem is *noncomputable*.[1]

computable

noncomputable

Alan Turing proved that noncomputable problems exist. The way to show that uncomputable problems exist is to find one, similarly to the way Gödel showed unprovable true statements exist by finding an unprovable true statement.

The problem Turing found is known as the *Halting Problem*:[2]

Halting Problem

Input: A string representing a Python program.

Output: If evaluating the input program would ever finish, output True. Otherwise, output False.

[1] The terms *decidable* and *undecidable* are sometimes used to mean the same things as computable and noncomputable.

[2] This problem is a variation on Turing's original problem, which assumed a procedure that takes one input. Of course, Turing did not define the problem using a Python program since Python had not yet been invented when Turing proved the Halting Problem was noncomputable in 1936. In fact, nothing resembling a programmable digital computer would emerge until several years later.

Suppose we had a procedure *halts* that solves the Halting Problem. The input to *halts* is a Python program expressed as a string.

For example, *halts*('(+ 2 3)') should evaluate to True, *halts*('while True: pass') should evaluate to False (the Python **pass** statement does nothing, but is needed to make the while loop syntactically correct), and

```
halts('''
    def fibo(n):
      if n == 1 or n == 2: return 1
      else: return fibo(n-1) + fibo(n-2)
    fibo(60)
  ''')
```

should evaluate to True. From the last example, it is clear that *halts* cannot be implemented by evaluating the expression and outputting True if it terminates. The problem is knowing when to give up and output False. As we analyzed in Chapter 7, evaluating *fibo*(60) would take trillions of years; in theory, though, it eventually finishes so *halts* should output True.

This argument is not sufficient to prove that *halts* is noncomputable. It just shows that one particular way of implementing *halts* would not work. To show that *halts* is noncomputable, we need to show that it is impossible to implement a *halts* procedure that would produce the correct output for all inputs in a finite amount of time.

Here is another example that suggests (but does not prove) the impossibility of *halts* (where *sumOfTwoPrimes* is defined as an algorithm that take a number as input and outputs True if the number is the sum of two prime numbers and False otherwise):

```
halts('n = 4; while sumOfTwoPrimes(n): n = n + 2')
```

This program halts if there exists an even number greater than 2 that is not the sum of two primes. We assume unbounded integers even though every actual computer has a limit on the largest number it can represent. Our computing model, though, uses an infinite tape, so there is no arbitrary limit on number sizes.

Knowing whether or not the program halts would settle an open problem known as Goldbach's Conjecture: *every even integer greater than 2 can be written as the sum of two primes.* Christian Goldbach proposed a form of the conjecture in a letter to Leonhard Euler in 1742. Euler refined it and believed it to be true, but couldn't prove it.

With a *halts* algorithm, we could settle the conjecture using the expression above: if the result is False, the conjecture is proven; if the result is True, the conjecture is disproved. We could use a *halts* algorithm like this to resolve many other open problems. This strongly suggests there is no *halts* algorithm, but does not prove it cannot exist.

Proving Noncomputability. Proving non-existence is requires more than just showing a hard problem could be solved if something exists. One way to prove non-existence of an X, is to show that if an X exists it leads to a contradiction.

We prove that the existence of a *halts* algorithm leads to a contradiction, so no *halts* algorithm exists.

We obtain the contradiction by showing one input for which the *halts* procedure could not possibly work correctly. Consider this procedure:

```
def paradox():
    if halts('paradox()'): while True: pass
```

The body of the *paradox* procedure is an if expression. The consequent expression is a never-ending loop.

The predicate expression cannot sensibly evaluate to either True or False:

halts('paradox()') ⇒ True
: If the predicate expression evaluates to True, the consequent block is evaluated producing a never-ending loop. Thus, if *halts*('paradox()') evaluates to True, the evaluation of an application of *paradox* never halts. But, this means the result of *halts*('paradox()') was incorrect.

halts('paradox()') ⇒ False
: If the predicate expression evaluates to False, the alternate block is evaluated. It is empty, so evaluation terminates. Thus, the evaluation of *paradox*() terminates, contradicting the result of *halts*('paradox()').

Either result for *halts*(`*paradox*()') leads to a contradiction! The only sensible thing *halts* could do for this input is to not produce a value. That means there is no algorithm that solves the Halting Problem. Any procedure we define to implement *halts* must sometimes either produce the wrong result or fail to produce a result at all (that is, run forever without producing a result). This means the Halting Problem is noncomputable.

There is one important hole in our proof: we argued that because *paradox* does not make sense, something in the definition of *paradox* must not exist and identified *halts* as the component that does not exist. This assumes that everything else we used to define *paradox* does exist.

This seems reasonable enough—they are built-in to Python so they seem to exist. But, perhaps the reason *paradox* leads to a contradiction is because True does not really exist or because it is not possible to implement an if expression that strictly follows the Python evaluation rules. Although we have been using these and they seems to always work fine, we have no formal model in which to argue that evaluating True always terminates or that an if expression means exactly what the evaluation rules say it does.

Our informal proof is also insufficient to prove the stronger claim that no algorithm exists to solve the halting problem. All we have shown is that no Python procedure exists that solves *halts*. Perhaps there is a procedure in some more powerful programming language in which it is possible to implement a solution to the Halting Problem. In fact, we will see that no more powerful programming language exists.

A convincing proof requires a formal model of computing. This is why Alan Turing developed a model of computation.

12.3 Universality

Recall the Turing Machine model from Chapter 6: a Turing Machine consists of an infinite tape divided into discrete square into which symbols from a fixed alphabet can be written, and a tape head that moves along the tape. On each step, the tape head can read the symbol in the current square, write a symbol in the current square, and move left or right one square or halt. The machine can keep track of a finite number of possible states, and determines which action to take based on a set of transition rules that specify the output symbol and head action for a given current state and read symbol.

Turing argued that this simple model corresponds to our intuition about what can be done using mechanical computation. Recall this was 1936, so the model for mechanical computation was not what a mechanical computer can do, but what a human computer can do. Turing argued that his model corresponded to what a human computer could do by following a systematic procedure: the infinite tape was as powerful as a two-dimensional sheet of paper or any other recording medium, the set of symbols must be finite otherwise it would not be possible to correctly distinguish all symbols, and the number of machine states must be finite because there is a limited amount a human can keep in mind at one time.

We can enumerate all possible Turing Machines. One way to see this is to devise a notation for writing down any Turing Machine. A Turing Machine is completely described by its alphabet, states and transition rules. We could write down any Turing Machine by numbering each state and listing each transition rule as a tuple of the current state, alphabet symbol, next state, output symbol, and tape direction. We can map each state and alphabet symbol to a number, and use this encoding to write down a unique number for every possible Turing Machine. Hence, we can enumerate all possible Turing Machines by just enumerating the positive integers. Most positive integers do not correspond to valid Turing Machines, but if we go through all the numbers we will eventually reach every possible Turing Machine.

This is step towards proving that some problems cannot be solved by any algorithm. The number of Turing Machines is less than the number of real numbers. Both numbers are infinite, but as explained in Section 1.2.2, Cantor's diagonalization proof showed that the real numbers are not countable. Any attempt to map the real numbers to the integers must fail to include all the real numbers. This means there are real numbers that cannot be produced by any Turing Machine: there are fewer Turing Machines than there are real numbers, so there must be some real numbers that cannot be produced by any Turing Machine.

Universal Turing Machine

The next step is to define the machine depicted in Figure 12.2. A *Universal Turing Machine* is a machine that takes as input a number that identifies a Turing Machine and simulates the specified Turing Machine running on initially empty input tape.

The Universal Turing Machine can simulate any Turing Machine. In his proof, Turing describes the transition rules for such a machine. It simulates the Turing Machine encoded by the input number. One can imagine doing this by using the tape to keep track of the state of the simulated machine. For each step, the universal machine searches the description of the input machine to find the ap-

Figure 12.2. Universal Turing Machine.

propriate rule. This is the rule for the current state of the simulated machine on the current input symbol of the simulated machine. The universal machine keeps track of the machine and tape state of the simulated machine, and simulates each step. Thus, there is a single Turing Machine that can simulate every Turing Machine.

Since a Universal Turing Machine can simulate every Turing Machine, and a Turing Machine can perform any computation according to our intuitive notion of computation, this means a Universal Turing Machine can perform all computations. Using the universal machine and a diagonalization argument similar to the one above for the real numbers, Turing reached a similar contradiction for a problem analogous to the Halting Problem for Python programs but for Turing Machines instead.

If we can simulate a Universal Turing Machine in a programming language, that language is a *universal programming language*. There is some program that can be written in that language to perform every possible computation.

universal programming language

To show that a programming language is universal, it is sufficient to show that it can simulate any Turing Machine, since a Turing Machine can perform every possible computation. To simulate a Universal Turing Machine, we need some way to keep track of the state of the tape (for example, the list datatypes in Scheme or Python would be adequate), a way to keep track of the internal machine state (a number can do this), and a way to execute the transition rules (we could define a procedure that does this using an if expression to make decisions about which transition rule to follow for each step), and a way to keep going (we can do this in Scheme with recursive applications). Thus, Scheme is a universal programming language: one can write a Scheme program to simulate a Universal Turing Machine, and thus, perform any mechanical computation.

12.4 Proving Non-Computability

We can show that a problem is computable by describing a procedure and proving that the procedure always terminates and always produces the correct answer. It is enough to provide a convincing argument that such a procedure exists; finding the actual procedure is not necessary (but often helps to make the argument more convincing).

To show that a problem is not computable, we need to show that *no* algorithm exists that solves the problem. Since there are an infinite number of possible procedures, we cannot just list all possible procedures and show why each one does not solve the problem. Instead, we need to construct an argument showing that if there were such an algorithm it would lead to a contradiction.

The core of our argument is based on knowing the Halting Problem is noncomputable. If a solution to some new problem P could be used to solve the Halting

Problem, then we know that P is also noncomputable. That is, no algorithm exists that can solve P since if such an algorithm exists it could be used to also solve the Halting Problem which we already know is impossible.

Reduction Proofs. The proof technique where we show that a solution for some problem P can be used to solve a different problem Q is known as a *reduction*.

reduction

reducible

A problem Q is *reducible* to a problem P if a solution to P could be used to solve Q. This means that problem Q is no harder than problem P, since a solution to problem Q leads to a solution to problem P.

Example 12.1: Prints-Three Problem

Consider the problem of determining if an application of a procedure would ever print 3:

Prints-Three

Input: A string representing a Python program.

Output: If evaluating the input program would print 3, output True; otherwise, output False.

We show the Prints-Three Problem is noncomputable by showing that it is as hard as the Halting Problem, which we already know is noncomputable.

Suppose we had an algorithm *printsThree* that solves the Prints-Three Problem. Then, we could define *halts* as:

```
def halts(p):
  return printsThree(p + '; print(3)')
```

The *printsThree* application would evaluate to True if evaluating the Python program specified by p would halt since that means the **print**(3) statement appended to p would be evaluated. On the other hand, if evaluating p would not halt, the added print statement never evaluated. As long as the program specified by p would never print 3, the application of *printsThree* should evaluate to False. Hence, if a *printsThree* algorithm exists, we would use it to implement an algorithm that solves the Halting Problem.

The one wrinkle is that the specified input program might print 3 itself. We can avoid this problem by transforming the input program so it would never print 3 itself, without otherwise altering its behavior. One way to do this would be to replace all occurrences of **print** (or any other built-in procedure that prints) in the string with a new procedure, *dontprint* that behaves like **print** but doesn't actually print out anything. Suppose the *replacePrints* procedure is defined to do this. Then, we could use *printsThree* to define *halts*:

```
def halts(p): return printsThree(replacePrints(p) + '; print(3)')
```

We know that the Halting Problem is noncomputable, so this means the Prints-Three Problem must also be noncomputable.

Exploration 12.1: Virus Detection

The Halting Problem and Prints-Three Problem are noncomputable, but do seem to be obviously important problems. It is useful to know if a procedure application will terminate in a reasonable amount of time, but the Halting Problem does not answer that question. It concerns the question of whether the procedure application will terminate in any finite amount of time, no matter how long it is. This example considers a problem for which it would be very useful to have a solution for it one existed.

A virus is a program that infects other programs. A virus spreads by copying its own code into the code of other programs, so when those programs are executed the virus will execute. In this manner, the virus spreads to infect more and more programs. A typical virus also includes a malicious payload so when it executes in addition to infecting other programs it also performs some damaging (corrupting data files) or annoying (popping up messages) behavior. The Is-Virus Problem is to determine if a procedure specification contains a virus:

Is-Virus

Input: A specification of a Python program.

Output: If the expression contains a virus (a code fragment that will infect other files) output True. Otherwise, output False.

We demonstrate the Is-Virus Problem is noncomputable using a similar strategy to the one we used for the Prints-Three Problem: we show how to define a *halts* algorithm given a hypothetical *isVirus* algorithm. Since we know *halts* is noncomputable, this shows there is no *isVirus* algorithm.

Assume *infectFiles* is a procedure that infects files, so the result of evaluating *isVirus*('infectFiles()') is True. We could define *halts* as:

```
def halts(p):
  return isVirus(p + '; infectFiles()')
```

This works as long as the program specified by *p* does not exhibit the file-infecting behavior. If it does, *p* could infect a file and never terminate, and *halts* would produce the wrong output. To solve this we need to do something like we did in the previous example to hide the printing behavior of the original program.

A rough definition of file-infecting behavior would be to consider any write to an executable file to be an infection. To avoid any file infections in the specific program, we replace all procedures that write to files with procedures that write to shadow copies of these files. For example, we could do this by creating a new temporary directory and prepend that path to all file names. We call this (assumed) procedure, *sandBox*, since it transforms the original program specification into one that would execute in a protected sandbox.

```
def halts(p): isVirus(sandBox(p) + '; infectFiles()')
```

Since we know there is no algorithm that solves the Halting Problem, this proves that there is no algorithm that solves the Is-Virus problem.

Virus scanners such as Symantec's Norton AntiVirus attempt to solve the Is-Virus Problem, but its non-computability means they are doomed to always fail. Virus scanners detect known viruses by scanning files for strings that match signatures in a database of known viruses. As long as the signature database is frequently updated they may be able to detect currently spreading viruses, but this approach cannot detect a new virus that will not match the signature of a previously known virus.

Sophisticated virus scanners employ more advanced techniques to attempt to detect complex viruses such as metamorphic viruses that alter their own code as they propagate to avoid detection. But, because the general Is-Virus Problem is noncomputable, we know that it is impossible to create a program that always terminates and that always correctly determines if an input procedure specification is a virus.

I am rather puzzled why you draw this distinction between proof finders and proof checkers. It seems to me rather unimportant as one can always get a proof finder from a proof checker, and the converse is almost true: the converse false if for instance one allows the proof finder to go through a proof in the ordinary way, and then, rejecting the steps, to write down the final formula as a 'proof' of itself. One can easily think up suitable restrictions on the idea of proof which will make this converse true and which agree well with our ideas of what a proof should be like. I am afraid this may be more confusing to you than enlightening.
Alan Turing, letter to Max Newman, 1940

Exercise 12.1. Is the Launches-Missiles Problem described below computable? Provide a convincing argument supporting your answer.

Launches-Missiles

Input: A specification of a procedure.

Output: If an application of the procedure would lead to the missiles being launched, outputs True. Otherwise, outputs False.

You may assume that the only thing that causes the missiles to be launched is an application of the *launchMissiles* procedure.

Exercise 12.2. Is the Same-Result Problem described below computable? Provide a convincing argument supporting your answer.

Same-Result

Input: Specifications of two procedures, P and Q.

Output: If an application of P terminates and produces the same value as applying Q, outputs True. If an application of P does not terminate, and an application of Q also does not terminate, outputs True. Otherwise, outputs False.

Exercise 12.3. Is the Check-Proof Problem described below computable? Provide a convincing argument supporting your answer.

Check-Proof

Input: A specification of an axiomatic system, a statement (the theorem), and a proof (a sequence of steps, each identifying the axiom that is applied).

Output: Outputs True if the proof is a valid proof of the theorem in the system, or False if it is not a valid proof.

Exercise 12.4. Is the Find-Finite-Proof Problem described below computable? Provide a convincing argument supporting your answer.

Find-Finite-Proof

Input: A specification of an axiomatic system, a statement (the theorem), and a maximum number of steps (max-steps).

Output: If there is a proof in the axiomatic system of the theorem that uses max-steps or fewer steps, outputs True. Otherwise, outputs False.

Exercise 12.5. [⋆] Is the Find-Proof Problem described below computable? Provide a convincing argument why it is or why it is not computable.

Find-Proof

Input: A specification of an axiomatic system, and a statement (the theorem).

Output: If there is a proof in the axiomatic system of the theorem, outputs True. Otherwise, outputs False.

Exploration 12.2: Busy Beavers

Consider the Busy-Beaver Problem (devised by Tibor Radó in 1962):

Busy-Beaver

Input: A positive integer, n.

Output: A number representing that maximum number of steps a Turing Machine with n states and a two-symbol tape alphabet can run starting on an empty tape before halting.

We use 0 and 1 for the two tape symbols, where the blank squares on the tape are interpreted as 0s (alternately, we could use *blank* and X as the symbols, but it is more natural to describe machines where symbols are 0 and 1, so we can think of the initially blank tape as containing all 0s).

For example, if the Busy Beaver input n is 1, the output should be 1. The best we can do with only one state is to halt on the first step. If the transition rule for a 0 input moves left, then it will reach another 0 square and continue forever without halting; similarly it if moves right.

For $n = 2$, there are more options to consider. The machine in Figure 12.3 runs for 6 steps before halting, and there is no two-state machine that runs for more steps. One way to support this claim would be to try simulating all possible two-state Turing Machines.

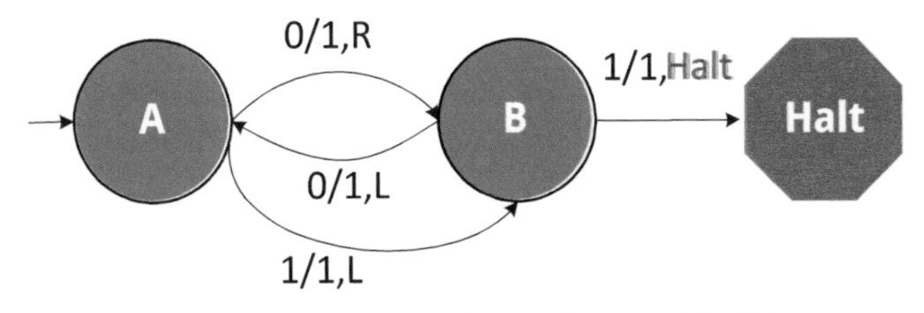

Figure 12.3. Two-state Busy Beaver Machine.

Busy Beaver numbers increase extremely quickly. The maximum number of steps for a three-state machine is 21, and for a four-state machine is 107. The value for a five-state machine is not yet known, but the best machine found to date runs for 47,176,870 steps! For six states, the best known result, discovered in 2007 by Terry Ligocki and Shawn Ligocki, is over 2879 decimal digits long.

We can prove the Busy Beaver Problem is noncomputable by reducing the Halting Problem to it. Suppose we had an algorithm, *bb*(n), that takes the number of states as input and outputs the corresponding Busy Beaver. Then, we could solve the Halting Problem for a Turing Machine:

TM Halting Problem

Input: A string representing a Turing Machine.

Output: If executing the input Turing Machine starting with a blank tape would ever finish, output True. Otherwise, output False.

The TM Halting Problem is different from the Halting Problem as we defined it earlier, so first we need to show that the TM Halting Problem is noncomputable by showing it could be used to solve the Python Halting Problem. Because Python is universal programming language, it is possible to transform any Turing Machine into a Python program. Once way to do this would be to write a Universal Turing Machine simulator in Python, and then create a Python program that first creates a tape containing the input Turing Machine description, and then calls the Universal Turing Machine simulator on that input. This shows that the TM Halting Problem is noncomputable.

Next, we show that an algorithm that solves the Busy Beaver Problem could be used to solve the TM Halting Problem. Here's how (in Pythonish pseudocode):

```
def haltsTM(m):
  states = numberOfStates(m)
  maxSteps = bb(states)
  state = 0
  tape = []
  for step in range(0, maxSteps):
    state, tape = simulateOneStep(m, state, tape)
    if halted(state): return True
  return False
```

The *simulateOneStep* procedure takes as inputs a Turing Machine description, its current state and tape, and simulates the next step on the machine. So, *haltsTM* simulates up to $bb(n)$ steps of the input machine m where n is the number of states in m. Since $bb(n)$ is the maximum number of steps a Turing Machine with n states can execute before halting, we know if m has not halted in the simulate before *maxSteps* is reached that the machine m will never halt, and can correctly return False. This means there is no algorithm that can solve the Busy Beaver Problem.

Exercise 12.6. Confirm that the machine showing in Figure 12.3 runs for 6 steps before halting.

Exercise 12.7. Prove the Beaver Bound problem described below is also noncomputable:

Beaver-Bound

Input: A positive integer, n.

Output: A number that is greater than the maximum number of steps a Turing Machine with n states and a two-symbol tape alphabet can run starting on an empty tape before halting.

A valid solution to the Beaver-Bound problem can produce any result for n as long as it is greater than the Busy Beaver value for n.

Exercise 12.8. [★★★] Find a 5-state Turing Machine that runs for more than 47,176,870 steps, or prove that no such machine exists.

12.5 Summary

Although today's computers can do amazing things, many of which could not even have been imagined twenty years ago, there are problems that can never be solved by computing. The Halting Problem is the most famous example: it is impossible to define a mechanical procedure that always terminates and correctly determines if the computation specified by its input would terminate. Once we know the Halting Problem is noncomputable, we can show that other problems are also noncomputable by illustrating how a solution to the other problem could be used to solve the Halting Problem which we know to be impossible.

Noncomputable problems frequently arise in practice. For example, identifying viruses, analyzing program paths, and constructing proofs, are all noncomputable problems.

Just because a problem is noncomputable does not mean we cannot produce useful programs that address the problem. These programs provide approximate solutions, which are often useful in practice. They produce the correct results on many inputs, but on some inputs must either fail to produce any result or produce an incorrect result.

Index

People

Made in the USA
Lexington, KY
10 April 2017